GNU Make Reference Manual

A catalogue record for this book is available from the Hong Kong Public Libraries.

Published by Samurai Media Limited.

Email: info@samuraimedia.org

ISBN 978-988-14435-1-9

Background Cover Image by https://www.flickr.com/people/webtreatsetc/

Short Contents

Table of Contents

5   Writing Recipes in Rules 41

6   How to Use Variables........................ 59

1 Overview of `make`

The `make` utility automatically determines which pieces of a large program need to be recompiled, and issues commands to recompile them. This manual describes GNU `make`, which was implemented by Richard Stallman and Roland McGrath. Development since Version 3.76 has been handled by Paul D. Smith.

GNU `make` conforms to section 6.2 of *IEEE Standard 1003.2-1992* (POSIX.2).

Our examples show C programs, since they are most common, but you can use `make` with any programming language whose compiler can be run with a shell command. Indeed, `make` is not limited to programs. You can use it to describe any task where some files must be updated automatically from others whenever the others change.

To prepare to use `make`, you must write a file called the *makefile* that describes the relationships among files in your program and provides commands for updating each file. In a program, typically, the executable file is updated from object files, which are in turn made by compiling source files.

Once a suitable makefile exists, each time you change some source files, this simple shell command:

    make

suffices to perform all necessary recompilations. The `make` program uses the makefile data base and the last-modification times of the files to decide which of the files need to be updated. For each of those files, it issues the recipes recorded in the data base.

You can provide command line arguments to `make` to control which files should be recompiled, or how. See Chapter 9 [How to Run `make`], page 99.

1.1 How to Read This Manual

If you are new to `make`, or are looking for a general introduction, read the first few sections of each chapter, skipping the later sections. In each chapter, the first few sections contain introductory or general information and the later sections contain specialized or technical information. The exception is Chapter 2 [An Introduction to Makefiles], page 3, all of which is introductory.

If you are familiar with other `make` programs, see Chapter 13 [Features of GNU `make`], page 143, which lists the enhancements GNU `make` has, and Chapter 14 [Incompatibilities and Missing Features], page 147, which explains the few things GNU `make` lacks that others have.

For a quick summary, see Section 9.7 [Options Summary], page 104, Appendix A [Quick Reference], page 165, and Section 4.8 [Special Targets], page 32.

1.2 Problems and Bugs

If you have problems with GNU `make` or think you've found a bug, please report it to the developers; we cannot promise to do anything but we might well want to fix it.

Before reporting a bug, make sure you've actually found a real bug. Carefully reread the documentation and see if it really says you can do what you're trying to do. If it's not clear whether you should be able to do something or not, report that too; it's a bug in the documentation!

Before reporting a bug or trying to fix it yourself, try to isolate it to the smallest possible makefile that reproduces the problem. Then send us the makefile and the exact results make gave you, including any error or warning messages. Please don't paraphrase these messages: it's best to cut and paste them into your report. When generating this small makefile, be sure to not use any non-free or unusual tools in your recipes: you can almost always emulate what such a tool would do with simple shell commands. Finally, be sure to explain what you expected to occur; this will help us decide whether the problem was really in the documentation.

Once you have a precise problem you can report it in one of two ways. Either send electronic mail to:

> `bug-make@gnu.org`

or use our Web-based project management tool, at:

> `http://savannah.gnu.org/projects/make/`

In addition to the information above, please be careful to include the version number of make you are using. You can get this information with the command 'make --version'. Be sure also to include the type of machine and operating system you are using. One way to obtain this information is by looking at the final lines of output from the command 'make --help'.

2 An Introduction to Makefiles

You need a file called a *makefile* to tell `make` what to do. Most often, the makefile tells `make` how to compile and link a program.

In this chapter, we will discuss a simple makefile that describes how to compile and link a text editor which consists of eight C source files and three header files. The makefile can also tell `make` how to run miscellaneous commands when explicitly asked (for example, to remove certain files as a clean-up operation). To see a more complex example of a makefile, see Appendix C [Complex Makefile], page 177.

When `make` recompiles the editor, each changed C source file must be recompiled. If a header file has changed, each C source file that includes the header file must be recompiled to be safe. Each compilation produces an object file corresponding to the source file. Finally, if any source file has been recompiled, all the object files, whether newly made or saved from previous compilations, must be linked together to produce the new executable editor.

2.1 What a Rule Looks Like

A simple makefile consists of "rules" with the following shape:

```
target ... : prerequisites ...
        recipe
        ...
        ...
```

A *target* is usually the name of a file that is generated by a program; examples of targets are executable or object files. A target can also be the name of an action to carry out, such as 'clean' (see Section 4.5 [Phony Targets], page 29).

A *prerequisite* is a file that is used as input to create the target. A target often depends on several files.

A *recipe* is an action that `make` carries out. A recipe may have more than one command, either on the same line or each on its own line. **Please note:** you need to put a tab character at the beginning of every recipe line! This is an obscurity that catches the unwary. If you prefer to prefix your recipes with a character other than tab, you can set the `.RECIPEPREFIX` variable to an alternate character (see Section 6.14 [Special Variables], page 73).

Usually a recipe is in a rule with prerequisites and serves to create a target file if any of the prerequisites change. However, the rule that specifies a recipe for the target need not have prerequisites. For example, the rule containing the delete command associated with the target 'clean' does not have prerequisites.

A *rule*, then, explains how and when to remake certain files which are the targets of the particular rule. `make` carries out the recipe on the prerequisites to create or update the target. A rule can also explain how and when to carry out an action. See Chapter 4 [Writing Rules], page 21.

A makefile may contain other text besides rules, but a simple makefile need only contain rules. Rules may look somewhat more complicated than shown in this template, but all fit the pattern more or less.

2.2 A Simple Makefile

Here is a straightforward makefile that describes the way an executable file called `edit` depends on eight object files which, in turn, depend on eight C source and three header files.

In this example, all the C files include `defs.h`, but only those defining editing commands include `command.h`, and only low level files that change the editor buffer include `buffer.h`.

```
edit : main.o kbd.o command.o display.o \
       insert.o search.o files.o utils.o
         cc -o edit main.o kbd.o command.o display.o \
                    insert.o search.o files.o utils.o

main.o : main.c defs.h
        cc -c main.c
kbd.o : kbd.c defs.h command.h
        cc -c kbd.c
command.o : command.c defs.h command.h
        cc -c command.c
display.o : display.c defs.h buffer.h
        cc -c display.c
insert.o : insert.c defs.h buffer.h
        cc -c insert.c
search.o : search.c defs.h buffer.h
        cc -c search.c
files.o : files.c defs.h buffer.h command.h
        cc -c files.c
utils.o : utils.c defs.h
        cc -c utils.c
clean :
        rm edit main.o kbd.o command.o display.o \
           insert.o search.o files.o utils.o
```

We split each long line into two lines using backslash/newline; this is like using one long line, but is easier to read. See Section 3.1.1 [Splitting Long Lines], page 12.

To use this makefile to create the executable file called `edit`, type:

```
make
```

To use this makefile to delete the executable file and all the object files from the directory, type:

```
make clean
```

In the example makefile, the targets include the executable file 'edit', and the object files 'main.o' and 'kbd.o'. The prerequisites are files such as 'main.c' and 'defs.h'. In fact, each '.o' file is both a target and a prerequisite. Recipes include 'cc -c main.c' and 'cc -c kbd.c'.

When a target is a file, it needs to be recompiled or relinked if any of its prerequisites change. In addition, any prerequisites that are themselves automatically generated should be updated first. In this example, `edit` depends on each of the eight object files; the object file `main.o` depends on the source file `main.c` and on the header file `defs.h`.

A recipe may follow each line that contains a target and prerequisites. These recipes say how to update the target file. A tab character (or whatever character is specified by the .RECIPEPREFIX variable; see Section 6.14 [Special Variables], page 73) must come at the beginning of every line in the recipe to distinguish recipes from other lines in the makefile. (Bear in mind that make does not know anything about how the recipes work. It is up to you to supply recipes that will update the target file properly. All make does is execute the recipe you have specified when the target file needs to be updated.)

The target 'clean' is not a file, but merely the name of an action. Since you normally do not want to carry out the actions in this rule, 'clean' is not a prerequisite of any other rule. Consequently, make never does anything with it unless you tell it specifically. Note that this rule not only is not a prerequisite, it also does not have any prerequisites, so the only purpose of the rule is to run the specified recipe. Targets that do not refer to files but are just actions are called *phony targets*. See Section 4.5 [Phony Targets], page 29, for information about this kind of target. See Section 5.5 [Errors in Recipes], page 49, to see how to cause make to ignore errors from rm or any other command.

2.3 How make Processes a Makefile

By default, make starts with the first target (not targets whose names start with '.'). This is called the *default goal*. (*Goals* are the targets that make strives ultimately to update. You can override this behavior using the command line (see Section 9.2 [Arguments to Specify the Goals], page 99) or with the .DEFAULT_GOAL special variable (see Section 6.14 [Other Special Variables], page 73).

In the simple example of the previous section, the default goal is to update the executable program edit; therefore, we put that rule first.

Thus, when you give the command:

```
make
```

make reads the makefile in the current directory and begins by processing the first rule. In the example, this rule is for relinking edit; but before make can fully process this rule, it must process the rules for the files that edit depends on, which in this case are the object files. Each of these files is processed according to its own rule. These rules say to update each '.o' file by compiling its source file. The recompilation must be done if the source file, or any of the header files named as prerequisites, is more recent than the object file, or if the object file does not exist.

The other rules are processed because their targets appear as prerequisites of the goal. If some other rule is not depended on by the goal (or anything it depends on, etc.), that rule is not processed, unless you tell make to do so (with a command such as make clean).

Before recompiling an object file, make considers updating its prerequisites, the source file and header files. This makefile does not specify anything to be done for them—the '.c' and '.h' files are not the targets of any rules—so make does nothing for these files. But make would update automatically generated C programs, such as those made by Bison or Yacc, by their own rules at this time.

After recompiling whichever object files need it, make decides whether to relink edit. This must be done if the file edit does not exist, or if any of the object files are newer than it. If an object file was just recompiled, it is now newer than edit, so edit is relinked.

Thus, if we change the file `insert.c` and run `make`, `make` will compile that file to update `insert.o`, and then link `edit`. If we change the file `command.h` and run `make`, `make` will recompile the object files `kbd.o`, `command.o` and `files.o` and then link the file `edit`.

2.4 Variables Make Makefiles Simpler

In our example, we had to list all the object files twice in the rule for `edit` (repeated here):

```
edit : main.o kbd.o command.o display.o \
            insert.o search.o files.o utils.o
    cc -o edit main.o kbd.o command.o display.o \
                insert.o search.o files.o utils.o
```

Such duplication is error-prone; if a new object file is added to the system, we might add it to one list and forget the other. We can eliminate the risk and simplify the makefile by using a variable. *Variables* allow a text string to be defined once and substituted in multiple places later (see Chapter 6 [How to Use Variables], page 59).

It is standard practice for every makefile to have a variable named `objects`, `OBJECTS`, `objs`, `OBJS`, `obj`, or `OBJ` which is a list of all object file names. We would define such a variable `objects` with a line like this in the makefile:

```
objects = main.o kbd.o command.o display.o \
            insert.o search.o files.o utils.o
```

Then, each place we want to put a list of the object file names, we can substitute the variable's value by writing '`$(objects)`' (see Chapter 6 [How to Use Variables], page 59).

Here is how the complete simple makefile looks when you use a variable for the object files:

```
objects = main.o kbd.o command.o display.o \
          insert.o search.o files.o utils.o

edit : $(objects)
        cc -o edit $(objects)
main.o : main.c defs.h
        cc -c main.c
kbd.o : kbd.c defs.h command.h
        cc -c kbd.c
command.o : command.c defs.h command.h
        cc -c command.c
display.o : display.c defs.h buffer.h
        cc -c display.c
insert.o : insert.c defs.h buffer.h
        cc -c insert.c
search.o : search.c defs.h buffer.h
        cc -c search.c
files.o : files.c defs.h buffer.h command.h
        cc -c files.c
utils.o : utils.c defs.h
        cc -c utils.c
clean :
        rm edit $(objects)
```

2.5 Letting make Deduce the Recipes

It is not necessary to spell out the recipes for compiling the individual C source files, because make can figure them out: it has an *implicit rule* for updating a '.o' file from a correspondingly named '.c' file using a 'cc -c' command. For example, it will use the recipe 'cc -c main.c -o main.o' to compile main.c into main.o. We can therefore omit the recipes from the rules for the object files. See Chapter 10 [Using Implicit Rules], page 111.

When a '.c' file is used automatically in this way, it is also automatically added to the list of prerequisites. We can therefore omit the '.c' files from the prerequisites, provided we omit the recipe.

Here is the entire example, with both of these changes, and a variable objects as suggested above:

```
objects = main.o kbd.o command.o display.o \
          insert.o search.o files.o utils.o

edit : $(objects)
        cc -o edit $(objects)

main.o : defs.h
kbd.o : defs.h command.h
command.o : defs.h command.h
display.o : defs.h buffer.h
insert.o : defs.h buffer.h
search.o : defs.h buffer.h
files.o : defs.h buffer.h command.h
utils.o : defs.h

.PHONY : clean
clean :
        rm edit $(objects)
```

This is how we would write the makefile in actual practice. (The complications associated with 'clean' are described elsewhere. See Section 4.5 [Phony Targets], page 29, and Section 5.5 [Errors in Recipes], page 49.)

Because implicit rules are so convenient, they are important. You will see them used frequently.

2.6 Another Style of Makefile

When the objects of a makefile are created only by implicit rules, an alternative style of makefile is possible. In this style of makefile, you group entries by their prerequisites instead of by their targets. Here is what one looks like:

```
objects = main.o kbd.o command.o display.o \
          insert.o search.o files.o utils.o

edit : $(objects)
        cc -o edit $(objects)

$(objects) : defs.h
kbd.o command.o files.o : command.h
display.o insert.o search.o files.o : buffer.h
```

Here defs.h is given as a prerequisite of all the object files; command.h and buffer.h are prerequisites of the specific object files listed for them.

Whether this is better is a matter of taste: it is more compact, but some people dislike it because they find it clearer to put all the information about each target in one place.

2.7 Rules for Cleaning the Directory

Compiling a program is not the only thing you might want to write rules for. Makefiles commonly tell how to do a few other things besides compiling a program: for example, how to delete all the object files and executables so that the directory is 'clean'.

Here is how we could write a make rule for cleaning our example editor:

```
clean:
        rm edit $(objects)
```

In practice, we might want to write the rule in a somewhat more complicated manner to handle unanticipated situations. We would do this:

```
.PHONY : clean
clean :
        -rm edit $(objects)
```

This prevents make from getting confused by an actual file called clean and causes it to continue in spite of errors from rm. (See Section 4.5 [Phony Targets], page 29, and Section 5.5 [Errors in Recipes], page 49.)

A rule such as this should not be placed at the beginning of the makefile, because we do not want it to run by default! Thus, in the example makefile, we want the rule for edit, which recompiles the editor, to remain the default goal.

Since clean is not a prerequisite of edit, this rule will not run at all if we give the command 'make' with no arguments. In order to make the rule run, we have to type 'make clean'. See Chapter 9 [How to Run make], page 99.

3 Writing Makefiles

The information that tells **make** how to recompile a system comes from reading a data base called the *makefile*.

3.1 What Makefiles Contain

Makefiles contain five kinds of things: *explicit rules*, *implicit rules*, *variable definitions*, *directives*, and *comments*. Rules, variables, and directives are described at length in later chapters.

- An *explicit rule* says when and how to remake one or more files, called the rule's *targets*. It lists the other files that the targets depend on, called the *prerequisites* of the target, and may also give a recipe to use to create or update the targets. See Chapter 4 [Writing Rules], page 21.

- An *implicit rule* says when and how to remake a class of files based on their names. It describes how a target may depend on a file with a name similar to the target and gives a recipe to create or update such a target. See Chapter 10 [Using Implicit Rules], page 111.

- A *variable definition* is a line that specifies a text string value for a variable that can be substituted into the text later. The simple makefile example shows a variable definition for **objects** as a list of all object files (see Section 2.4 [Variables Make Makefiles Simpler], page 6).

- A *directive* is an instruction for **make** to do something special while reading the makefile. These include:

  - Reading another makefile (see Section 3.3 [Including Other Makefiles], page 13).

  - Deciding (based on the values of variables) whether to use or ignore a part of the makefile (see Chapter 7 [Conditional Parts of Makefiles], page 77).

  - Defining a variable from a verbatim string containing multiple lines (see Section 6.8 [Defining Multi-Line Variables], page 69).

- '#' in a line of a makefile starts a *comment*. It and the rest of the line are ignored, except that a trailing backslash not escaped by another backslash will continue the comment across multiple lines. A line containing just a comment (with perhaps spaces before it) is effectively blank, and is ignored. If you want a literal #, escape it with a backslash (e.g., \#). Comments may appear on any line in the makefile, although they are treated specially in certain situations.

  You cannot use comments within variable references or function calls: any instance of # will be treated literally (rather than as the start of a comment) inside a variable reference or function call.

  Comments within a recipe are passed to the shell, just as with any other recipe text. The shell decides how to interpret it: whether or not this is a comment is up to the shell.

  Within a **define** directive, comments are not ignored during the definition of the variable, but rather kept intact in the value of the variable. When the variable is expanded they will either be treated as **make** comments or as recipe text, depending on the context in which the variable is evaluated.

3.1.1 Splitting Long Lines

Makefiles use a "line-based" syntax in which the newline character is special and marks the end of a statement. GNU make has no limit on the length of a statement line, up to the amount of memory in your computer.

However, it is difficult to read lines which are too long to display without wrapping or scrolling. So, you can format your makefiles for readability by adding newlines into the middle of a statement: you do this by escaping the internal newlines with a backslash (\) character. Where we need to make a distinction we will refer to "physical lines" as a single line ending with a newline (regardless of whether it is escaped) and a "logical line" being a complete statement including all escaped newlines up to the first non-escaped newline.

The way in which backslash/newline combinations are handled depends on whether the statement is a recipe line or a non-recipe line. Handling of backslash/newline in a recipe line is discussed later (see Section 5.1.1 [Splitting Recipe Lines], page 41).

Outside of recipe lines, backslash/newlines are converted into a single space character. Once that is done, all whitespace around the backslash/newline is condensed into a single space: this includes all whitespace preceding the backslash, all whitespace at the beginning of the line after the backslash/newline, and any consecutive backslash/newline combinations.

If the .POSIX special target is defined then backslash/newline handling is modified slightly to conform to POSIX.2: first, whitespace preceding a backslash is not removed and second, consecutive backslash/newlines are not condensed.

3.2 What Name to Give Your Makefile

By default, when make looks for the makefile, it tries the following names, in order: GNUmakefile, makefile and Makefile.

Normally you should call your makefile either makefile or Makefile. (We recommend Makefile because it appears prominently near the beginning of a directory listing, right near other important files such as README.) The first name checked, GNUmakefile, is not recommended for most makefiles. You should use this name if you have a makefile that is specific to GNU make, and will not be understood by other versions of make. Other make programs look for makefile and Makefile, but not GNUmakefile.

If make finds none of these names, it does not use any makefile. Then you must specify a goal with a command argument, and make will attempt to figure out how to remake it using only its built-in implicit rules. See Chapter 10 [Using Implicit Rules], page 111.

If you want to use a nonstandard name for your makefile, you can specify the makefile name with the '-f' or '--file' option. The arguments '-f name' or '--file=name' tell make to read the file name as the makefile. If you use more than one '-f' or '--file' option, you can specify several makefiles. All the makefiles are effectively concatenated in the order specified. The default makefile names GNUmakefile, makefile and Makefile are not checked automatically if you specify '-f' or '--file'.

3.3 Including Other Makefiles

The `include` directive tells `make` to suspend reading the current makefile and read one or more other makefiles before continuing. The directive is a line in the makefile that looks like this:

```
include filenames...
```

filenames can contain shell file name patterns. If *filenames* is empty, nothing is included and no error is printed.

Extra spaces are allowed and ignored at the beginning of the line, but the first character must not be a tab (or the value of `.RECIPEPREFIX`)—if the line begins with a tab, it will be considered a recipe line. Whitespace is required between `include` and the file names, and between file names; extra whitespace is ignored there and at the end of the directive. A comment starting with '#' is allowed at the end of the line. If the file names contain any variable or function references, they are expanded. See Chapter 6 [How to Use Variables], page 59.

For example, if you have three `.mk` files, `a.mk`, `b.mk`, and `c.mk`, and `$(bar)` expands to `bish bash`, then the following expression

```
include foo *.mk $(bar)
```

is equivalent to

```
include foo a.mk b.mk c.mk bish bash
```

When `make` processes an `include` directive, it suspends reading of the containing makefile and reads from each listed file in turn. When that is finished, `make` resumes reading the makefile in which the directive appears.

One occasion for using `include` directives is when several programs, handled by individual makefiles in various directories, need to use a common set of variable definitions (see Section 6.5 [Setting Variables], page 65) or pattern rules (see Section 10.5 [Defining and Redefining Pattern Rules], page 118).

Another such occasion is when you want to generate prerequisites from source files automatically; the prerequisites can be put in a file that is included by the main makefile. This practice is generally cleaner than that of somehow appending the prerequisites to the end of the main makefile as has been traditionally done with other versions of `make`. See Section 4.13 [Automatic Prerequisites], page 38.

If the specified name does not start with a slash, and the file is not found in the current directory, several other directories are searched. First, any directories you have specified with the '-I' or '--include-dir' option are searched (see Section 9.7 [Summary of Options], page 104). Then the following directories (if they exist) are searched, in this order: *prefix*/include (normally `/usr/local/include`[1]) `/usr/gnu/include`, `/usr/local/include`, `/usr/include`.

If an included makefile cannot be found in any of these directories, a warning message is generated, but it is not an immediately fatal error; processing of the makefile containing the `include` continues. Once it has finished reading makefiles, `make` will try to remake any that are out of date or don't exist. See Section 3.5 [How Makefiles Are Remade], page 14.

---

[1] GNU Make compiled for MS-DOS and MS-Windows behaves as if *prefix* has been defined to be the root of the DJGPP tree hierarchy.

Only after it has tried to find a way to remake a makefile and failed, will make diagnose the missing makefile as a fatal error.

If you want make to simply ignore a makefile which does not exist or cannot be remade, with no error message, use the -include directive instead of include, like this:

        -include filenames...

This acts like include in every way except that there is no error (not even a warning) if any of the filenames (or any prerequisites of any of the filenames) do not exist or cannot be remade.

For compatibility with some other make implementations, sinclude is another name for -include.

3.4 The Variable MAKEFILES

If the environment variable MAKEFILES is defined, make considers its value as a list of names (separated by whitespace) of additional makefiles to be read before the others. This works much like the include directive: various directories are searched for those files (see Section 3.3 [Including Other Makefiles], page 13). In addition, the default goal is never taken from one of these makefiles (or any makefile included by them) and it is not an error if the files listed in MAKEFILES are not found.

The main use of MAKEFILES is in communication between recursive invocations of make (see Section 5.7 [Recursive Use of make], page 50). It usually is not desirable to set the environment variable before a top-level invocation of make, because it is usually better not to mess with a makefile from outside. However, if you are running make without a specific makefile, a makefile in MAKEFILES can do useful things to help the built-in implicit rules work better, such as defining search paths (see Section 4.4 [Directory Search], page 25).

Some users are tempted to set MAKEFILES in the environment automatically on login, and program makefiles to expect this to be done. This is a very bad idea, because such makefiles will fail to work if run by anyone else. It is much better to write explicit include directives in the makefiles. See Section 3.3 [Including Other Makefiles], page 13.

3.5 How Makefiles Are Remade

Sometimes makefiles can be remade from other files, such as RCS or SCCS files. If a makefile can be remade from other files, you probably want make to get an up-to-date version of the makefile to read in.

To this end, after reading in all makefiles, make will consider each as a goal target and attempt to update it. If a makefile has a rule which says how to update it (found either in that very makefile or in another one) or if an implicit rule applies to it (see Chapter 10 [Using Implicit Rules], page 111), it will be updated if necessary. After all makefiles have been checked, if any have actually been changed, make starts with a clean slate and reads all the makefiles over again. (It will also attempt to update each of them over again, but normally this will not change them again, since they are already up to date.)

If you know that one or more of your makefiles cannot be remade and you want to keep make from performing an implicit rule search on them, perhaps for efficiency reasons, you can use any normal method of preventing implicit rule look-up to do so. For example, you can write an explicit rule with the makefile as the target, and an empty recipe (see Section 5.9 [Using Empty Recipes], page 57).

If the makefiles specify a double-colon rule to remake a file with a recipe but no prerequisites, that file will always be remade (see Section 4.12 [Double-Colon], page 38). In the case of makefiles, a makefile that has a double-colon rule with a recipe but no prerequisites will be remade every time make is run, and then again after make starts over and reads the makefiles in again. This would cause an infinite loop: make would constantly remake the makefile, and never do anything else. So, to avoid this, make will **not** attempt to remake makefiles which are specified as targets of a double-colon rule with a recipe but no prerequisites.

If you do not specify any makefiles to be read with '-f' or '--file' options, make will try the default makefile names; see Section 3.2 [What Name to Give Your Makefile], page 12. Unlike makefiles explicitly requested with '-f' or '--file' options, make is not certain that these makefiles should exist. However, if a default makefile does not exist but can be created by running make rules, you probably want the rules to be run so that the makefile can be used.

Therefore, if none of the default makefiles exists, make will try to make each of them in the same order in which they are searched for (see Section 3.2 [What Name to Give Your Makefile], page 12) until it succeeds in making one, or it runs out of names to try. Note that it is not an error if make cannot find or make any makefile; a makefile is not always necessary.

When you use the '-t' or '--touch' option (see Section 9.3 [Instead of Executing Recipes], page 101), you would not want to use an out-of-date makefile to decide which targets to touch. So the '-t' option has no effect on updating makefiles; they are really updated even if '-t' is specified. Likewise, '-q' (or '--question') and '-n' (or '--just-print') do not prevent updating of makefiles, because an out-of-date makefile would result in the wrong output for other targets. Thus, 'make -f mfile -n foo' will update mfile, read it in, and then print the recipe to update foo and its prerequisites without running it. The recipe printed for foo will be the one specified in the updated contents of mfile.

However, on occasion you might actually wish to prevent updating of even the makefiles. You can do this by specifying the makefiles as goals in the command line as well as specifying them as makefiles. When the makefile name is specified explicitly as a goal, the options '-t' and so on do apply to them.

Thus, 'make -f mfile -n mfile foo' would read the makefile mfile, print the recipe needed to update it without actually running it, and then print the recipe needed to update foo without running that. The recipe for foo will be the one specified by the existing contents of mfile.

3.6 Overriding Part of Another Makefile

Sometimes it is useful to have a makefile that is mostly just like another makefile. You can often use the 'include' directive to include one in the other, and add more targets or variable definitions. However, it is invalid for two makefiles to give different recipes for the same target. But there is another way.

In the containing makefile (the one that wants to include the other), you can use a match-anything pattern rule to say that to remake any target that cannot be made from the information in the containing makefile, make should look in another makefile. See Section 10.5 [Pattern Rules], page 118, for more information on pattern rules.

For example, if you have a makefile called Makefile that says how to make the target 'foo' (and other targets), you can write a makefile called GNUmakefile that contains:

```
foo:
        frobnicate > foo

%: force
        @$(MAKE) -f Makefile $@
force: ;
```

If you say 'make foo', make will find GNUmakefile, read it, and see that to make foo, it needs to run the recipe 'frobnicate > foo'. If you say 'make bar', make will find no way to make bar in GNUmakefile, so it will use the recipe from the pattern rule: 'make -f Makefile bar'. If Makefile provides a rule for updating bar, make will apply the rule. And likewise for any other target that GNUmakefile does not say how to make.

The way this works is that the pattern rule has a pattern of just '%', so it matches any target whatever. The rule specifies a prerequisite force, to guarantee that the recipe will be run even if the target file already exists. We give the force target an empty recipe to prevent make from searching for an implicit rule to build it—otherwise it would apply the same match-anything rule to force itself and create a prerequisite loop!

3.7 How make Reads a Makefile

GNU make does its work in two distinct phases. During the first phase it reads all the makefiles, included makefiles, etc. and internalizes all the variables and their values, implicit and explicit rules, and constructs a dependency graph of all the targets and their prerequisites. During the second phase, make uses these internal structures to determine what targets will need to be rebuilt and to invoke the rules necessary to do so.

It's important to understand this two-phase approach because it has a direct impact on how variable and function expansion happens; this is often a source of some confusion when writing makefiles. Here we will present a summary of the phases in which expansion happens for different constructs within the makefile. We say that expansion is *immediate* if it happens during the first phase: in this case make will expand any variables or functions in that section of a construct as the makefile is parsed. We say that expansion is *deferred* if expansion is not performed immediately. Expansion of a deferred construct is not performed until either the construct appears later in an immediate context, or until the second phase.

You may not be familiar with some of these constructs yet. You can reference this section as you become familiar with them, in later chapters.

Variable Assignment

Variable definitions are parsed as follows:

```
immediate = deferred
immediate ?= deferred
immediate := immediate
immediate ::= immediate
immediate += deferred or immediate
```

```
immediate != immediate

define immediate
  deferred
endef

define immediate =
  deferred
endef

define immediate ?=
  deferred
endef

define immediate :=
  immediate
endef

define immediate ::=
  immediate
endef

define immediate +=
  deferred or immediate
endef

define immediate !=
  immediate
endef
```

For the append operator, '+=', the right-hand side is considered immediate if the variable was previously set as a simple variable (':=' or '::='), and deferred otherwise.

For the shell assignment operator, '!=', the right-hand side is evaluated immediately and handed to the shell. The result is stored in the variable named on the left, and that variable becomes a simple variable (and will thus be re-evaluated on each reference).

Conditional Directives

Conditional directives are parsed immediately. This means, for example, that automatic variables cannot be used in conditional directives, as automatic variables are not set until the recipe for that rule is invoked. If you need to use automatic variables in a conditional directive you *must* move the condition into the recipe and use shell conditional syntax instead.

Rule Definition

A rule is always expanded the same way, regardless of the form:

```
immediate : immediate ; deferred
        deferred
```

That is, the target and prerequisite sections are expanded immediately, and the recipe used to construct the target is always deferred. This general rule is true for explicit rules, pattern rules, suffix rules, static pattern rules, and simple prerequisite definitions.

3.8 Secondary Expansion

In the previous section we learned that GNU make works in two distinct phases: a read-in phase and a target-update phase (see Section 3.7 [How make Reads a Makefile], page 16). GNU make also has the ability to enable a *second expansion* of the prerequisites (only) for some or all targets defined in the makefile. In order for this second expansion to occur, the special target .SECONDEXPANSION must be defined before the first prerequisite list that makes use of this feature.

If that special target is defined then in between the two phases mentioned above, right at the end of the read-in phase, all the prerequisites of the targets defined after the special target are expanded a *second time*. In most circumstances this secondary expansion will have no effect, since all variable and function references will have been expanded during the initial parsing of the makefiles. In order to take advantage of the secondary expansion phase of the parser, then, it's necessary to *escape* the variable or function reference in the makefile. In this case the first expansion merely un-escapes the reference but doesn't expand it, and expansion is left to the secondary expansion phase. For example, consider this makefile:

```
.SECONDEXPANSION:
ONEVAR = onefile
TWOVAR = twofile
myfile: $(ONEVAR) $$(TWOVAR)
```

After the first expansion phase the prerequisites list of the myfile target will be onefile and $(TWOVAR); the first (unescaped) variable reference to *ONEVAR* is expanded, while the second (escaped) variable reference is simply unescaped, without being recognized as a variable reference. Now during the secondary expansion the first word is expanded again but since it contains no variable or function references it remains the value onefile, while the second word is now a normal reference to the variable *TWOVAR*, which is expanded to the value twofile. The final result is that there are two prerequisites, onefile and twofile.

Obviously, this is not a very interesting case since the same result could more easily have been achieved simply by having both variables appear, unescaped, in the prerequisites list. One difference becomes apparent if the variables are reset; consider this example:

```
.SECONDEXPANSION:
AVAR = top
onefile: $(AVAR)
twofile: $$(AVAR)
AVAR = bottom
```

Here the prerequisite of onefile will be expanded immediately, and resolve to the value top, while the prerequisite of twofile will not be full expanded until the secondary expansion and yield a value of bottom.

This is marginally more exciting, but the true power of this feature only becomes apparent when you discover that secondary expansions always take place within the scope of the automatic variables for that target. This means that you can use variables such as $@,

$*, etc. during the second expansion and they will have their expected values, just as in the recipe. All you have to do is defer the expansion by escaping the $. Also, secondary expansion occurs for both explicit and implicit (pattern) rules. Knowing this, the possible uses for this feature increase dramatically. For example:

```
.SECONDEXPANSION:
main_OBJS := main.o try.o test.o
lib_OBJS := lib.o api.o

main lib: $$($$@_OBJS)
```

Here, after the initial expansion the prerequisites of both the `main` and `lib` targets will be `$($@_OBJS)`. During the secondary expansion, the `$@` variable is set to the name of the target and so the expansion for the `main` target will yield `$(main_OBJS)`, or `main.o try.o test.o`, while the secondary expansion for the `lib` target will yield `$(lib_OBJS)`, or `lib.o api.o`.

You can also mix in functions here, as long as they are properly escaped:

```
main_SRCS := main.c try.c test.c
lib_SRCS := lib.c api.c

.SECONDEXPANSION:
main lib: $$(patsubst %.c,%.o,$$($$@_SRCS))
```

This version allows users to specify source files rather than object files, but gives the same resulting prerequisites list as the previous example.

Evaluation of automatic variables during the secondary expansion phase, especially of the target name variable `$$@`, behaves similarly to evaluation within recipes. However, there are some subtle differences and "corner cases" which come into play for the different types of rule definitions that `make` understands. The subtleties of using the different automatic variables are described below.

Secondary Expansion of Explicit Rules

During the secondary expansion of explicit rules, `$$@` and `$$%` evaluate, respectively, to the file name of the target and, when the target is an archive member, the target member name. The `$$<` variable evaluates to the first prerequisite in the first rule for this target. `$$^` and `$$+` evaluate to the list of all prerequisites of rules *that have already appeared* for the same target (`$$+` with repetitions and `$$^` without). The following example will help illustrate these behaviors:

```
.SECONDEXPANSION:

foo: foo.1 bar.1 $$< $$^ $$+     # line #1

foo: foo.2 bar.2 $$< $$^ $$+     # line #2

foo: foo.3 bar.3 $$< $$^ $$+     # line #3
```

In the first prerequisite list, all three variables (`$$<`, `$$^`, and `$$+`) expand to the empty string. In the second, they will have values `foo.1`, `foo.1 bar.1`, and `foo.1 bar.1` respectively. In the third they will have values `foo.1`, `foo.1 bar.1 foo.2 bar.2`, and `foo.1 bar.1 foo.2 bar.2 foo.1 foo.1 bar.1 foo.1 bar.1` respectively.

Rules undergo secondary expansion in makefile order, except that the rule with the recipe is always evaluated last.

The variables `$$?` and `$$*` are not available and expand to the empty string.

Secondary Expansion of Static Pattern Rules

Rules for secondary expansion of static pattern rules are identical to those for explicit rules, above, with one exception: for static pattern rules the `$$*` variable is set to the pattern stem. As with explicit rules, `$$?` is not available and expands to the empty string.

Secondary Expansion of Implicit Rules

As `make` searches for an implicit rule, it substitutes the stem and then performs secondary expansion for every rule with a matching target pattern. The value of the automatic variables is derived in the same fashion as for static pattern rules. As an example:

```
.SECONDEXPANSION:

foo: bar

foo foz: fo%: bo%

%oo: $$< $$^ $$+ $$*
```

When the implicit rule is tried for target `foo`, `$$<` expands to `bar`, `$$^` expands to `bar boo`, `$$+` also expands to `bar boo`, and `$$*` expands to `f`.

Note that the directory prefix (D), as described in Section 10.8 [Implicit Rule Search Algorithm], page 127, is appended (after expansion) to all the patterns in the prerequisites list. As an example:

```
.SECONDEXPANSION:

/tmp/foo.o:

%.o: $$(addsuffix /%.c,foo bar) foo.h
        @echo $^
```

The prerequisite list printed, after the secondary expansion and directory prefix reconstruction, will be `/tmp/foo/foo.c /tmp/bar/foo.c foo.h`. If you are not interested in this reconstruction, you can use `$$*` instead of `%` in the prerequisites list.

4 Writing Rules

A *rule* appears in the makefile and says when and how to remake certain files, called the rule's *targets* (most often only one per rule). It lists the other files that are the *prerequisites* of the target, and the *recipe* to use to create or update the target.

The order of rules is not significant, except for determining the *default goal*: the target for make to consider, if you do not otherwise specify one. The default goal is the target of the first rule in the first makefile. If the first rule has multiple targets, only the first target is taken as the default. There are two exceptions: a target starting with a period is not a default unless it contains one or more slashes, '/', as well; and, a target that defines a pattern rule has no effect on the default goal. (See Section 10.5 [Defining and Redefining Pattern Rules], page 118.)

Therefore, we usually write the makefile so that the first rule is the one for compiling the entire program or all the programs described by the makefile (often with a target called 'all'). See Section 9.2 [Arguments to Specify the Goals], page 99.

4.1 Rule Syntax

In general, a rule looks like this:

```
targets : prerequisites
        recipe
        . . .
```

or like this:

```
targets : prerequisites ; recipe
        recipe
        . . .
```

The *targets* are file names, separated by spaces. Wildcard characters may be used (see Section 4.3 [Using Wildcard Characters in File Names], page 23) and a name of the form a(m) represents member *m* in archive file *a* (see Section 11.1 [Archive Members as Targets], page 129). Usually there is only one target per rule, but occasionally there is a reason to have more (see Section 4.9 [Multiple Targets in a Rule], page 34).

The *recipe* lines start with a tab character (or the first character in the value of the .RECIPEPREFIX variable; see Section 6.14 [Special Variables], page 73). The first recipe line may appear on the line after the prerequisites, with a tab character, or may appear on the same line, with a semicolon. Either way, the effect is the same. There are other differences in the syntax of recipes. See Chapter 5 [Writing Recipes in Rules], page 41.

Because dollar signs are used to start make variable references, if you really want a dollar sign in a target or prerequisite you must write two of them, '$$' (see Chapter 6 [How to Use Variables], page 59). If you have enabled secondary expansion (see Section 3.8 [Secondary Expansion], page 18) and you want a literal dollar sign in the prerequisites list, you must actually write *four* dollar signs ('$$$$').

You may split a long line by inserting a backslash followed by a newline, but this is not required, as make places no limit on the length of a line in a makefile.

A rule tells make two things: when the targets are out of date, and how to update them when necessary.

The criterion for being out of date is specified in terms of the *prerequisites*, which consist of file names separated by spaces. (Wildcards and archive members (see Chapter 11 [Archives], page 129) are allowed here too.) A target is out of date if it does not exist or if it is older than any of the prerequisites (by comparison of last-modification times). The idea is that the contents of the target file are computed based on information in the prerequisites, so if any of the prerequisites changes, the contents of the existing target file are no longer necessarily valid.

How to update is specified by a *recipe*. This is one or more lines to be executed by the shell (normally 'sh'), but with some extra features (see Chapter 5 [Writing Recipes in Rules], page 41).

4.2 Types of Prerequisites

There are actually two different types of prerequisites understood by GNU `make`: normal prerequisites such as described in the previous section, and *order-only* prerequisites. A normal prerequisite makes two statements: first, it imposes an order in which recipes will be invoked: the recipes for all prerequisites of a target will be completed before the recipe for the target is run. Second, it imposes a dependency relationship: if any prerequisite is newer than the target, then the target is considered out-of-date and must be rebuilt.

Normally, this is exactly what you want: if a target's prerequisite is updated, then the target should also be updated.

Occasionally, however, you have a situation where you want to impose a specific ordering on the rules to be invoked *without* forcing the target to be updated if one of those rules is executed. In that case, you want to define *order-only* prerequisites. Order-only prerequisites can be specified by placing a pipe symbol (|) in the prerequisites list: any prerequisites to the left of the pipe symbol are normal; any prerequisites to the right are order-only:

```
targets : normal-prerequisites | order-only-prerequisites
```

The normal prerequisites section may of course be empty. Also, you may still declare multiple lines of prerequisites for the same target: they are appended appropriately (normal prerequisites are appended to the list of normal prerequisites; order-only prerequisites are appended to the list of order-only prerequisites). Note that if you declare the same file to be both a normal and an order-only prerequisite, the normal prerequisite takes precedence (since they have a strict superset of the behavior of an order-only prerequisite).

Consider an example where your targets are to be placed in a separate directory, and that directory might not exist before `make` is run. In this situation, you want the directory to be created before any targets are placed into it but, because the timestamps on directories change whenever a file is added, removed, or renamed, we certainly don't want to rebuild all the targets whenever the directory's timestamp changes. One way to manage this is with order-only prerequisites: make the directory an order-only prerequisite on all the targets:

```
OBJDIR := objdir
OBJS := $(addprefix $(OBJDIR)/,foo.o bar.o baz.o)

$(OBJDIR)/%.o : %.c
        $(COMPILE.c) $(OUTPUT_OPTION) $<

all: $(OBJS)
```

```
$(OBJS): | $(OBJDIR)

$(OBJDIR):
        mkdir $(OBJDIR)
```

Now the rule to create the `objdir` directory will be run, if needed, before any '`.o`' is built, but no '`.o`' will be built because the `objdir` directory timestamp changed.

4.3 Using Wildcard Characters in File Names

A single file name can specify many files using *wildcard characters*. The wildcard characters in `make` are '`*`', '`?`' and '`[...]`', the same as in the Bourne shell. For example, `*.c` specifies a list of all the files (in the working directory) whose names end in '`.c`'.

The character '`~`' at the beginning of a file name also has special significance. If alone, or followed by a slash, it represents your home directory. For example `~/bin` expands to `/home/you/bin`. If the '`~`' is followed by a word, the string represents the home directory of the user named by that word. For example `~john/bin` expands to `/home/john/bin`. On systems which don't have a home directory for each user (such as MS-DOS or MS-Windows), this functionality can be simulated by setting the environment variable *HOME*.

Wildcard expansion is performed by `make` automatically in targets and in prerequisites. In recipes, the shell is responsible for wildcard expansion. In other contexts, wildcard expansion happens only if you request it explicitly with the `wildcard` function.

The special significance of a wildcard character can be turned off by preceding it with a backslash. Thus, `foo\*bar` would refer to a specific file whose name consists of '`foo`', an asterisk, and '`bar`'.

4.3.1 Wildcard Examples

Wildcards can be used in the recipe of a rule, where they are expanded by the shell. For example, here is a rule to delete all the object files:

```
clean:
        rm -f *.o
```

Wildcards are also useful in the prerequisites of a rule. With the following rule in the makefile, '`make print`' will print all the '`.c`' files that have changed since the last time you printed them:

```
print: *.c
        lpr -p $?
        touch print
```

This rule uses `print` as an empty target file; see Section 4.7 [Empty Target Files to Record Events], page 31. (The automatic variable '`$?`' is used to print only those files that have changed; see Section 10.5.3 [Automatic Variables], page 120.)

Wildcard expansion does not happen when you define a variable. Thus, if you write this:

```
objects = *.o
```

then the value of the variable `objects` is the actual string '`*.o`'. However, if you use the value of `objects` in a target or prerequisite, wildcard expansion will take place there. If you use the value of `objects` in a recipe, the shell may perform wildcard expansion when the recipe runs. To set `objects` to the expansion, instead use:

```
objects := $(wildcard *.o)
```

See Section 4.3.3 [Wildcard Function], page 24.

4.3.2 Pitfalls of Using Wildcards

Now here is an example of a naive way of using wildcard expansion, that does not do what you would intend. Suppose you would like to say that the executable file `foo` is made from all the object files in the directory, and you write this:

```
objects = *.o

foo : $(objects)
        cc -o foo $(CFLAGS) $(objects)
```

The value of `objects` is the actual string '`*.o`'. Wildcard expansion happens in the rule for `foo`, so that each *existing* '`.o`' file becomes a prerequisite of `foo` and will be recompiled if necessary.

But what if you delete all the '`.o`' files? When a wildcard matches no files, it is left as it is, so then `foo` will depend on the oddly-named file `*.o`. Since no such file is likely to exist, `make` will give you an error saying it cannot figure out how to make `*.o`. This is not what you want!

Actually it is possible to obtain the desired result with wildcard expansion, but you need more sophisticated techniques, including the `wildcard` function and string substitution. These are described in the following section.

Microsoft operating systems (MS-DOS and MS-Windows) use backslashes to separate directories in pathnames, like so:

```
c:\foo\bar\baz.c
```

This is equivalent to the Unix-style `c:/foo/bar/baz.c` (the `c:` part is the so-called drive letter). When `make` runs on these systems, it supports backslashes as well as the Unix-style forward slashes in pathnames. However, this support does *not* include the wildcard expansion, where backslash is a quote character. Therefore, you *must* use Unix-style slashes in these cases.

4.3.3 The Function `wildcard`

Wildcard expansion happens automatically in rules. But wildcard expansion does not normally take place when a variable is set, or inside the arguments of a function. If you want to do wildcard expansion in such places, you need to use the `wildcard` function, like this:

```
$(wildcard pattern...)
```

This string, used anywhere in a makefile, is replaced by a space-separated list of names of existing files that match one of the given file name patterns. If no existing file name matches a pattern, then that pattern is omitted from the output of the `wildcard` function. Note that this is different from how unmatched wildcards behave in rules, where they are used verbatim rather than ignored (see Section 4.3.2 [Wildcard Pitfall], page 24).

One use of the `wildcard` function is to get a list of all the C source files in a directory, like this:

```
$(wildcard *.c)
```

We can change the list of C source files into a list of object files by replacing the '.c' suffix with '.o' in the result, like this:

```
$(patsubst %.c,%.o,$(wildcard *.c))
```

(Here we have used another function, `patsubst`. See Section 8.2 [Functions for String Substitution and Analysis], page 84.)

Thus, a makefile to compile all C source files in the directory and then link them together could be written as follows:

```
objects := $(patsubst %.c,%.o,$(wildcard *.c))

foo : $(objects)
        cc -o foo $(objects)
```

(This takes advantage of the implicit rule for compiling C programs, so there is no need to write explicit rules for compiling the files. See Section 6.2 [The Two Flavors of Variables], page 60, for an explanation of ':=', which is a variant of '='.)

4.4 Searching Directories for Prerequisites

For large systems, it is often desirable to put sources in a separate directory from the binaries. The *directory search* features of make facilitate this by searching several directories automatically to find a prerequisite. When you redistribute the files among directories, you do not need to change the individual rules, just the search paths.

4.4.1 VPATH: Search Path for All Prerequisites

The value of the make variable VPATH specifies a list of directories that make should search. Most often, the directories are expected to contain prerequisite files that are not in the current directory; however, make uses VPATH as a search list for both prerequisites and targets of rules.

Thus, if a file that is listed as a target or prerequisite does not exist in the current directory, make searches the directories listed in VPATH for a file with that name. If a file is found in one of them, that file may become the prerequisite (see below). Rules may then specify the names of files in the prerequisite list as if they all existed in the current directory. See Section 4.4.4 [Writing Recipes with Directory Search], page 27.

In the VPATH variable, directory names are separated by colons or blanks. The order in which directories are listed is the order followed by make in its search. (On MS-DOS and MS-Windows, semi-colons are used as separators of directory names in VPATH, since the colon can be used in the pathname itself, after the drive letter.)

For example,

```
VPATH = src:../headers
```

specifies a path containing two directories, `src` and `../headers`, which make searches in that order.

With this value of VPATH, the following rule,

```
foo.o : foo.c
```

is interpreted as if it were written like this:

```
foo.o : src/foo.c
```

assuming the file `foo.c` does not exist in the current directory but is found in the directory `src`.

4.4.2 The vpath Directive

Similar to the `VPATH` variable, but more selective, is the `vpath` directive (note lower case), which allows you to specify a search path for a particular class of file names: those that match a particular pattern. Thus you can supply certain search directories for one class of file names and other directories (or none) for other file names.

There are three forms of the `vpath` directive:

vpath *pattern directories*

> Specify the search path *directories* for file names that match *pattern*.
>
> The search path, *directories*, is a list of directories to be searched, separated by colons (semi-colons on MS-DOS and MS-Windows) or blanks, just like the search path used in the `VPATH` variable.

vpath *pattern*

> Clear out the search path associated with *pattern*.

vpath

> Clear all search paths previously specified with `vpath` directives.

A `vpath` pattern is a string containing a '%' character. The string must match the file name of a prerequisite that is being searched for, the '%' character matching any sequence of zero or more characters (as in pattern rules; see Section 10.5 [Defining and Redefining Pattern Rules], page 118). For example, `%.h` matches files that end in `.h`. (If there is no '%', the pattern must match the prerequisite exactly, which is not useful very often.)

'%' characters in a `vpath` directive's pattern can be quoted with preceding backslashes ('\'). Backslashes that would otherwise quote '%' characters can be quoted with more backslashes. Backslashes that quote '%' characters or other backslashes are removed from the pattern before it is compared to file names. Backslashes that are not in danger of quoting '%' characters go unmolested.

When a prerequisite fails to exist in the current directory, if the *pattern* in a `vpath` directive matches the name of the prerequisite file, then the *directories* in that directive are searched just like (and before) the directories in the `VPATH` variable.

For example,

```
vpath %.h ../headers
```

tells `make` to look for any prerequisite whose name ends in `.h` in the directory `../headers` if the file is not found in the current directory.

If several `vpath` patterns match the prerequisite file's name, then `make` processes each matching `vpath` directive one by one, searching all the directories mentioned in each directive. `make` handles multiple `vpath` directives in the order in which they appear in the makefile; multiple directives with the same pattern are independent of each other.

Thus,

```
vpath %.c foo
vpath %   blish
vpath %.c bar
```

will look for a file ending in '.c' in foo, then blish, then bar, while

```
vpath %.c foo:bar
vpath %   blish
```

will look for a file ending in '.c' in foo, then bar, then blish.

4.4.3 How Directory Searches are Performed

When a prerequisite is found through directory search, regardless of type (general or selective), the pathname located may not be the one that make actually provides you in the prerequisite list. Sometimes the path discovered through directory search is thrown away.

The algorithm make uses to decide whether to keep or abandon a path found via directory search is as follows:

1. If a target file does not exist at the path specified in the makefile, directory search is performed.

2. If the directory search is successful, that path is kept and this file is tentatively stored as the target.

3. All prerequisites of this target are examined using this same method.

4. After processing the prerequisites, the target may or may not need to be rebuilt:

    a. If the target does *not* need to be rebuilt, the path to the file found during directory search is used for any prerequisite lists which contain this target. In short, if make doesn't need to rebuild the target then you use the path found via directory search.

    b. If the target *does* need to be rebuilt (is out-of-date), the pathname found during directory search is *thrown away*, and the target is rebuilt using the file name specified in the makefile. In short, if make must rebuild, then the target is rebuilt locally, not in the directory found via directory search.

This algorithm may seem complex, but in practice it is quite often exactly what you want.

Other versions of make use a simpler algorithm: if the file does not exist, and it is found via directory search, then that pathname is always used whether or not the target needs to be built. Thus, if the target is rebuilt it is created at the pathname discovered during directory search.

If, in fact, this is the behavior you want for some or all of your directories, you can use the GPATH variable to indicate this to make.

GPATH has the same syntax and format as VPATH (that is, a space- or colon-delimited list of pathnames). If an out-of-date target is found by directory search in a directory that also appears in GPATH, then that pathname is not thrown away. The target is rebuilt using the expanded path.

4.4.4 Writing Recipes with Directory Search

When a prerequisite is found in another directory through directory search, this cannot change the recipe of the rule; they will execute as written. Therefore, you must write the recipe with care so that it will look for the prerequisite in the directory where make finds it.

This is done with the *automatic variables* such as '$^' (see Section 10.5.3 [Automatic Variables], page 120). For instance, the value of '$^' is a list of all the prerequisites of the rule, including the names of the directories in which they were found, and the value of '$@' is the target. Thus:

```
foo.o : foo.c
        cc -c $(CFLAGS) $^ -o $@
```

(The variable CFLAGS exists so you can specify flags for C compilation by implicit rules; we use it here for consistency so it will affect all C compilations uniformly; see Section 10.3 [Variables Used by Implicit Rules], page 115.)

Often the prerequisites include header files as well, which you do not want to mention in the recipe. The automatic variable '$<' is just the first prerequisite:

```
VPATH = src:../headers
foo.o : foo.c defs.h hack.h
        cc -c $(CFLAGS) $< -o $@
```

4.4.5 Directory Search and Implicit Rules

The search through the directories specified in VPATH or with vpath also happens during consideration of implicit rules (see Chapter 10 [Using Implicit Rules], page 111).

For example, when a file foo.o has no explicit rule, make considers implicit rules, such as the built-in rule to compile foo.c if that file exists. If such a file is lacking in the current directory, the appropriate directories are searched for it. If foo.c exists (or is mentioned in the makefile) in any of the directories, the implicit rule for C compilation is applied.

The recipes of implicit rules normally use automatic variables as a matter of necessity; consequently they will use the file names found by directory search with no extra effort.

4.4.6 Directory Search for Link Libraries

Directory search applies in a special way to libraries used with the linker. This special feature comes into play when you write a prerequisite whose name is of the form '-lname'. (You can tell something strange is going on here because the prerequisite is normally the name of a file, and the *file name* of a library generally looks like libname.a, not like '-lname'.)

When a prerequisite's name has the form '-lname', make handles it specially by searching for the file libname.so, and, if it is not found, for the file libname.a in the current directory, in directories specified by matching vpath search paths and the VPATH search path, and then in the directories /lib, /usr/lib, and *prefix*/lib (normally /usr/local/lib, but MS-DOS/MS-Windows versions of make behave as if *prefix* is defined to be the root of the DJGPP installation tree).

For example, if there is a /usr/lib/libcurses.a library on your system (and no /usr/lib/libcurses.so file), then

```
foo : foo.c -lcurses
        cc $^ -o $@
```

would cause the command 'cc foo.c /usr/lib/libcurses.a -o foo' to be executed when foo is older than foo.c or than /usr/lib/libcurses.a.

Although the default set of files to be searched for is libname.so and libname.a, this is customizable via the .LIBPATTERNS variable. Each word in the value of this variable is a pattern string. When a prerequisite like '-l*name*' is seen, make will replace the percent in each pattern in the list with *name* and perform the above directory searches using each library file name.

The default value for .LIBPATTERNS is 'lib%.so lib%.a', which provides the default behavior described above.

You can turn off link library expansion completely by setting this variable to an empty value.

4.5 Phony Targets

A phony target is one that is not really the name of a file; rather it is just a name for a recipe to be executed when you make an explicit request. There are two reasons to use a phony target: to avoid a conflict with a file of the same name, and to improve performance.

If you write a rule whose recipe will not create the target file, the recipe will be executed every time the target comes up for remaking. Here is an example:

```
clean:
        rm *.o temp
```

Because the rm command does not create a file named clean, probably no such file will ever exist. Therefore, the rm command will be executed every time you say 'make clean'.

In this example, the clean target will not work properly if a file named clean is ever created in this directory. Since it has no prerequisites, clean would always be considered up to date and its recipe would not be executed. To avoid this problem you can explicitly declare the target to be phony by making it a prerequisite of the special target .PHONY (see Section 4.8 [Special Built-in Target Names], page 32) as follows:

```
.PHONY: clean
clean:
        rm *.o temp
```

Once this is done, 'make clean' will run the recipe regardless of whether there is a file named clean.

Phony targets are also useful in conjunction with recursive invocations of make (see Section 5.7 [Recursive Use of make], page 50). In this situation the makefile will often contain a variable which lists a number of sub-directories to be built. A simplistic way to handle this is to define one rule with a recipe that loops over the sub-directories, like this:

```
SUBDIRS = foo bar baz

subdirs:
        for dir in $(SUBDIRS); do \
          $(MAKE) -C $$dir; \
        done
```

There are problems with this method, however. First, any error detected in a sub-make is ignored by this rule, so it will continue to build the rest of the directories even when one fails. This can be overcome by adding shell commands to note the error and exit, but then it will do so even if make is invoked with the -k option, which is unfortunate. Second, and perhaps more importantly, you cannot take advantage of make's ability to build targets in parallel (see Section 5.4 [Parallel Execution], page 47), since there is only one rule.

By declaring the sub-directories as .PHONY targets (you must do this as the sub-directory obviously always exists; otherwise it won't be built) you can remove these problems:

```
SUBDIRS = foo bar baz

.PHONY: subdirs $(SUBDIRS)

subdirs: $(SUBDIRS)

$(SUBDIRS):
        $(MAKE) -C $@

foo: baz
```

Here we've also declared that the foo sub-directory cannot be built until after the baz sub-directory is complete; this kind of relationship declaration is particularly important when attempting parallel builds.

The implicit rule search (see Chapter 10 [Implicit Rules], page 111) is skipped for .PHONY targets. This is why declaring a target as .PHONY is good for performance, even if you are not worried about the actual file existing.

A phony target should not be a prerequisite of a real target file; if it is, its recipe will be run every time make goes to update that file. As long as a phony target is never a prerequisite of a real target, the phony target recipe will be executed only when the phony target is a specified goal (see Section 9.2 [Arguments to Specify the Goals], page 99).

Phony targets can have prerequisites. When one directory contains multiple programs, it is most convenient to describe all of the programs in one makefile ./Makefile. Since the target remade by default will be the first one in the makefile, it is common to make this a phony target named 'all' and give it, as prerequisites, all the individual programs. For example:

```
all : prog1 prog2 prog3
.PHONY : all

prog1 : prog1.o utils.o
        cc -o prog1 prog1.o utils.o

prog2 : prog2.o
        cc -o prog2 prog2.o

prog3 : prog3.o sort.o utils.o
        cc -o prog3 prog3.o sort.o utils.o
```

Now you can say just 'make' to remake all three programs, or specify as arguments the ones to remake (as in 'make prog1 prog3'). Phoniness is not inherited: the prerequisites of a phony target are not themselves phony, unless explicitly declared to be so.

When one phony target is a prerequisite of another, it serves as a subroutine of the other. For example, here 'make cleanall' will delete the object files, the difference files, and the file program:

```
.PHONY: cleanall cleanobj cleandiff
```

```
cleanall : cleanobj cleandiff
        rm program

cleanobj :
        rm *.o

cleandiff :
        rm *.diff
```

4.6 Rules without Recipes or Prerequisites

If a rule has no prerequisites or recipe, and the target of the rule is a nonexistent file, then `make` imagines this target to have been updated whenever its rule is run. This implies that all targets depending on this one will always have their recipe run.

An example will illustrate this:

```
clean: FORCE
        rm $(objects)
FORCE:
```

Here the target 'FORCE' satisfies the special conditions, so the target `clean` that depends on it is forced to run its recipe. There is nothing special about the name 'FORCE', but that is one name commonly used this way.

As you can see, using 'FORCE' this way has the same results as using '.PHONY: clean'.

Using '.PHONY' is more explicit and more efficient. However, other versions of `make` do not support '.PHONY'; thus 'FORCE' appears in many makefiles. See Section 4.5 [Phony Targets], page 29.

4.7 Empty Target Files to Record Events

The *empty target* is a variant of the phony target; it is used to hold recipes for an action that you request explicitly from time to time. Unlike a phony target, this target file can really exist; but the file's contents do not matter, and usually are empty.

The purpose of the empty target file is to record, with its last-modification time, when the rule's recipe was last executed. It does so because one of the commands in the recipe is a `touch` command to update the target file.

The empty target file should have some prerequisites (otherwise it doesn't make sense). When you ask to remake the empty target, the recipe is executed if any prerequisite is more recent than the target; in other words, if a prerequisite has changed since the last time you remade the target. Here is an example:

```
print: foo.c bar.c
        lpr -p $?
        touch print
```

With this rule, 'make print' will execute the `lpr` command if either source file has changed since the last 'make print'. The automatic variable '$?' is used to print only those files that have changed (see Section 10.5.3 [Automatic Variables], page 120).

4.8 Special Built-in Target Names

Certain names have special meanings if they appear as targets.

.PHONY

>   The prerequisites of the special target .PHONY are considered to be phony targets. When it is time to consider such a target, make will run its recipe unconditionally, regardless of whether a file with that name exists or what its last-modification time is. See Section 4.5 [Phony Targets], page 29.

.SUFFIXES

>   The prerequisites of the special target .SUFFIXES are the list of suffixes to be used in checking for suffix rules. See Section 10.7 [Old-Fashioned Suffix Rules], page 125.

.DEFAULT

>   The recipe specified for .DEFAULT is used for any target for which no rules are found (either explicit rules or implicit rules). See Section 10.6 [Last Resort], page 125. If a .DEFAULT recipe is specified, every file mentioned as a prerequisite, but not as a target in a rule, will have that recipe executed on its behalf. See Section 10.8 [Implicit Rule Search Algorithm], page 127.

.PRECIOUS

>   The targets which .PRECIOUS depends on are given the following special treatment: if make is killed or interrupted during the execution of their recipes, the target is not deleted. See Section 5.6 [Interrupting or Killing make], page 50. Also, if the target is an intermediate file, it will not be deleted after it is no longer needed, as is normally done. See Section 10.4 [Chains of Implicit Rules], page 117. In this latter respect it overlaps with the .SECONDARY special target.
>
>   You can also list the target pattern of an implicit rule (such as '%.o') as a prerequisite file of the special target .PRECIOUS to preserve intermediate files created by rules whose target patterns match that file's name.

.INTERMEDIATE

>   The targets which .INTERMEDIATE depends on are treated as intermediate files. See Section 10.4 [Chains of Implicit Rules], page 117. .INTERMEDIATE with no prerequisites has no effect.

.SECONDARY

>   The targets which .SECONDARY depends on are treated as intermediate files, except that they are never automatically deleted. See Section 10.4 [Chains of Implicit Rules], page 117.
>
>   .SECONDARY with no prerequisites causes all targets to be treated as secondary (i.e., no target is removed because it is considered intermediate).

.SECONDEXPANSION

>   If .SECONDEXPANSION is mentioned as a target anywhere in the makefile, then all prerequisite lists defined *after* it appears will be expanded a second time after all makefiles have been read in. See Section 3.8 [Secondary Expansion], page 18.

`.DELETE_ON_ERROR`

> If `.DELETE_ON_ERROR` is mentioned as a target anywhere in the makefile, then `make` will delete the target of a rule if it has changed and its recipe exits with a nonzero exit status, just as it does when it receives a signal. See Section 5.5 [Errors in Recipes], page 49.

`.IGNORE`

> If you specify prerequisites for `.IGNORE`, then `make` will ignore errors in execution of the recipe for those particular files. The recipe for `.IGNORE` (if any) is ignored.
>
> If mentioned as a target with no prerequisites, `.IGNORE` says to ignore errors in execution of recipes for all files. This usage of '`.IGNORE`' is supported only for historical compatibility. Since this affects every recipe in the makefile, it is not very useful; we recommend you use the more selective ways to ignore errors in specific recipes. See Section 5.5 [Errors in Recipes], page 49.

`.LOW_RESOLUTION_TIME`

> If you specify prerequisites for `.LOW_RESOLUTION_TIME`, `make` assumes that these files are created by commands that generate low resolution time stamps. The recipe for the `.LOW_RESOLUTION_TIME` target are ignored.
>
> The high resolution file time stamps of many modern file systems lessen the chance of `make` incorrectly concluding that a file is up to date. Unfortunately, some hosts do not provide a way to set a high resolution file time stamp, so commands like '`cp -p`' that explicitly set a file's time stamp must discard its sub-second part. If a file is created by such a command, you should list it as a prerequisite of `.LOW_RESOLUTION_TIME` so that `make` does not mistakenly conclude that the file is out of date. For example:
>
> ```
>         .LOW_RESOLUTION_TIME: dst
>         dst: src
>                   cp -p src dst
> ```
>
> Since '`cp -p`' discards the sub-second part of `src`'s time stamp, `dst` is typically slightly older than `src` even when it is up to date. The `.LOW_RESOLUTION_TIME` line causes `make` to consider `dst` to be up to date if its time stamp is at the start of the same second that `src`'s time stamp is in.
>
> Due to a limitation of the archive format, archive member time stamps are always low resolution. You need not list archive members as prerequisites of `.LOW_RESOLUTION_TIME`, as `make` does this automatically.

`.SILENT`

> If you specify prerequisites for `.SILENT`, then `make` will not print the recipe used to remake those particular files before executing them. The recipe for `.SILENT` is ignored.
>
> If mentioned as a target with no prerequisites, `.SILENT` says not to print any recipes before executing them. This usage of '`.SILENT`' is supported only for historical compatibility. We recommend you use the more selective ways to silence specific recipes. See Section 5.2 [Recipe Echoing], page 43. If you want to silence all recipes for a particular run of `make`, use the '`-s`' or '`--silent`' option (see Section 9.7 [Options Summary], page 104).

`.EXPORT_ALL_VARIABLES`

> Simply by being mentioned as a target, this tells `make` to export all variables to child processes by default. See Section 5.7.2 [Communicating Variables to a Sub-make], page 52.

`.NOTPARALLEL`

> If `.NOTPARALLEL` is mentioned as a target, then this invocation of `make` will be run serially, even if the '`-j`' option is given. Any recursively invoked `make` command will still run recipes in parallel (unless its makefile also contains this target). Any prerequisites on this target are ignored.

`.ONESHELL`

> If `.ONESHELL` is mentioned as a target, then when a target is built all lines of the recipe will be given to a single invocation of the shell rather than each line being invoked separately (see Section 5.3 [Recipe Execution], page 44).

`.POSIX`

> If `.POSIX` is mentioned as a target, then the makefile will be parsed and run in POSIX-conforming mode. This does *not* mean that only POSIX-conforming makefiles will be accepted: all advanced GNU `make` features are still available. Rather, this target causes `make` to behave as required by POSIX in those areas where `make`'s default behavior differs.
>
> In particular, if this target is mentioned then recipes will be invoked as if the shell had been passed the `-e` flag: the first failing command in a recipe will cause the recipe to fail immediately.

Any defined implicit rule suffix also counts as a special target if it appears as a target, and so does the concatenation of two suffixes, such as '`.c.o`'. These targets are suffix rules, an obsolete way of defining implicit rules (but a way still widely used). In principle, any target name could be special in this way if you break it in two and add both pieces to the suffix list. In practice, suffixes normally begin with '`.`', so these special target names also begin with '`.`'. See Section 10.7 [Old-Fashioned Suffix Rules], page 125.

4.9 Multiple Targets in a Rule

A rule with multiple targets is equivalent to writing many rules, each with one target, and all identical aside from that. The same recipe applies to all the targets, but its effect may vary because you can substitute the actual target name into the recipe using '`$@`'. The rule contributes the same prerequisites to all the targets also.

This is useful in two cases.

- You want just prerequisites, no recipe. For example:

  ```
  kbd.o command.o files.o: command.h
  ```

  gives an additional prerequisite to each of the three object files mentioned.

- Similar recipes work for all the targets. The recipes do not need to be absolutely identical, since the automatic variable '`$@`' can be used to substitute the particular target to be remade into the commands (see Section 10.5.3 [Automatic Variables], page 120). For example:

```
bigoutput littleoutput : text.g
        generate text.g -$(subst output,,$@) > $@
```

is equivalent to

```
bigoutput : text.g
        generate text.g -big > bigoutput
littleoutput : text.g
        generate text.g -little > littleoutput
```

Here we assume the hypothetical program `generate` makes two types of output, one if given '`-big`' and one if given '`-little`'. See Section 8.2 [Functions for String Substitution and Analysis], page 84, for an explanation of the `subst` function.

Suppose you would like to vary the prerequisites according to the target, much as the variable '`$@`' allows you to vary the recipe. You cannot do this with multiple targets in an ordinary rule, but you can do it with a *static pattern rule*. See Section 4.11 [Static Pattern Rules], page 36.

4.10 Multiple Rules for One Target

One file can be the target of several rules. All the prerequisites mentioned in all the rules are merged into one list of prerequisites for the target. If the target is older than any prerequisite from any rule, the recipe is executed.

There can only be one recipe to be executed for a file. If more than one rule gives a recipe for the same file, `make` uses the last one given and prints an error message. (As a special case, if the file's name begins with a dot, no error message is printed. This odd behavior is only for compatibility with other implementations of `make`... you should avoid using it). Occasionally it is useful to have the same target invoke multiple recipes which are defined in different parts of your makefile; you can use *double-colon rules* (see Section 4.12 [Double-Colon], page 38) for this.

An extra rule with just prerequisites can be used to give a few extra prerequisites to many files at once. For example, makefiles often have a variable, such as `objects`, containing a list of all the compiler output files in the system being made. An easy way to say that all of them must be recompiled if `config.h` changes is to write the following:

```
objects = foo.o bar.o
foo.o : defs.h
bar.o : defs.h test.h
$(objects) : config.h
```

This could be inserted or taken out without changing the rules that really specify how to make the object files, making it a convenient form to use if you wish to add the additional prerequisite intermittently.

Another wrinkle is that the additional prerequisites could be specified with a variable that you set with a command line argument to `make` (see Section 9.5 [Overriding Variables], page 103). For example,

```
extradeps=
$(objects) : $(extradeps)
```

means that the command '`make extradeps=foo.h`' will consider `foo.h` as a prerequisite of each object file, but plain '`make`' will not.

If none of the explicit rules for a target has a recipe, then `make` searches for an applicable implicit rule to find one see Chapter 10 [Using Implicit Rules], page 111).

4.11 Static Pattern Rules

Static pattern rules are rules which specify multiple targets and construct the prerequisite names for each target based on the target name. They are more general than ordinary rules with multiple targets because the targets do not have to have identical prerequisites. Their prerequisites must be *analogous*, but not necessarily *identical*.

4.11.1 Syntax of Static Pattern Rules

Here is the syntax of a static pattern rule:

```
targets ...: target-pattern: prereq-patterns ...
        recipe
        ...
```

The *targets* list specifies the targets that the rule applies to. The targets can contain wildcard characters, just like the targets of ordinary rules (see Section 4.3 [Using Wildcard Characters in File Names], page 23).

The *target-pattern* and *prereq-patterns* say how to compute the prerequisites of each target. Each target is matched against the *target-pattern* to extract a part of the target name, called the *stem*. This stem is substituted into each of the *prereq-patterns* to make the prerequisite names (one from each *prereq-pattern*).

Each pattern normally contains the character '%' just once. When the *target-pattern* matches a target, the '%' can match any part of the target name; this part is called the *stem*. The rest of the pattern must match exactly. For example, the target `foo.o` matches the pattern '%.o', with 'foo' as the stem. The targets `foo.c` and `foo.out` do not match that pattern.

The prerequisite names for each target are made by substituting the stem for the '%' in each prerequisite pattern. For example, if one prerequisite pattern is `%.c`, then substitution of the stem 'foo' gives the prerequisite name `foo.c`. It is legitimate to write a prerequisite pattern that does not contain '%'; then this prerequisite is the same for all targets.

'%' characters in pattern rules can be quoted with preceding backslashes ('\'). Backslashes that would otherwise quote '%' characters can be quoted with more backslashes. Backslashes that quote '%' characters or other backslashes are removed from the pattern before it is compared to file names or has a stem substituted into it. Backslashes that are not in danger of quoting '%' characters go unmolested. For example, the pattern `the\%weird\\%pattern\\` has 'the%weird\' preceding the operative '%' character, and 'pattern\\' following it. The final two backslashes are left alone because they cannot affect any '%' character.

Here is an example, which compiles each of `foo.o` and `bar.o` from the corresponding `.c` file:

```
objects = foo.o bar.o

all: $(objects)

$(objects): %.o: %.c
        $(CC) -c $(CFLAGS) $< -o $@
```

Here '$<' is the automatic variable that holds the name of the prerequisite and '$@' is the automatic variable that holds the name of the target; see Section 10.5.3 [Automatic Variables], page 120.

Each target specified must match the target pattern; a warning is issued for each target that does not. If you have a list of files, only some of which will match the pattern, you can use the **filter** function to remove non-matching file names (see Section 8.2 [Functions for String Substitution and Analysis], page 84):

```
files = foo.elc bar.o lose.o

$(filter %.o,$(files)): %.o: %.c
        $(CC) -c $(CFLAGS) $< -o $@
$(filter %.elc,$(files)): %.elc: %.el
        emacs -f batch-byte-compile $<
```

In this example the result of '$(filter %.o,$(files))' is bar.o lose.o, and the first static pattern rule causes each of these object files to be updated by compiling the corresponding C source file. The result of '$(filter %.elc,$(files))' is foo.elc, so that file is made from foo.el.

Another example shows how to use $* in static pattern rules:

```
bigoutput littleoutput : %output : text.g
        generate text.g -$* > $@
```

When the generate command is run, $* will expand to the stem, either 'big' or 'little'.

4.11.2 Static Pattern Rules versus Implicit Rules

A static pattern rule has much in common with an implicit rule defined as a pattern rule (see Section 10.5 [Defining and Redefining Pattern Rules], page 118). Both have a pattern for the target and patterns for constructing the names of prerequisites. The difference is in how **make** decides *when* the rule applies.

An implicit rule *can* apply to any target that matches its pattern, but it *does* apply only when the target has no recipe otherwise specified, and only when the prerequisites can be found. If more than one implicit rule appears applicable, only one applies; the choice depends on the order of rules.

By contrast, a static pattern rule applies to the precise list of targets that you specify in the rule. It cannot apply to any other target and it invariably does apply to each of the targets specified. If two conflicting rules apply, and both have recipes, that's an error.

The static pattern rule can be better than an implicit rule for these reasons:

- You may wish to override the usual implicit rule for a few files whose names cannot be categorized syntactically but can be given in an explicit list.

- If you cannot be sure of the precise contents of the directories you are using, you may not be sure which other irrelevant files might lead make to use the wrong implicit rule. The choice might depend on the order in which the implicit rule search is done. With static pattern rules, there is no uncertainty: each rule applies to precisely the targets specified.

4.12 Double-Colon Rules

Double-colon rules are explicit rules written with '::' instead of ':' after the target names. They are handled differently from ordinary rules when the same target appears in more than one rule. Pattern rules with double-colons have an entirely different meaning (see Section 10.5.5 [Match-Anything Rules], page 123).

When a target appears in multiple rules, all the rules must be the same type: all ordinary, or all double-colon. If they are double-colon, each of them is independent of the others. Each double-colon rule's recipe is executed if the target is older than any prerequisites of that rule. If there are no prerequisites for that rule, its recipe is always executed (even if the target already exists). This can result in executing none, any, or all of the double-colon rules.

Double-colon rules with the same target are in fact completely separate from one another. Each double-colon rule is processed individually, just as rules with different targets are processed.

The double-colon rules for a target are executed in the order they appear in the makefile. However, the cases where double-colon rules really make sense are those where the order of executing the recipes would not matter.

Double-colon rules are somewhat obscure and not often very useful; they provide a mechanism for cases in which the method used to update a target differs depending on which prerequisite files caused the update, and such cases are rare.

Each double-colon rule should specify a recipe; if it does not, an implicit rule will be used if one applies. See Chapter 10 [Using Implicit Rules], page 111.

4.13 Generating Prerequisites Automatically

In the makefile for a program, many of the rules you need to write often say only that some object file depends on some header file. For example, if main.c uses defs.h via an #include, you would write:

```
main.o: defs.h
```

You need this rule so that make knows that it must remake main.o whenever defs.h changes. You can see that for a large program you would have to write dozens of such rules in your makefile. And, you must always be very careful to update the makefile every time you add or remove an #include.

To avoid this hassle, most modern C compilers can write these rules for you, by looking at the #include lines in the source files. Usually this is done with the '-M' option to the compiler. For example, the command:

```
cc -M main.c
```

generates the output:

```
main.o : main.c defs.h
```

Thus you no longer have to write all those rules yourself. The compiler will do it for you.

Note that such a rule constitutes mentioning `main.o` in a makefile, so it can never be considered an intermediate file by implicit rule search. This means that `make` won't ever remove the file after using it; see Section 10.4 [Chains of Implicit Rules], page 117.

With old `make` programs, it was traditional practice to use this compiler feature to generate prerequisites on demand with a command like 'make depend'. That command would create a file `depend` containing all the automatically-generated prerequisites; then the makefile could use `include` to read them in (see Section 3.3 [Include], page 13).

In GNU `make`, the feature of remaking makefiles makes this practice obsolete—you need never tell `make` explicitly to regenerate the prerequisites, because it always regenerates any makefile that is out of date. See Section 3.5 [Remaking Makefiles], page 14.

The practice we recommend for automatic prerequisite generation is to have one makefile corresponding to each source file. For each source file *name*`.c` there is a makefile *name*`.d` which lists what files the object file *name*`.o` depends on. That way only the source files that have changed need to be rescanned to produce the new prerequisites.

Here is the pattern rule to generate a file of prerequisites (i.e., a makefile) called *name*`.d` from a C source file called *name*`.c`:

```
%.d: %.c
        @set -e; rm -f $@; \
        $(CC) -M $(CPPFLAGS) $< > $@.$$$$; \
        sed 's,\($*\)\.o[ :]*,\1.o $@ : ,g' < $@.$$$$ > $@; \
        rm -f $@.$$$$
```

See Section 10.5 [Pattern Rules], page 118, for information on defining pattern rules. The '-e' flag to the shell causes it to exit immediately if the $(CC) command (or any other command) fails (exits with a nonzero status).

With the GNU C compiler, you may wish to use the '-MM' flag instead of '-M'. This omits prerequisites on system header files. See Section "Options Controlling the Preprocessor" in *Using GNU CC*, for details.

The purpose of the `sed` command is to translate (for example):

```
main.o : main.c defs.h
```

into:

```
main.o main.d : main.c defs.h
```

This makes each '.d' file depend on all the source and header files that the corresponding '.o' file depends on. `make` then knows it must regenerate the prerequisites whenever any of the source or header files changes.

Once you've defined the rule to remake the '.d' files, you then use the `include` directive to read them all in. See Section 3.3 [Include], page 13. For example:

```
sources = foo.c bar.c


include $(sources:.c=.d)
```

(This example uses a substitution variable reference to translate the list of source files 'foo.c bar.c' into a list of prerequisite makefiles, 'foo.d bar.d'. See Section 6.3.1 [Substitution Refs], page 62, for full information on substitution references.) Since the '.d' files are makefiles like any others, `make` will remake them as necessary with no further work from you. See Section 3.5 [Remaking Makefiles], page 14.

Note that the '.d' files contain target definitions; you should be sure to place the `include` directive *after* the first, default goal in your makefiles or run the risk of having a random object file become the default goal. See Section 2.3 [How Make Works], page 5.

5 Writing Recipes in Rules

The recipe of a rule consists of one or more shell command lines to be executed, one at a time, in the order they appear. Typically, the result of executing these commands is that the target of the rule is brought up to date.

Users use many different shell programs, but recipes in makefiles are always interpreted by `/bin/sh` unless the makefile specifies otherwise. See Section 5.3 [Recipe Execution], page 44.

5.1 Recipe Syntax

Makefiles have the unusual property that there are really two distinct syntaxes in one file. Most of the makefile uses **make** syntax (see Chapter 3 [Writing Makefiles], page 11). However, recipes are meant to be interpreted by the shell and so they are written using shell syntax. The **make** program does not try to understand shell syntax: it performs only a very few specific translations on the content of the recipe before handing it to the shell.

Each line in the recipe must start with a tab (or the first character in the value of the `.RECIPEPREFIX` variable; see Section 6.14 [Special Variables], page 73), except that the first recipe line may be attached to the target-and-prerequisites line with a semicolon in between. *Any* line in the makefile that begins with a tab and appears in a "rule context" (that is, after a rule has been started until another rule or variable definition) will be considered part of a recipe for that rule. Blank lines and lines of just comments may appear among the recipe lines; they are ignored.

Some consequences of these rules include:

- A blank line that begins with a tab is not blank: it's an empty recipe (see Section 5.9 [Empty Recipes], page 57).

- A comment in a recipe is not a **make** comment; it will be passed to the shell as-is. Whether the shell treats it as a comment or not depends on your shell.

- A variable definition in a "rule context" which is indented by a tab as the first character on the line, will be considered part of a recipe, not a **make** variable definition, and passed to the shell.

- A conditional expression (`ifdef`, `ifeq`, etc. see Section 7.2 [Syntax of Conditionals], page 78) in a "rule context" which is indented by a tab as the first character on the line, will be considered part of a recipe and be passed to the shell.

5.1.1 Splitting Recipe Lines

One of the few ways in which **make** does interpret recipes is checking for a backslash just before the newline. As in normal makefile syntax, a single logical recipe line can be split into multiple physical lines in the makefile by placing a backslash before each newline. A sequence of lines like this is considered a single recipe line, and one instance of the shell will be invoked to run it.

However, in contrast to how they are treated in other places in a makefile (see Section 3.1.1 [Splitting Long Lines], page 12), backslash/newline pairs are *not* removed from the recipe. Both the backslash and the newline characters are preserved and passed to the shell. How the backslash/newline is interpreted depends on your shell. If the first character of the next line after the backslash/newline is the recipe prefix character (a tab by default; see Section 6.14 [Special Variables], page 73), then that character (and only that character) is removed. Whitespace is never added to the recipe.

For example, the recipe for the all target in this makefile:

```
all :
        @echo no\
space
        @echo no\
        space
        @echo one \
        space
        @echo one\
         space
```

consists of four separate shell commands where the output is:

```
nospace
nospace
one space
one space
```

As a more complex example, this makefile:

```
all : ; @echo 'hello \
        world' ; echo "hello \
    world"
```

will invoke one shell with a command of:

```
echo 'hello \
world' ; echo "hello \
    world"
```

which, according to shell quoting rules, will yield the following output:

```
hello \
world
hello    world
```

Notice how the backslash/newline pair was removed inside the string quoted with double quotes ("..."), but not from the string quoted with single quotes ('...'). This is the way the default shell (/bin/sh) handles backslash/newline pairs. If you specify a different shell in your makefiles it may treat them differently.

Sometimes you want to split a long line inside of single quotes, but you don't want the backslash/newline to appear in the quoted content. This is often the case when passing scripts to languages such as Perl, where extraneous backslashes inside the script can change its meaning or even be a syntax error. One simple way of handling this is to place the quoted string, or even the entire command, into a make variable then use the variable in the recipe. In this situation the newline quoting rules for makefiles will be used, and the backslash/newline will be removed. If we rewrite our example above using this method:

```
HELLO = 'hello \
world'

all : ; @echo $(HELLO)
```

we will get output like this:

```
hello world
```

If you like, you can also use target-specific variables (see Section 6.11 [Target-specific Variable Values], page 71) to obtain a tighter correspondence between the variable and the recipe that uses it.

5.1.2 Using Variables in Recipes

The other way in which **make** processes recipes is by expanding any variable references in them (see Section 6.1 [Reference], page 59). This occurs after make has finished reading all the makefiles and the target is determined to be out of date; so, the recipes for targets which are not rebuilt are never expanded.

Variable and function references in recipes have identical syntax and semantics to references elsewhere in the makefile. They also have the same quoting rules: if you want a dollar sign to appear in your recipe, you must double it ('$$'). For shells like the default shell, that use dollar signs to introduce variables, it's important to keep clear in your mind whether the variable you want to reference is a **make** variable (use a single dollar sign) or a shell variable (use two dollar signs). For example:

```
LIST = one two three
all:
        for i in $(LIST); do \
            echo $$i; \
        done
```

results in the following command being passed to the shell:

```
for i in one two three; do \
    echo $i; \
done
```

which generates the expected result:

```
one
two
three
```

5.2 Recipe Echoing

Normally **make** prints each line of the recipe before it is executed. We call this *echoing* because it gives the appearance that you are typing the lines yourself.

When a line starts with '@', the echoing of that line is suppressed. The '@' is discarded before the line is passed to the shell. Typically you would use this for a command whose only effect is to print something, such as an **echo** command to indicate progress through the makefile:

```
@echo About to make distribution files
```

When **make** is given the flag '-n' or '--just-print' it only echoes most recipes, without executing them. See Section 9.7 [Summary of Options], page 104. In this case even the recipe lines starting with '@' are printed. This flag is useful for finding out which recipes **make** thinks are necessary without actually doing them.

The '-s' or '--silent' flag to make prevents all echoing, as if all recipes started with
'@'. A rule in the makefile for the special target .SILENT without prerequisites has the same
effect (see Section 4.8 [Special Built-in Target Names], page 32). .SILENT is essentially
obsolete since '@' is more flexible.

5.3 Recipe Execution

When it is time to execute recipes to update a target, they are executed by invoking a new
sub-shell for each line of the recipe, unless the .ONESHELL special target is in effect (see
Section 5.3.1 [Using One Shell], page 44) (In practice, make may take shortcuts that do not
affect the results.)

Please note: this implies that setting shell variables and invoking shell commands such
as cd that set a context local to each process will not affect the following lines in the recipe.[1]
If you want to use cd to affect the next statement, put both statements in a single recipe
line. Then make will invoke one shell to run the entire line, and the shell will execute the
statements in sequence. For example:

```
foo : bar/lose
        cd $(@D) && gobble $(@F) > ../$@
```

Here we use the shell AND operator (&&) so that if the cd command fails, the script will fail
without trying to invoke the gobble command in the wrong directory, which could cause
problems (in this case it would certainly cause ../foo to be truncated, at least).

5.3.1 Using One Shell

Sometimes you would prefer that all the lines in the recipe be passed to a single invocation
of the shell. There are generally two situations where this is useful: first, it can improve
performance in makefiles where recipes consist of many command lines, by avoiding extra
processes. Second, you might want newlines to be included in your recipe command (for
example perhaps you are using a very different interpreter as your SHELL). If the .ONESHELL
special target appears anywhere in the makefile then *all* recipe lines for each target will be
provided to a single invocation of the shell. Newlines between recipe lines will be preserved.
For example:

```
.ONESHELL:
foo : bar/lose
        cd $(@D)
        gobble $(@F) > ../$@
```

would now work as expected even though the commands are on different recipe lines.

If .ONESHELL is provided, then only the first line of the recipe will be checked for the
special prefix characters ('@', '-', and '+'). Subsequent lines will include the special characters in the recipe line when the SHELL is invoked. If you want your recipe to start with
one of these special characters you'll need to arrange for them to not be the first characters
on the first line, perhaps by adding a comment or similar. For example, this would be a
syntax error in Perl because the first '@' is removed by make:

---

[1] On MS-DOS, the value of current working directory is **global**, so changing it *will* affect the following
recipe lines on those systems.

```
.ONESHELL:
SHELL = /usr/bin/perl
.SHELLFLAGS = -e
show :
        @f = qw(a b c);
        print "@f\n";
```

However, either of these alternatives would work properly:

```
.ONESHELL:
SHELL = /usr/bin/perl
.SHELLFLAGS = -e
show :
        # Make sure "@" is not the first character on the first line
        @f = qw(a b c);
        print "@f\n";
```

or

```
.ONESHELL:
SHELL = /usr/bin/perl
.SHELLFLAGS = -e
show :
        my @f = qw(a b c);
        print "@f\n";
```

As a special feature, if SHELL is determined to be a POSIX-style shell, the special prefix characters in "internal" recipe lines will *removed* before the recipe is processed. This feature is intended to allow existing makefiles to add the .ONESHELL special target and still run properly without extensive modifications. Since the special prefix characters are not legal at the beginning of a line in a POSIX shell script this is not a loss in functionality. For example, this works as expected:

```
.ONESHELL:
foo : bar/lose
        @cd $(@D)
        @gobble $(@F) > ../$@
```

Even with this special feature, however, makefiles with .ONESHELL will behave differently in ways that could be noticeable. For example, normally if any line in the recipe fails, that causes the rule to fail and no more recipe lines are processed. Under .ONESHELL a failure of any but the final recipe line will not be noticed by make. You can modify .SHELLFLAGS to add the -e option to the shell which will cause any failure anywhere in the command line to cause the shell to fail, but this could itself cause your recipe to behave differently. Ultimately you may need to harden your recipe lines to allow them to work with .ONESHELL.

5.3.2 Choosing the Shell

The program used as the shell is taken from the variable SHELL. If this variable is not set in your makefile, the program /bin/sh is used as the shell. The argument(s) passed to the shell are taken from the variable .SHELLFLAGS. The default value of .SHELLFLAGS is -c normally, or -ec in POSIX-conforming mode.

Unlike most variables, the variable SHELL is never set from the environment. This is because the SHELL environment variable is used to specify your personal choice of shell program for interactive use. It would be very bad for personal choices like this to affect the functioning of makefiles. See Section 6.10 [Variables from the Environment], page 70.

Furthermore, when you do set SHELL in your makefile that value is *not* exported in the environment to recipe lines that make invokes. Instead, the value inherited from the user's environment, if any, is exported. You can override this behavior by explicitly exporting SHELL (see Section 5.7.2 [Communicating Variables to a Sub-make], page 52), forcing it to be passed in the environment to recipe lines.

However, on MS-DOS and MS-Windows the value of SHELL in the environment **is** used, since on those systems most users do not set this variable, and therefore it is most likely set specifically to be used by make. On MS-DOS, if the setting of SHELL is not suitable for make, you can set the variable MAKESHELL to the shell that make should use; if set it will be used as the shell instead of the value of SHELL.

Choosing a Shell in DOS and Windows

Choosing a shell in MS-DOS and MS-Windows is much more complex than on other systems.

On MS-DOS, if SHELL is not set, the value of the variable COMSPEC (which is always set) is used instead.

The processing of lines that set the variable SHELL in Makefiles is different on MS-DOS. The stock shell, command.com, is ridiculously limited in its functionality and many users of make tend to install a replacement shell. Therefore, on MS-DOS, make examines the value of SHELL, and changes its behavior based on whether it points to a Unix-style or DOS-style shell. This allows reasonable functionality even if SHELL points to command.com.

If SHELL points to a Unix-style shell, make on MS-DOS additionally checks whether that shell can indeed be found; if not, it ignores the line that sets SHELL. In MS-DOS, GNU make searches for the shell in the following places:

1. In the precise place pointed to by the value of SHELL. For example, if the makefile specifies 'SHELL = /bin/sh', make will look in the directory /bin on the current drive.

2. In the current directory.

3. In each of the directories in the PATH variable, in order.

In every directory it examines, make will first look for the specific file (sh in the example above). If this is not found, it will also look in that directory for that file with one of the known extensions which identify executable files. For example .exe, .com, .bat, .btm, .sh, and some others.

If any of these attempts is successful, the value of SHELL will be set to the full pathname of the shell as found. However, if none of these is found, the value of SHELL will not be changed, and thus the line that sets it will be effectively ignored. This is so make will only support features specific to a Unix-style shell if such a shell is actually installed on the system where make runs.

Note that this extended search for the shell is limited to the cases where SHELL is set from the Makefile; if it is set in the environment or command line, you are expected to set it to the full pathname of the shell, exactly as things are on Unix.

The effect of the above DOS-specific processing is that a Makefile that contains 'SHELL = /bin/sh' (as many Unix makefiles do), will work on MS-DOS unaltered if you have e.g. sh.exe installed in some directory along your PATH.

5.4 Parallel Execution

GNU make knows how to execute several recipes at once. Normally, make will execute only one recipe at a time, waiting for it to finish before executing the next. However, the '-j' or '--jobs' option tells make to execute many recipes simultaneously. You can inhibit parallelism in a particular makefile with the .NOTPARALLEL pseudo-target (see Section 4.8 [Special Targets], page 32).

On MS-DOS, the '-j' option has no effect, since that system doesn't support multi-processing.

If the '-j' option is followed by an integer, this is the number of recipes to execute at once; this is called the number of *job slots*. If there is nothing looking like an integer after the '-j' option, there is no limit on the number of job slots. The default number of job slots is one, which means serial execution (one thing at a time).

Handling recursive make invocations raises issues for parallel execution. For more information on this, see Section 5.7.3 [Communicating Options to a Sub-make], page 54.

If a recipe fails (is killed by a signal or exits with a nonzero status), and errors are not ignored for that recipe (see Section 5.5 [Errors in Recipes], page 49), the remaining recipe lines to remake the same target will not be run. If a recipe fails and the '-k' or '--keep-going' option was not given (see Section 9.7 [Summary of Options], page 104), make aborts execution. If make terminates for any reason (including a signal) with child processes running, it waits for them to finish before actually exiting.

When the system is heavily loaded, you will probably want to run fewer jobs than when it is lightly loaded. You can use the '-l' option to tell make to limit the number of jobs to run at once, based on the load average. The '-l' or '--max-load' option is followed by a floating-point number. For example,

```
-l 2.5
```

will not let make start more than one job if the load average is above 2.5. The '-l' option with no following number removes the load limit, if one was given with a previous '-l' option.

More precisely, when make goes to start up a job, and it already has at least one job running, it checks the current load average; if it is not lower than the limit given with '-l', make waits until the load average goes below that limit, or until all the other jobs finish.

By default, there is no load limit.

5.4.1 Output During Parallel Execution

When running several recipes in parallel the output from each recipe appears as soon as it is generated, with the result that messages from different recipes may be interspersed, sometimes even appearing on the same line. This can make reading the output very difficult.

To avoid this you can use the '--output-sync' ('-O') option. This option instructs make to save the output from the commands it invokes and print it all once the commands are completed. Additionally, if there are multiple recursive make invocations running in parallel, they will communicate so that only one of them is generating output at a time.

If working directory printing is enabled (see Section 5.7.4 [The '--print-directory' Option], page 55), the enter/leave messages are printed around each output grouping. If you prefer not to see these messages add the '--no-print-directory' option to MAKEFLAGS.

There are four levels of granularity when synchronizing output, specified by giving an argument to the option (e.g., '-Oline' or '--output-sync=recurse').

none   This is the default: all output is sent directly as it is generated and no synchronization is performed.

line   Output from each individual line of the recipe is grouped and printed as soon as that line is complete. If a recipe consists of multiple lines, they may be interspersed with lines from other recipes.

target   Output from the entire recipe for each target is grouped and printed once the target is complete. This is the default if the --output-sync or -O option is given with no argument.

recurse   Output from each recursive invocation of make is grouped and printed once the recursive invocation is complete.

Regardless of the mode chosen, the total build time will be the same. The only difference is in how the output appears.

The 'target' and 'recurse' modes both collect the output of the entire recipe of a target and display it uninterrupted when the recipe completes. The difference between them is in how recipes that contain recursive invocations of make are treated (see Section 5.7 [Recursive Use of make], page 50). For all recipes which have no recursive lines, the 'target' and 'recurse' modes behave identically.

If the 'recurse' mode is chosen, recipes that contain recursive make invocations are treated the same as other targets: the output from the recipe, including the output from the recursive make, is saved and printed after the entire recipe is complete. This ensures output from all the targets built by a given recursive make instance are grouped together, which may make the output easier to understand. However it also leads to long periods of time during the build where no output is seen, followed by large bursts of output. If you are not watching the build as it proceeds, but instead viewing a log of the build after the fact, this may be the best option for you.

If you are watching the output, the long gaps of quiet during the build can be frustrating. The 'target' output synchronization mode detects when make is going to be invoked recursively, using the standard methods, and it will not synchronize the output of those lines. The recursive make will perform the synchronization for its targets and the output from each will be displayed immediately when it completes. Be aware that output from recursive lines of the recipe are not synchronized (for example if the recursive line prints a message before running make, that message will not be synchronized).

The 'line' mode can be useful for front-ends that are watching the output of make to track when recipes are started and completed.

Some programs invoked by make may behave differently if they determine they're writing output to a terminal versus a file (often described as "interactive" vs. "non-interactive" modes). For example, many programs that can display colorized output will not do so if they determine they are not writing to a terminal. If your makefile invokes a program like this then using the output synchronization options will cause the program to believe it's running in "non-interactive" mode even though the output will ultimately go to the terminal.

5.4.2 Input During Parallel Execution

Two processes cannot both take input from the same device at the same time. To make sure that only one recipe tries to take input from the terminal at once, `make` will invalidate the standard input streams of all but one running recipe. If another recipe attempts to read from standard input it will usually incur a fatal error (a 'Broken pipe' signal).

It is unpredictable which recipe will have a valid standard input stream (which will come from the terminal, or wherever you redirect the standard input of `make`). The first recipe run will always get it first, and the first recipe started after that one finishes will get it next, and so on.

We will change how this aspect of `make` works if we find a better alternative. In the mean time, you should not rely on any recipe using standard input at all if you are using the parallel execution feature; but if you are not using this feature, then standard input works normally in all recipes.

5.5 Errors in Recipes

After each shell invocation returns, `make` looks at its exit status. If the shell completed successfully (the exit status is zero), the next line in the recipe is executed in a new shell; after the last line is finished, the rule is finished.

If there is an error (the exit status is nonzero), `make` gives up on the current rule, and perhaps on all rules.

Sometimes the failure of a certain recipe line does not indicate a problem. For example, you may use the `mkdir` command to ensure that a directory exists. If the directory already exists, `mkdir` will report an error, but you probably want `make` to continue regardless.

To ignore errors in a recipe line, write a '-' at the beginning of the line's text (after the initial tab). The '-' is discarded before the line is passed to the shell for execution.

For example,

```
clean:
        -rm -f *.o
```

This causes `make` to continue even if `rm` is unable to remove a file.

When you run `make` with the '-i' or '--ignore-errors' flag, errors are ignored in all recipes of all rules. A rule in the makefile for the special target .IGNORE has the same effect, if there are no prerequisites. These ways of ignoring errors are obsolete because '-' is more flexible.

When errors are to be ignored, because of either a '-' or the '-i' flag, `make` treats an error return just like success, except that it prints out a message that tells you the status code the shell exited with, and says that the error has been ignored.

When an error happens that `make` has not been told to ignore, it implies that the current target cannot be correctly remade, and neither can any other that depends on it either directly or indirectly. No further recipes will be executed for these targets, since their preconditions have not been achieved.

Normally make gives up immediately in this circumstance, returning a nonzero status. However, if the '-k' or '--keep-going' flag is specified, make continues to consider the other prerequisites of the pending targets, remaking them if necessary, before it gives up and returns nonzero status. For example, after an error in compiling one object file, 'make -k' will continue compiling other object files even though it already knows that linking them will be impossible. See Section 9.7 [Summary of Options], page 104.

The usual behavior assumes that your purpose is to get the specified targets up to date; once make learns that this is impossible, it might as well report the failure immediately. The '-k' option says that the real purpose is to test as many of the changes made in the program as possible, perhaps to find several independent problems so that you can correct them all before the next attempt to compile. This is why Emacs' compile command passes the '-k' flag by default.

Usually when a recipe line fails, if it has changed the target file at all, the file is corrupted and cannot be used—or at least it is not completely updated. Yet the file's time stamp says that it is now up to date, so the next time make runs, it will not try to update that file. The situation is just the same as when the shell is killed by a signal; see Section 5.6 [Interrupts], page 50. So generally the right thing to do is to delete the target file if the recipe fails after beginning to change the file. make will do this if .DELETE_ON_ERROR appears as a target. This is almost always what you want make to do, but it is not historical practice; so for compatibility, you must explicitly request it.

5.6 Interrupting or Killing make

If make gets a fatal signal while a shell is executing, it may delete the target file that the recipe was supposed to update. This is done if the target file's last-modification time has changed since make first checked it.

The purpose of deleting the target is to make sure that it is remade from scratch when make is next run. Why is this? Suppose you type *Ctrl-c* while a compiler is running, and it has begun to write an object file foo.o. The *Ctrl-c* kills the compiler, resulting in an incomplete file whose last-modification time is newer than the source file foo.c. But make also receives the *Ctrl-c* signal and deletes this incomplete file. If make did not do this, the next invocation of make would think that foo.o did not require updating—resulting in a strange error message from the linker when it tries to link an object file half of which is missing.

You can prevent the deletion of a target file in this way by making the special target .PRECIOUS depend on it. Before remaking a target, make checks to see whether it appears on the prerequisites of .PRECIOUS, and thereby decides whether the target should be deleted if a signal happens. Some reasons why you might do this are that the target is updated in some atomic fashion, or exists only to record a modification-time (its contents do not matter), or must exist at all times to prevent other sorts of trouble.

5.7 Recursive Use of make

Recursive use of make means using make as a command in a makefile. This technique is useful when you want separate makefiles for various subsystems that compose a larger system. For example, suppose you have a sub-directory `subdir` which has its own makefile, and you would like the containing directory's makefile to run `make` on the sub-directory. You can do it by writing this:

```
subsystem:
        cd subdir && $(MAKE)
```

or, equivalently, this (see Section 9.7 [Summary of Options], page 104):

```
subsystem:
        $(MAKE) -C subdir
```

You can write recursive `make` commands just by copying this example, but there are many things to know about how they work and why, and about how the sub-`make` relates to the top-level `make`. You may also find it useful to declare targets that invoke recursive `make` commands as '`.PHONY`' (for more discussion on when this is useful, see Section 4.5 [Phony Targets], page 29).

For your convenience, when GNU `make` starts (after it has processed any `-C` options) it sets the variable `CURDIR` to the pathname of the current working directory. This value is never touched by `make` again: in particular note that if you include files from other directories the value of `CURDIR` does not change. The value has the same precedence it would have if it were set in the makefile (by default, an environment variable `CURDIR` will not override this value). Note that setting this variable has no impact on the operation of `make` (it does not cause `make` to change its working directory, for example).

5.7.1 How the `MAKE` Variable Works

Recursive `make` commands should always use the variable `MAKE`, not the explicit command name '`make`', as shown here:

```
subsystem:
        cd subdir && $(MAKE)
```

The value of this variable is the file name with which `make` was invoked. If this file name was `/bin/make`, then the recipe executed is '`cd subdir && /bin/make`'. If you use a special version of `make` to run the top-level makefile, the same special version will be executed for recursive invocations.

As a special feature, using the variable `MAKE` in the recipe of a rule alters the effects of the '`-t`' ('`--touch`'), '`-n`' ('`--just-print`'), or '`-q`' ('`--question`') option. Using the `MAKE` variable has the same effect as using a '`+`' character at the beginning of the recipe line. See Section 9.3 [Instead of Executing the Recipes], page 101. This special feature is only enabled if the `MAKE` variable appears directly in the recipe: it does not apply if the `MAKE` variable is referenced through expansion of another variable. In the latter case you must use the '`+`' token to get these special effects.

Consider the command '`make -t`' in the above example. (The '`-t`' option marks targets as up to date without actually running any recipes; see Section 9.3 [Instead of Execution], page 101.) Following the usual definition of '`-t`', a '`make -t`' command in the example would create a file named `subsystem` and do nothing else. What you really want it to do is run '`cd subdir && make -t`'; but that would require executing the recipe, and '`-t`' says not to execute recipes.

The special feature makes this do what you want: whenever a recipe line of a rule contains the variable `MAKE`, the flags '`-t`', '`-n`' and '`-q`' do not apply to that line. Recipe lines containing `MAKE` are executed normally despite the presence of a flag that causes most recipes not to be run. The usual `MAKEFLAGS` mechanism passes the flags to the sub-make (see Section 5.7.3 [Communicating Options to a Sub-make], page 54), so your request to touch the files, or print the recipes, is propagated to the subsystem.

5.7.2 Communicating Variables to a Sub-make

Variable values of the top-level `make` can be passed to the sub-`make` through the environment by explicit request. These variables are defined in the sub-`make` as defaults, but they do not override variables defined in the makefile used by the sub-`make` unless you use the '`-e`' switch (see Section 9.7 [Summary of Options], page 104).

To pass down, or *export*, a variable, `make` adds the variable and its value to the environment for running each line of the recipe. The sub-`make`, in turn, uses the environment to initialize its table of variable values. See Section 6.10 [Variables from the Environment], page 70.

Except by explicit request, `make` exports a variable only if it is either defined in the environment initially or set on the command line, and if its name consists only of letters, numbers, and underscores. Some shells cannot cope with environment variable names consisting of characters other than letters, numbers, and underscores.

The value of the `make` variable `SHELL` is not exported. Instead, the value of the `SHELL` variable from the invoking environment is passed to the sub-`make`. You can force `make` to export its value for `SHELL` by using the `export` directive, described below. See Section 5.3.2 [Choosing the Shell], page 45.

The special variable `MAKEFLAGS` is always exported (unless you unexport it). `MAKEFILES` is exported if you set it to anything.

`make` automatically passes down variable values that were defined on the command line, by putting them in the `MAKEFLAGS` variable. See the next section.

Variables are *not* normally passed down if they were created by default by `make` (see Section 10.3 [Variables Used by Implicit Rules], page 115). The sub-`make` will define these for itself.

If you want to export specific variables to a sub-`make`, use the `export` directive, like this:

```
export variable ...
```

If you want to *prevent* a variable from being exported, use the `unexport` directive, like this:

```
unexport variable ...
```

In both of these forms, the arguments to `export` and `unexport` are expanded, and so could be variables or functions which expand to a (list of) variable names to be (un)exported.

As a convenience, you can define a variable and export it at the same time by doing:

```
export variable = value
```

has the same result as:

```
variable = value
export variable
```

and

```
export variable := value
```

has the same result as:

```
variable := value
export variable
```

Likewise,

```
export variable += value
```

is just like:

```
variable += value
export variable
```

See Section 6.6 [Appending More Text to Variables], page 66.

You may notice that the `export` and `unexport` directives work in `make` in the same way they work in the shell, `sh`.

If you want all variables to be exported by default, you can use `export` by itself:

```
export
```

This tells `make` that variables which are not explicitly mentioned in an `export` or `unexport` directive should be exported. Any variable given in an `unexport` directive will still *not* be exported. If you use `export` by itself to export variables by default, variables whose names contain characters other than alphanumerics and underscores will not be exported unless specifically mentioned in an `export` directive.

The behavior elicited by an `export` directive by itself was the default in older versions of GNU `make`. If your makefiles depend on this behavior and you want to be compatible with old versions of `make`, you can write a rule for the special target `.EXPORT_ALL_VARIABLES` instead of using the `export` directive. This will be ignored by old `makes`, while the `export` directive will cause a syntax error.

Likewise, you can use `unexport` by itself to tell `make` *not* to export variables by default. Since this is the default behavior, you would only need to do this if `export` had been used by itself earlier (in an included makefile, perhaps). You **cannot** use `export` and `unexport` by themselves to have variables exported for some recipes and not for others. The last `export` or `unexport` directive that appears by itself determines the behavior for the entire run of `make`.

As a special feature, the variable `MAKELEVEL` is changed when it is passed down from level to level. This variable's value is a string which is the depth of the level as a decimal number. The value is '0' for the top-level `make`; '1' for a sub-`make`, '2' for a sub-sub-`make`, and so on. The incrementation happens when `make` sets up the environment for a recipe.

The main use of `MAKELEVEL` is to test it in a conditional directive (see Chapter 7 [Conditional Parts of Makefiles], page 77); this way you can write a makefile that behaves one way if run recursively and another way if run directly by you.

You can use the variable `MAKEFILES` to cause all sub-`make` commands to use additional makefiles. The value of `MAKEFILES` is a whitespace-separated list of file names. This variable, if defined in the outer-level makefile, is passed down through the environment; then it serves as a list of extra makefiles for the sub-`make` to read before the usual or specified ones. See Section 3.4 [The Variable `MAKEFILES`], page 14.

5.7.3 Communicating Options to a Sub-make

Flags such as '-s' and '-k' are passed automatically to the sub-make through the variable MAKEFLAGS. This variable is set up automatically by make to contain the flag letters that make received. Thus, if you do 'make -ks' then MAKEFLAGS gets the value 'ks'.

As a consequence, every sub-make gets a value for MAKEFLAGS in its environment. In response, it takes the flags from that value and processes them as if they had been given as arguments. See Section 9.7 [Summary of Options], page 104.

Likewise variables defined on the command line are passed to the sub-make through MAKEFLAGS. Words in the value of MAKEFLAGS that contain '=', make treats as variable definitions just as if they appeared on the command line. See Section 9.5 [Overriding Variables], page 103.

The options '-C', '-f', '-o', and '-W' are not put into MAKEFLAGS; these options are not passed down.

The '-j' option is a special case (see Section 5.4 [Parallel Execution], page 47). If you set it to some numeric value 'N' and your operating system supports it (most any UNIX system will; others typically won't), the parent make and all the sub-makes will communicate to ensure that there are only 'N' jobs running at the same time between them all. Note that any job that is marked recursive (see Section 9.3 [Instead of Executing Recipes], page 101) doesn't count against the total jobs (otherwise we could get 'N' sub-makes running and have no slots left over for any real work!)

If your operating system doesn't support the above communication, then '-j 1' is always put into MAKEFLAGS instead of the value you specified. This is because if the '-j' option were passed down to sub-makes, you would get many more jobs running in parallel than you asked for. If you give '-j' with no numeric argument, meaning to run as many jobs as possible in parallel, this is passed down, since multiple infinities are no more than one.

If you do not want to pass the other flags down, you must change the value of MAKEFLAGS, like this:

```
subsystem:
        cd subdir && $(MAKE) MAKEFLAGS=
```

The command line variable definitions really appear in the variable MAKEOVERRIDES, and MAKEFLAGS contains a reference to this variable. If you do want to pass flags down normally, but don't want to pass down the command line variable definitions, you can reset MAKEOVERRIDES to empty, like this:

```
MAKEOVERRIDES =
```

This is not usually useful to do. However, some systems have a small fixed limit on the size of the environment, and putting so much information into the value of MAKEFLAGS can exceed it. If you see the error message 'Arg list too long', this may be the problem. (For strict compliance with POSIX.2, changing MAKEOVERRIDES does not affect MAKEFLAGS if the special target '.POSIX' appears in the makefile. You probably do not care about this.)

A similar variable MFLAGS exists also, for historical compatibility. It has the same value as MAKEFLAGS except that it does not contain the command line variable definitions, and it always begins with a hyphen unless it is empty (MAKEFLAGS begins with a hyphen only when it begins with an option that has no single-letter version, such as

'--warn-undefined-variables'). MFLAGS was traditionally used explicitly in the recursive make command, like this:

```
subsystem:
        cd subdir && $(MAKE) $(MFLAGS)
```

but now MAKEFLAGS makes this usage redundant. If you want your makefiles to be compatible with old make programs, use this technique; it will work fine with more modern make versions too.

The MAKEFLAGS variable can also be useful if you want to have certain options, such as '-k' (see Section 9.7 [Summary of Options], page 104), set each time you run make. You simply put a value for MAKEFLAGS in your environment. You can also set MAKEFLAGS in a makefile, to specify additional flags that should also be in effect for that makefile. (Note that you cannot use MFLAGS this way. That variable is set only for compatibility; make does not interpret a value you set for it in any way.)

When make interprets the value of MAKEFLAGS (either from the environment or from a makefile), it first prepends a hyphen if the value does not already begin with one. Then it chops the value into words separated by blanks, and parses these words as if they were options given on the command line (except that '-C', '-f', '-h', '-o', '-W', and their long-named versions are ignored; and there is no error for an invalid option).

If you do put MAKEFLAGS in your environment, you should be sure not to include any options that will drastically affect the actions of make and undermine the purpose of make-files and of make itself. For instance, the '-t', '-n', and '-q' options, if put in one of these variables, could have disastrous consequences and would certainly have at least surprising and probably annoying effects.

If you'd like to run other implementations of make in addition to GNU make, and hence do not want to add GNU make-specific flags to the MAKEFLAGS variable, you can add them to the GNUMAKEFLAGS variable instead. This variable is parsed just before MAKEFLAGS, in the same way as MAKEFLAGS. When make constructs MAKEFLAGS to pass to a recursive make it will include all flags, even those taken from GNUMAKEFLAGS. As a result, after parsing GNUMAKEFLAGS GNU make sets this variable to the empty string to avoid duplicating flags during recursion.

It's best to use GNUMAKEFLAGS only with flags which won't materially change the behavior of your makefiles. If your makefiles require GNU make anyway then simply use MAKEFLAGS. Flags such as '--no-print-directory' or '--output-sync' may be appropriate for GNUMAKEFLAGS.

5.7.4 The '--print-directory' Option

If you use several levels of recursive make invocations, the '-w' or '--print-directory' option can make the output a lot easier to understand by showing each directory as make starts processing it and as make finishes processing it. For example, if 'make -w' is run in the directory /u/gnu/make, make will print a line of the form:

```
make: Entering directory '/u/gnu/make'.
```

before doing anything else, and a line of the form:

```
make: Leaving directory '/u/gnu/make'.
```

when processing is completed.

Normally, you do not need to specify this option because 'make' does it for you: '-w' is turned on automatically when you use the '-C' option, and in sub-makes. make will not automatically turn on '-w' if you also use '-s', which says to be silent, or if you use '--no-print-directory' to explicitly disable it.

5.8 Defining Canned Recipes

When the same sequence of commands is useful in making various targets, you can define it as a canned sequence with the **define** directive, and refer to the canned sequence from the recipes for those targets. The canned sequence is actually a variable, so the name must not conflict with other variable names.

Here is an example of defining a canned recipe:

```
define run-yacc =
yacc $(firstword $^)
mv y.tab.c $@
endef
```

Here run-yacc is the name of the variable being defined; **endef** marks the end of the definition; the lines in between are the commands. The **define** directive does not expand variable references and function calls in the canned sequence; the '$' characters, parentheses, variable names, and so on, all become part of the value of the variable you are defining. See Section 6.8 [Defining Multi-Line Variables], page 69, for a complete explanation of **define**.

The first command in this example runs Yacc on the first prerequisite of whichever rule uses the canned sequence. The output file from Yacc is always named y.tab.c. The second command moves the output to the rule's target file name.

To use the canned sequence, substitute the variable into the recipe of a rule. You can substitute it like any other variable (see Section 6.1 [Basics of Variable References], page 59). Because variables defined by **define** are recursively expanded variables, all the variable references you wrote inside the **define** are expanded now. For example:

```
foo.c : foo.y
        $(run-yacc)
```

'foo.y' will be substituted for the variable '$^' when it occurs in run-yacc's value, and 'foo.c' for '$@'.

This is a realistic example, but this particular one is not needed in practice because make has an implicit rule to figure out these commands based on the file names involved (see Chapter 10 [Using Implicit Rules], page 111).

In recipe execution, each line of a canned sequence is treated just as if the line appeared on its own in the rule, preceded by a tab. In particular, make invokes a separate sub-shell for each line. You can use the special prefix characters that affect command lines ('@', '-', and '+') on each line of a canned sequence. See Chapter 5 [Writing Recipes in Rules], page 41. For example, using this canned sequence:

```
define frobnicate =
@echo "frobnicating target $@"
frob-step-1 $< -o $@-step-1
frob-step-2 $@-step-1 -o $@
endef
```

`make` will not echo the first line, the `echo` command. But it *will* echo the following two recipe lines.

On the other hand, prefix characters on the recipe line that refers to a canned sequence apply to every line in the sequence. So the rule:

```
frob.out: frob.in
        @$(frobnicate)
```

does not echo *any* recipe lines. (See Section 5.2 [Recipe Echoing], page 43, for a full explanation of '@'.)

5.9 Using Empty Recipes

It is sometimes useful to define recipes which do nothing. This is done simply by giving a recipe that consists of nothing but whitespace. For example:

```
target: ;
```

defines an empty recipe for `target`. You could also use a line beginning with a recipe prefix character to define an empty recipe, but this would be confusing because such a line looks empty.

You may be wondering why you would want to define a recipe that does nothing. The only reason this is useful is to prevent a target from getting implicit recipes (from implicit rules or the `.DEFAULT` special target; see Chapter 10 [Implicit Rules], page 111 and see Section 10.6 [Defining Last-Resort Default Rules], page 125).

You may be inclined to define empty recipes for targets that are not actual files, but only exist so that their prerequisites can be remade. However, this is not the best way to do that, because the prerequisites may not be remade properly if the target file actually does exist. See Section 4.5 [Phony Targets], page 29, for a better way to do this.

6 How to Use Variables

A *variable* is a name defined in a makefile to represent a string of text, called the variable's *value*. These values are substituted by explicit request into targets, prerequisites, recipes, and other parts of the makefile. (In some other versions of make, variables are called *macros*.)

Variables and functions in all parts of a makefile are expanded when read, except for in recipes, the right-hand sides of variable definitions using '=', and the bodies of variable definitions using the **define** directive.

Variables can represent lists of file names, options to pass to compilers, programs to run, directories to look in for source files, directories to write output in, or anything else you can imagine.

A variable name may be any sequence of characters not containing ':', '#', '=', or white-space. However, variable names containing characters other than letters, numbers, and underscores should be considered carefully, as in some shells they cannot be passed through the environment to a sub-**make** (see Section 5.7.2 [Communicating Variables to a Sub-make], page 52). Variable names beginning with '.' and an uppercase letter may be given special meaning in future versions of **make**.

Variable names are case-sensitive. The names 'foo', 'FOO', and 'Foo' all refer to different variables.

It is traditional to use upper case letters in variable names, but we recommend using lower case letters for variable names that serve internal purposes in the makefile, and reserving upper case for parameters that control implicit rules or for parameters that the user should override with command options (see Section 9.5 [Overriding Variables], page 103).

A few variables have names that are a single punctuation character or just a few characters. These are the *automatic variables*, and they have particular specialized uses. See Section 10.5.3 [Automatic Variables], page 120.

6.1 Basics of Variable References

To substitute a variable's value, write a dollar sign followed by the name of the variable in parentheses or braces: either '$(foo)' or '${foo}' is a valid reference to the variable foo. This special significance of '$' is why you must write '$$' to have the effect of a single dollar sign in a file name or recipe.

Variable references can be used in any context: targets, prerequisites, recipes, most directives, and new variable values. Here is an example of a common case, where a variable holds the names of all the object files in a program:

```
objects = program.o foo.o utils.o
program : $(objects)
        cc -o program $(objects)

$(objects) : defs.h
```

Variable references work by strict textual substitution. Thus, the rule

```
foo = c
prog.o : prog.$(foo)
        $(foo)$(foo) -$(foo) prog.$(foo)
```

could be used to compile a C program `prog.c`. Since spaces before the variable value are
ignored in variable assignments, the value of `foo` is precisely 'c'. (Don't actually write your
makefiles this way!)

A dollar sign followed by a character other than a dollar sign, open-parenthesis or open-
brace treats that single character as the variable name. Thus, you could reference the
variable x with '`$x`'. However, this practice is strongly discouraged, except in the case of
the automatic variables (see Section 10.5.3 [Automatic Variables], page 120).

6.2 The Two Flavors of Variables

There are two ways that a variable in GNU `make` can have a value; we call them the two
flavors of variables. The two flavors are distinguished in how they are defined and in what
they do when expanded.

The first flavor of variable is a *recursively expanded* variable. Variables of this sort are
defined by lines using '`=`' (see Section 6.5 [Setting Variables], page 65) or by the **define**
directive (see Section 6.8 [Defining Multi-Line Variables], page 69). The value you specify is
installed verbatim; if it contains references to other variables, these references are expanded
whenever this variable is substituted (in the course of expanding some other string). When
this happens, it is called *recursive expansion*.

For example,

```
foo = $(bar)
bar = $(ugh)
ugh = Huh?


all:;echo $(foo)
```

will echo 'Huh?': '`$(foo)`' expands to '`$(bar)`' which expands to '`$(ugh)`' which finally
expands to 'Huh?'.

This flavor of variable is the only sort supported by most other versions of `make`. It has
its advantages and its disadvantages. An advantage (most would say) is that:

```
CFLAGS = $(include_dirs) -O
include_dirs = -Ifoo -Ibar
```

will do what was intended: when '`CFLAGS`' is expanded in a recipe, it will expand to '`-Ifoo
-Ibar -O`'. A major disadvantage is that you cannot append something on the end of a
variable, as in

```
CFLAGS = $(CFLAGS) -O
```

because it will cause an infinite loop in the variable expansion. (Actually `make` detects the
infinite loop and reports an error.)

Another disadvantage is that any functions (see Chapter 8 [Functions for Transforming
Text], page 83) referenced in the definition will be executed every time the variable is
expanded. This makes `make` run slower; worse, it causes the `wildcard` and `shell` functions
to give unpredictable results because you cannot easily control when they are called, or
even how many times.

To avoid all the problems and inconveniences of recursively expanded variables, there is
another flavor: simply expanded variables.

Simply expanded variables are defined by lines using ':=' or '::=' (see Section 6.5 [Setting Variables], page 65). Both forms are equivalent in GNU make; however only the '::=' form is described by the POSIX standard (support for '::=' was added to the POSIX standard in 2012, so older versions of make won't accept this form either).

The value of a simply expanded variable is scanned once and for all, expanding any references to other variables and functions, when the variable is defined. The actual value of the simply expanded variable is the result of expanding the text that you write. It does not contain any references to other variables; it contains their values *as of the time this variable was defined*. Therefore,

```
x := foo
y := $(x) bar
x := later
```

is equivalent to

```
y := foo bar
x := later
```

When a simply expanded variable is referenced, its value is substituted verbatim.

Here is a somewhat more complicated example, illustrating the use of ':=' in conjunction with the shell function. (See Section 8.13 [The shell Function], page 97.) This example also shows use of the variable MAKELEVEL, which is changed when it is passed down from level to level. (See Section 5.7.2 [Communicating Variables to a Sub-make], page 52, for information about MAKELEVEL.)

```
ifeq (0,${MAKELEVEL})
whoami    := $(shell whoami)
host-type := $(shell arch)
MAKE := ${MAKE} host-type=${host-type} whoami=${whoami}
endif
```

An advantage of this use of ':=' is that a typical 'descend into a directory' recipe then looks like this:

```
${subdirs}:
        ${MAKE} -C $@ all
```

Simply expanded variables generally make complicated makefile programming more predictable because they work like variables in most programming languages. They allow you to redefine a variable using its own value (or its value processed in some way by one of the expansion functions) and to use the expansion functions much more efficiently (see Chapter 8 [Functions for Transforming Text], page 83).

You can also use them to introduce controlled leading whitespace into variable values. Leading whitespace characters are discarded from your input before substitution of variable references and function calls; this means you can include leading spaces in a variable value by protecting them with variable references, like this:

```
nullstring :=
space := $(nullstring) # end of the line
```

Here the value of the variable space is precisely one space. The comment '# end of the line' is included here just for clarity. Since trailing space characters are *not* stripped from variable values, just a space at the end of the line would have the same effect (but be rather hard to read). If you put whitespace at the end of a variable value, it is a good idea to put a comment like that at the end of the line to make your intent clear. Conversely, if you do *not* want any whitespace characters at the end of your variable value, you must remember not to put a random comment on the end of the line after some whitespace, such as this:

```
dir := /foo/bar    # directory to put the frobs in
```

Here the value of the variable `dir` is '`/foo/bar` ' (with four trailing spaces), which was probably not the intention. (Imagine something like '`$(dir)/file`' with this definition!)

There is another assignment operator for variables, '`?=`'. This is called a conditional variable assignment operator, because it only has an effect if the variable is not yet defined. This statement:

```
FOO ?= bar
```

is exactly equivalent to this (see Section 8.10 [The `origin` Function], page 94):

```
ifeq ($(origin FOO), undefined)
  FOO = bar
endif
```

Note that a variable set to an empty value is still defined, so '`?=`' will not set that variable.

6.3 Advanced Features for Reference to Variables

This section describes some advanced features you can use to reference variables in more flexible ways.

6.3.1 Substitution References

A *substitution reference* substitutes the value of a variable with alterations that you specify. It has the form '`$(var:a=b)`' (or '`${var:a=b}`') and its meaning is to take the value of the variable *var*, replace every *a* at the end of a word with *b* in that value, and substitute the resulting string.

When we say "at the end of a word", we mean that *a* must appear either followed by whitespace or at the end of the value in order to be replaced; other occurrences of *a* in the value are unaltered. For example:

```
foo := a.o b.o c.o
bar := $(foo:.o=.c)
```

sets '`bar`' to '`a.c b.c c.c`'. See Section 6.5 [Setting Variables], page 65.

A substitution reference is actually an abbreviation for use of the `patsubst` expansion function (see Section 8.2 [Functions for String Substitution and Analysis], page 84). We provide substitution references as well as `patsubst` for compatibility with other implementations of `make`.

Another type of substitution reference lets you use the full power of the `patsubst` function. It has the same form '`$(var:a=b)`' described above, except that now *a* must contain a single '`%`' character. This case is equivalent to '`$(patsubst a,b,$(var))`'. See Section 8.2 [Functions for String Substitution and Analysis], page 84, for a description of the `patsubst` function.

For example:

```
foo := a.o b.o c.o
bar := $(foo:%.o=%.c)
```

sets 'bar' to 'a.c b.c c.c'.

6.3.2 Computed Variable Names

Computed variable names are a complicated concept needed only for sophisticated makefile programming. For most purposes you need not consider them, except to know that making a variable with a dollar sign in its name might have strange results. However, if you are the type that wants to understand everything, or you are actually interested in what they do, read on.

Variables may be referenced inside the name of a variable. This is called a *computed variable name* or a *nested variable reference*. For example,

```
x = y
y = z
a := $($(x))
```

defines a as 'z': the '$(x)' inside '$($(x))' expands to 'y', so '$($(x))' expands to '$(y)' which in turn expands to 'z'. Here the name of the variable to reference is not stated explicitly; it is computed by expansion of '$(x)'. The reference '$(x)' here is nested within the outer variable reference.

The previous example shows two levels of nesting, but any number of levels is possible. For example, here are three levels:

```
x = y
y = z
z = u
a := $($($(x)))
```

Here the innermost '$(x)' expands to 'y', so '$($(x))' expands to '$(y)' which in turn expands to 'z'; now we have '$(z)', which becomes 'u'.

References to recursively-expanded variables within a variable name are re-expanded in the usual fashion. For example:

```
x = $(y)
y = z
z = Hello
a := $($(x))
```

defines a as 'Hello': '$($(x))' becomes '$($(y))' which becomes '$(z)' which becomes 'Hello'.

Nested variable references can also contain modified references and function invocations (see Chapter 8 [Functions for Transforming Text], page 83), just like any other reference. For example, using the **subst** function (see Section 8.2 [Functions for String Substitution and Analysis], page 84):

```
x = variable1
variable2 := Hello
y = $(subst 1,2,$(x))
z = y
a := $($($(z)))
```

eventually defines a as 'Hello'. It is doubtful that anyone would ever want to write a nested reference as convoluted as this one, but it works: '$($($(z)))' expands to '$($(y))' which becomes '$($(subst 1,2,$(x)))'. This gets the value 'variable1' from x and changes it by substitution to 'variable2', so that the entire string becomes '$(variable2)', a simple variable reference whose value is 'Hello'.

A computed variable name need not consist entirely of a single variable reference. It can contain several variable references, as well as some invariant text. For example,

```
a_dirs := dira dirb
1_dirs := dir1 dir2

a_files := filea fileb
1_files := file1 file2

ifeq "$(use_a)" "yes"
a1 := a
else
a1 := 1
endif

ifeq "$(use_dirs)" "yes"
df := dirs
else
df := files
endif

dirs := $($(a1)_$(df))
```

will give dirs the same value as a_dirs, 1_dirs, a_files or 1_files depending on the settings of use_a and use_dirs.

Computed variable names can also be used in substitution references:

```
a_objects := a.o b.o c.o
1_objects := 1.o 2.o 3.o

sources := $($(a1)_objects:.o=.c)
```

defines sources as either 'a.c b.c c.c' or '1.c 2.c 3.c', depending on the value of a1.

The only restriction on this sort of use of nested variable references is that they cannot specify part of the name of a function to be called. This is because the test for a recognized function name is done before the expansion of nested references. For example,

```
ifdef do_sort
func := sort
else
func := strip
endif

bar := a d b g q c

foo := $($(func) $(bar))
```

attempts to give 'foo' the value of the variable 'sort a d b g q c' or 'strip a d b g q c', rather than giving 'a d b g q c' as the argument to either the sort or the strip function. This restriction could be removed in the future if that change is shown to be a good idea.

You can also use computed variable names in the left-hand side of a variable assignment, or in a define directive, as in:

```
dir = foo
$(dir)_sources := $(wildcard $(dir)/*.c)
define $(dir)_print =
lpr $($(dir)_sources)
endef
```

This example defines the variables 'dir', 'foo_sources', and 'foo_print'.

Note that *nested variable references* are quite different from *recursively expanded variables* (see Section 6.2 [The Two Flavors of Variables], page 60), though both are used together in complex ways when doing makefile programming.

6.4 How Variables Get Their Values

Variables can get values in several different ways:

- You can specify an overriding value when you run make. See Section 9.5 [Overriding Variables], page 103.

- You can specify a value in the makefile, either with an assignment (see Section 6.5 [Setting Variables], page 65) or with a verbatim definition (see Section 6.8 [Defining Multi-Line Variables], page 69).

- Variables in the environment become make variables. See Section 6.10 [Variables from the Environment], page 70.

- Several *automatic* variables are given new values for each rule. Each of these has a single conventional use. See Section 10.5.3 [Automatic Variables], page 120.

- Several variables have constant initial values. See Section 10.3 [Variables Used by Implicit Rules], page 115.

6.5 Setting Variables

To set a variable from the makefile, write a line starting with the variable name followed by '=' ':=', or '::='. Whatever follows the '=', ':=', or '::=' on the line becomes the value. For example,

```
objects = main.o foo.o bar.o utils.o
```

defines a variable named `objects`. Whitespace around the variable name and immediately after the '=' is ignored.

Variables defined with '=' are *recursively expanded* variables. Variables defined with ':=' or '::=' are *simply expanded* variables; these definitions can contain variable references which will be expanded before the definition is made. See Section 6.2 [The Two Flavors of Variables], page 60.

The variable name may contain function and variable references, which are expanded when the line is read to find the actual variable name to use.

There is no limit on the length of the value of a variable except the amount of memory on the computer. You can split the value of a variable into multiple physical lines for readability (see Section 3.1.1 [Splitting Long Lines], page 12).

Most variable names are considered to have the empty string as a value if you have never set them. Several variables have built-in initial values that are not empty, but you can set them in the usual ways (see Section 10.3 [Variables Used by Implicit Rules], page 115). Several special variables are set automatically to a new value for each rule; these are called the *automatic* variables (see Section 10.5.3 [Automatic Variables], page 120).

If you'd like a variable to be set to a value only if it's not already set, then you can use the shorthand operator '?=' instead of '='. These two settings of the variable 'FOO' are identical (see Section 8.10 [The `origin` Function], page 94):

```
FOO ?= bar
```

and

```
ifeq ($(origin FOO), undefined)
FOO = bar
endif
```

The shell assignment operator '!=' can be used to execute a program and set a variable to its output. This operator first evaluates the right-hand side, then passes that result to the shell for execution. If the result of the execution ends in a newline, that one newline is removed; all other newlines are replaced by spaces. The resulting string is then placed into the named recursively-expanded variable. For example:

```
hash != printf '\043'
file_list != find . -name '*.c'
```

If the result of the execution could produce a `$`, and you don't intend what follows that to be interpreted as a make variable or function reference, then you must replace every `$` with `$$` as part of the execution. Alternatively, you can set a simply expanded variable to the result of running a program using the `shell` function call. See Section 8.13 [The `shell` Function], page 97. For example:

```
hash := $(shell printf '\043')
var := $(shell find . -name "*.c")
```

6.6 Appending More Text to Variables

Often it is useful to add more text to the value of a variable already defined. You do this with a line containing '+=', like this:

```
objects += another.o
```

This takes the value of the variable `objects`, and adds the text 'another.o' to it (preceded by a single space). Thus:

```
objects = main.o foo.o bar.o utils.o
objects += another.o
```

sets `objects` to 'main.o foo.o bar.o utils.o another.o'.

Using '+=' is similar to:

```
objects = main.o foo.o bar.o utils.o
objects := $(objects) another.o
```

but differs in ways that become important when you use more complex values.

When the variable in question has not been defined before, '+=' acts just like normal '=': it defines a recursively-expanded variable. However, when there *is* a previous definition, exactly what '+=' does depends on what flavor of variable you defined originally. See Section 6.2 [The Two Flavors of Variables], page 60, for an explanation of the two flavors of variables.

When you add to a variable's value with '+=', `make` acts essentially as if you had included the extra text in the initial definition of the variable. If you defined it first with ':=' or '::=', making it a simply-expanded variable, '+=' adds to that simply-expanded definition, and expands the new text before appending it to the old value just as ':=' does (see Section 6.5 [Setting Variables], page 65, for a full explanation of ':=' or '::='). In fact,

```
variable := value
variable += more
```

is exactly equivalent to:

```
variable := value
variable := $(variable) more
```

On the other hand, when you use '+=' with a variable that you defined first to be recursively-expanded using plain '=', `make` does something a bit different. Recall that when you define a recursively-expanded variable, `make` does not expand the value you set for variable and function references immediately. Instead it stores the text verbatim, and saves these variable and function references to be expanded later, when you refer to the new variable (see Section 6.2 [The Two Flavors of Variables], page 60). When you use '+=' on a recursively-expanded variable, it is this unexpanded text to which `make` appends the new text you specify.

```
variable = value
variable += more
```

is roughly equivalent to:

```
temp = value
variable = $(temp) more
```

except that of course it never defines a variable called `temp`. The importance of this comes when the variable's old value contains variable references. Take this common example:

```
CFLAGS = $(includes) -O
...
CFLAGS += -pg # enable profiling
```

The first line defines the **CFLAGS** variable with a reference to another variable, **includes**. (CFLAGS is used by the rules for C compilation; see Section 10.2 [Catalogue of Built-In Rules], page 112.) Using '=' for the definition makes **CFLAGS** a recursively-expanded variable, meaning '**$(includes) -O**' is *not* expanded when **make** processes the definition of **CFLAGS**. Thus, **includes** need not be defined yet for its value to take effect. It only has to be defined before any reference to **CFLAGS**. If we tried to append to the value of **CFLAGS** without using '+=', we might do it like this:

```
CFLAGS := $(CFLAGS) -pg # enable profiling
```

This is pretty close, but not quite what we want. Using ':=' redefines **CFLAGS** as a simply-expanded variable; this means **make** expands the text '**$(CFLAGS) -pg**' before setting the variable. If **includes** is not yet defined, we get ' **-O -pg**', and a later definition of **includes** will have no effect. Conversely, by using '+=' we set **CFLAGS** to the *unexpanded* value '**$(includes) -O -pg**'. Thus we preserve the reference to **includes**, so if that variable gets defined at any later point, a reference like '**$(CFLAGS)**' still uses its value.

6.7 The override Directive

If a variable has been set with a command argument (see Section 9.5 [Overriding Variables], page 103), then ordinary assignments in the makefile are ignored. If you want to set the variable in the makefile even though it was set with a command argument, you can use an **override** directive, which is a line that looks like this:

```
override variable = value
```

or

```
override variable := value
```

To append more text to a variable defined on the command line, use:

```
override variable += more text
```

See Section 6.6 [Appending More Text to Variables], page 66.

Variable assignments marked with the **override** flag have a higher priority than all other assignments, except another **override**. Subsequent assignments or appends to this variable which are not marked **override** will be ignored.

The **override** directive was not invented for escalation in the war between makefiles and command arguments. It was invented so you can alter and add to values that the user specifies with command arguments.

For example, suppose you always want the '-g' switch when you run the C compiler, but you would like to allow the user to specify the other switches with a command argument just as usual. You could use this **override** directive:

```
override CFLAGS += -g
```

You can also use **override** directives with **define** directives. This is done as you might expect:

```
override define foo =
bar
endef
```

See the next section for information about **define**.

6.8 Defining Multi-Line Variables

Another way to set the value of a variable is to use the `define` directive. This directive has an unusual syntax which allows newline characters to be included in the value, which is convenient for defining both canned sequences of commands (see Section 5.8 [Defining Canned Recipes], page 56), and also sections of makefile syntax to use with `eval` (see Section 8.9 [Eval Function], page 93).

The `define` directive is followed on the same line by the name of the variable being defined and an (optional) assignment operator, and nothing more. The value to give the variable appears on the following lines. The end of the value is marked by a line containing just the word `endef`. Aside from this difference in syntax, `define` works just like any other variable definition. The variable name may contain function and variable references, which are expanded when the directive is read to find the actual variable name to use.

You may omit the variable assignment operator if you prefer. If omitted, `make` assumes it to be '=' and creates a recursively-expanded variable (see Section 6.2 [The Two Flavors of Variables], page 60). When using a '+=' operator, the value is appended to the previous value as with any other append operation: with a single space separating the old and new values.

You may nest `define` directives: `make` will keep track of nested directives and report an error if they are not all properly closed with `endef`. Note that lines beginning with the recipe prefix character are considered part of a recipe, so any `define` or `endef` strings appearing on such a line will not be considered `make` directives.

```
define two-lines =
echo foo
echo $(bar)
endef
```

The value in an ordinary assignment cannot contain a newline; but the newlines that separate the lines of the value in a `define` become part of the variable's value (except for the final newline which precedes the `endef` and is not considered part of the value).

When used in a recipe, the previous example is functionally equivalent to this:

```
two-lines = echo foo; echo $(bar)
```

since two commands separated by semicolon behave much like two separate shell commands. However, note that using two separate lines means `make` will invoke the shell twice, running an independent sub-shell for each line. See Section 5.3 [Recipe Execution], page 44.

If you want variable definitions made with `define` to take precedence over command-line variable definitions, you can use the `override` directive together with `define`:

```
override define two-lines =
foo
$(bar)
endef
```

See Section 6.7 [The `override` Directive], page 68.

6.9 Undefining Variables

If you want to clear a variable, setting its value to empty is usually sufficient. Expanding such a variable will yield the same result (empty string) regardless of whether it was set or not. However, if you are using the `flavor` (see Section 8.11 [Flavor Function], page 95) and `origin` (see Section 8.10 [Origin Function], page 94) functions, there is a difference between a variable that was never set and a variable with an empty value. In such situations you may want to use the `undefine` directive to make a variable appear as if it was never set. For example:

```
foo := foo
bar = bar

undefine foo
undefine bar

$(info $(origin foo))
$(info $(flavor bar))
```

This example will print "undefined" for both variables.

If you want to undefine a command-line variable definition, you can use the `override` directive together with `undefine`, similar to how this is done for variable definitions:

```
override undefine CFLAGS
```

6.10 Variables from the Environment

Variables in `make` can come from the environment in which `make` is run. Every environment variable that `make` sees when it starts up is transformed into a `make` variable with the same name and value. However, an explicit assignment in the makefile, or with a command argument, overrides the environment. (If the '-e' flag is specified, then values from the environment override assignments in the makefile. See Section 9.7 [Summary of Options], page 104. But this is not recommended practice.)

Thus, by setting the variable `CFLAGS` in your environment, you can cause all C compilations in most makefiles to use the compiler switches you prefer. This is safe for variables with standard or conventional meanings because you know that no makefile will use them for other things. (Note this is not totally reliable; some makefiles set `CFLAGS` explicitly and therefore are not affected by the value in the environment.)

When `make` runs a recipe, variables defined in the makefile are placed into the environment of each shell. This allows you to pass values to sub-`make` invocations (see Section 5.7 [Recursive Use of `make`], page 50). By default, only variables that came from the environment or the command line are passed to recursive invocations. You can use the `export` directive to pass other variables. See Section 5.7.2 [Communicating Variables to a Submake], page 52, for full details.

Other use of variables from the environment is not recommended. It is not wise for makefiles to depend for their functioning on environment variables set up outside their control, since this would cause different users to get different results from the same makefile. This is against the whole purpose of most makefiles.

Such problems would be especially likely with the variable `SHELL`, which is normally present in the environment to specify the user's choice of interactive shell. It would be very undesirable for this choice to affect `make`; so, `make` handles the `SHELL` environment variable in a special way; see Section 5.3.2 [Choosing the Shell], page 45.

6.11 Target-specific Variable Values

Variable values in `make` are usually global; that is, they are the same regardless of where they are evaluated (unless they're reset, of course). One exception to that is automatic variables (see Section 10.5.3 [Automatic Variables], page 120).

The other exception is *target-specific variable values*. This feature allows you to define different values for the same variable, based on the target that `make` is currently building. As with automatic variables, these values are only available within the context of a target's recipe (and in other target-specific assignments).

Set a target-specific variable value like this:

```
target ... : variable-assignment
```

Target-specific variable assignments can be prefixed with any or all of the special keywords `export`, `override`, or `private`; these apply their normal behavior to this instance of the variable only.

Multiple *target* values create a target-specific variable value for each member of the target list individually.

The *variable-assignment* can be any valid form of assignment; recursive ('='), simple (':=' or '::='), appending ('+='), or conditional ('?='). All variables that appear within the *variable-assignment* are evaluated within the context of the target: thus, any previously-defined target-specific variable values will be in effect. Note that this variable is actually distinct from any "global" value: the two variables do not have to have the same flavor (recursive vs. simple).

Target-specific variables have the same priority as any other makefile variable. Variables provided on the command line (and in the environment if the '-e' option is in force) will take precedence. Specifying the `override` directive will allow the target-specific variable value to be preferred.

There is one more special feature of target-specific variables: when you define a target-specific variable that variable value is also in effect for all prerequisites of this target, and all their prerequisites, etc. (unless those prerequisites override that variable with their own target-specific variable value). So, for example, a statement like this:

```
prog : CFLAGS = -g
prog : prog.o foo.o bar.o
```

will set CFLAGS to '-g' in the recipe for `prog`, but it will also set CFLAGS to '-g' in the recipes that create `prog.o`, `foo.o`, and `bar.o`, and any recipes which create their prerequisites.

Be aware that a given prerequisite will only be built once per invocation of make, at most. If the same file is a prerequisite of multiple targets, and each of those targets has a different value for the same target-specific variable, then the first target to be built will cause that prerequisite to be built and the prerequisite will inherit the target-specific value from the first target. It will ignore the target-specific values from any other targets.

6.12 Pattern-specific Variable Values

In addition to target-specific variable values (see Section 6.11 [Target-specific Variable Values], page 71), GNU `make` supports pattern-specific variable values. In this form, the variable is defined for any target that matches the pattern specified.

Set a pattern-specific variable value like this:

```
pattern ... : variable-assignment
```

where *pattern* is a %-pattern. As with target-specific variable values, multiple *pattern* values create a pattern-specific variable value for each pattern individually. The *variable-assignment* can be any valid form of assignment. Any command line variable setting will take precedence, unless `override` is specified.

For example:

```
%.o : CFLAGS = -O
```

will assign `CFLAGS` the value of '-O' for all targets matching the pattern `%.o`.

If a target matches more than one pattern, the matching pattern-specific variables with longer stems are interpreted first. This results in more specific variables taking precedence over the more generic ones, for example:

```
%.o: %.c
        $(CC) -c $(CFLAGS) $(CPPFLAGS) $< -o $@

lib/%.o: CFLAGS := -fPIC -g
%.o: CFLAGS := -g

all: foo.o lib/bar.o
```

In this example the first definition of the `CFLAGS` variable will be used to update `lib/bar.o` even though the second one also applies to this target. Pattern-specific variables which result in the same stem length are considered in the order in which they were defined in the makefile.

Pattern-specific variables are searched after any target-specific variables defined explicitly for that target, and before target-specific variables defined for the parent target.

6.13 Suppressing Inheritance

As described in previous sections, `make` variables are inherited by prerequisites. This capability allows you to modify the behavior of a prerequisite based on which targets caused it to be rebuilt. For example, you might set a target-specific variable on a `debug` target, then running 'make debug' will cause that variable to be inherited by all prerequisites of `debug`, while just running 'make all' (for example) would not have that assignment.

Sometimes, however, you may not want a variable to be inherited. For these situations, `make` provides the `private` modifier. Although this modifier can be used with any variable assignment, it makes the most sense with target- and pattern-specific variables. Any variable marked `private` will be visible to its local target but will not be inherited by prerequisites of that target. A global variable marked `private` will be visible in the global scope but will not be inherited by any target, and hence will not be visible in any recipe.

As an example, consider this makefile:

```
EXTRA_CFLAGS =

prog: private EXTRA_CFLAGS = -L/usr/local/lib
prog: a.o b.o
```

Due to the `private` modifier, `a.o` and `b.o` will not inherit the `EXTRA_CFLAGS` variable assignment from the `prog` target.

6.14 Other Special Variables

GNU make supports some variables that have special properties.

MAKEFILE_LIST

Contains the name of each makefile that is parsed by make, in the order in which it was parsed. The name is appended just before make begins to parse the makefile. Thus, if the first thing a makefile does is examine the last word in this variable, it will be the name of the current makefile. Once the current makefile has used include, however, the last word will be the just-included makefile.

If a makefile named Makefile has this content:

```
name1 := $(lastword $(MAKEFILE_LIST))

include inc.mk

name2 := $(lastword $(MAKEFILE_LIST))

all:
        @echo name1 = $(name1)
        @echo name2 = $(name2)
```

then you would expect to see this output:

```
name1 = Makefile
name2 = inc.mk
```

.DEFAULT_GOAL

Sets the default goal to be used if no targets were specified on the command line (see Section 9.2 [Arguments to Specify the Goals], page 99). The .DEFAULT_GOAL variable allows you to discover the current default goal, restart the default goal selection algorithm by clearing its value, or to explicitly set the default goal. The following example illustrates these cases:

```
# Query the default goal.
ifeq ($(.DEFAULT_GOAL),)
  $(warning no default goal is set)
endif

.PHONY: foo
foo: ; @echo $@

$(warning default goal is $(.DEFAULT_GOAL))

# Reset the default goal.
.DEFAULT_GOAL :=

.PHONY: bar
bar: ; @echo $@

$(warning default goal is $(.DEFAULT_GOAL))

# Set our own.
.DEFAULT_GOAL := foo
```

This makefile prints:

```
no default goal is set
default goal is foo
default goal is bar
foo
```

Note that assigning more than one target name to .DEFAULT_GOAL is invalid and will result in an error.

MAKE_RESTARTS

This variable is set only if this instance of make has restarted (see Section 3.5 [How Makefiles Are Remade], page 14): it will contain the number of times this instance has restarted. Note this is not the same as recursion (counted by the MAKELEVEL variable). You should not set, modify, or export this variable.

MAKE_TERMOUT
MAKE_TERMERR

When make starts it will check whether stdout and stderr will show their output on a terminal. If so, it will set MAKE_TERMOUT and MAKE_TERMERR, respectively, to the name of the terminal device (or true if this cannot be determined). If set these variables will be marked for export. These variables will not be changed by make and they will not be modified if already set.

These values can be used (particularly in combination with output synchronization (see Section 5.4.1 [Output During Parallel Execution], page 47) to determine whether make itself is writing to a terminal; they can be tested to decide whether to force recipe commands to generate colorized output for example.

If you invoke a sub-make and redirect its stdout or stderr it is your responsibility to reset or unexport these variables as well, if your makefiles rely on them.

`.RECIPEPREFIX`

The first character of the value of this variable is used as the character make assumes is introducing a recipe line. If the variable is empty (as it is by default) that character is the standard tab character. For example, this is a valid makefile:

```
.RECIPEPREFIX = >
all:
> @echo Hello, world
```

The value of `.RECIPEPREFIX` can be changed multiple times; once set it stays in effect for all rules parsed until it is modified.

`.VARIABLES`

Expands to a list of the *names* of all global variables defined so far. This includes variables which have empty values, as well as built-in variables (see Section 10.3 [Variables Used by Implicit Rules], page 115), but does not include any variables which are only defined in a target-specific context. Note that any value you assign to this variable will be ignored; it will always return its special value.

`.FEATURES`

Expands to a list of special features supported by this version of **make**. Possible values include, but are not limited to:

'`archives`'

Supports **ar** (archive) files using special file name syntax. See Chapter 11 [Using **make** to Update Archive Files], page 129.

'`check-symlink`'

Supports the `-L` (`--check-symlink-times`) flag. See Section 9.7 [Summary of Options], page 104.

'`else-if`'   Supports "else if" non-nested conditionals. See Section 7.2 [Syntax of Conditionals], page 78.

'`jobserver`'

Supports "job server" enhanced parallel builds. See Section 5.4 [Parallel Execution], page 47.

'`oneshell`'

Supports the `.ONESHELL` special target. See Section 5.3.1 [Using One Shell], page 44.

'`order-only`'

Supports order-only prerequisites. See Section 4.2 [Types of Prerequisites], page 22.

'`second-expansion`'

Supports secondary expansion of prerequisite lists.

'`shortest-stem`'

Uses the "shortest stem" method of choosing which pattern, of multiple applicable options, will be used. See Section 10.5.4 [How Patterns Match], page 122.

'target-specific'

> Supports target-specific and pattern-specific variable assignments.
> See Section 6.11 [Target-specific Variable Values], page 71.

'undefine'

> Supports the **undefine** directive. See Section 6.9 [Undefine Directive], page 69.

'guile' Has GNU Guile available as an embedded extension language. See Section 12.1 [GNU Guile Integration], page 133.

'load'   Supports dynamically loadable objects for creating custom extensions. See Section 12.2 [Loading Dynamic Objects], page 135.

.INCLUDE_DIRS

> Expands to a list of directories that **make** searches for included makefiles (see Section 3.3 [Including Other Makefiles], page 13).

7 Conditional Parts of Makefiles

A *conditional* directive causes part of a makefile to be obeyed or ignored depending on the values of variables. Conditionals can compare the value of one variable to another, or the value of a variable to a constant string. Conditionals control what `make` actually "sees" in the makefile, so they *cannot* be used to control recipes at the time of execution.

7.1 Example of a Conditional

The following example of a conditional tells `make` to use one set of libraries if the `CC` variable is 'gcc', and a different set of libraries otherwise. It works by controlling which of two recipe lines will be used for the rule. The result is that 'CC=gcc' as an argument to `make` changes not only which compiler is used but also which libraries are linked.

```
libs_for_gcc = -lgnu
normal_libs =

foo: $(objects)
ifeq ($(CC),gcc)
        $(CC) -o foo $(objects) $(libs_for_gcc)
else
        $(CC) -o foo $(objects) $(normal_libs)
endif
```

This conditional uses three directives: one `ifeq`, one `else` and one `endif`.

The `ifeq` directive begins the conditional, and specifies the condition. It contains two arguments, separated by a comma and surrounded by parentheses. Variable substitution is performed on both arguments and then they are compared. The lines of the makefile following the `ifeq` are obeyed if the two arguments match; otherwise they are ignored.

The `else` directive causes the following lines to be obeyed if the previous conditional failed. In the example above, this means that the second alternative linking command is used whenever the first alternative is not used. It is optional to have an `else` in a conditional.

The `endif` directive ends the conditional. Every conditional must end with an `endif`. Unconditional makefile text follows.

As this example illustrates, conditionals work at the textual level: the lines of the conditional are treated as part of the makefile, or ignored, according to the condition. This is why the larger syntactic units of the makefile, such as rules, may cross the beginning or the end of the conditional.

When the variable `CC` has the value 'gcc', the above example has this effect:

```
foo: $(objects)
        $(CC) -o foo $(objects) $(libs_for_gcc)
```

When the variable `CC` has any other value, the effect is this:

```
foo: $(objects)
        $(CC) -o foo $(objects) $(normal_libs)
```

Equivalent results can be obtained in another way by conditionalizing a variable assignment and then using the variable unconditionally:

```
libs_for_gcc = -lgnu
normal_libs =

ifeq ($(CC),gcc)
  libs=$(libs_for_gcc)
else
  libs=$(normal_libs)
endif


foo: $(objects)
        $(CC) -o foo $(objects) $(libs)
```

7.2 Syntax of Conditionals

The syntax of a simple conditional with no else is as follows:

```
conditional-directive
text-if-true
endif
```

The *text-if-true* may be any lines of text, to be considered as part of the makefile if the condition is true. If the condition is false, no text is used instead.

The syntax of a complex conditional is as follows:

```
conditional-directive
text-if-true
else
text-if-false
endif
```

or:

```
conditional-directive-one
text-if-one-is-true
else conditional-directive-two
text-if-two-is-true
else
text-if-one-and-two-are-false
endif
```

There can be as many "else *conditional-directive*" clauses as necessary. Once a given condition is true, *text-if-true* is used and no other clause is used; if no condition is true then *text-if-false* is used. The *text-if-true* and *text-if-false* can be any number of lines of text.

The syntax of the *conditional-directive* is the same whether the conditional is simple or complex; after an else or not. There are four different directives that test different conditions. Here is a table of them:

```
ifeq (arg1, arg2)
ifeq 'arg1' 'arg2'
ifeq "arg1" "arg2"
ifeq "arg1" 'arg2'
ifeq 'arg1' "arg2"
```

> Expand all variable references in *arg1* and *arg2* and compare them. If they are identical, the *text-if-true* is effective; otherwise, the *text-if-false*, if any, is effective.
>
> Often you want to test if a variable has a non-empty value. When the value results from complex expansions of variables and functions, expansions you would consider empty may actually contain whitespace characters and thus are not seen as empty. However, you can use the **strip** function (see Section 8.2 [Text Functions], page 84) to avoid interpreting whitespace as a non-empty value. For example:
>
> ```
> ifeq ($(strip $(foo)),)
> text-if-empty
> endif
> ```
>
> will evaluate *text-if-empty* even if the expansion of $(foo) contains whitespace characters.

```
ifneq (arg1, arg2)
ifneq 'arg1' 'arg2'
ifneq "arg1" "arg2"
ifneq "arg1" 'arg2'
ifneq 'arg1' "arg2"
```

> Expand all variable references in *arg1* and *arg2* and compare them. If they are different, the *text-if-true* is effective; otherwise, the *text-if-false*, if any, is effective.

ifdef *variable-name*

> The **ifdef** form takes the *name* of a variable as its argument, not a reference to a variable. The value of that variable has a non-empty value, the *text-if-true* is effective; otherwise, the *text-if-false*, if any, is effective. Variables that have never been defined have an empty value. The text *variable-name* is expanded, so it could be a variable or function that expands to the name of a variable. For example:
>
> ```
> bar = true
> foo = bar
> ifdef $(foo)
> frobozz = yes
> endif
> ```
>
> The variable reference $(foo) is expanded, yielding **bar**, which is considered to be the name of a variable. The variable **bar** is not expanded, but its value is examined to determine if it is non-empty.
>
> Note that **ifdef** only tests whether a variable has a value. It does not expand the variable to see if that value is nonempty. Consequently, tests using **ifdef**

return true for all definitions except those like foo =. To test for an empty
value, use ifeq ($(foo),). For example,

```
bar =
foo = $(bar)
ifdef foo
frobozz = yes
else
frobozz = no
endif
```

sets 'frobozz' to 'yes', while:

```
foo =
ifdef foo
frobozz = yes
else
frobozz = no
endif
```

sets 'frobozz' to 'no'.

ifndef *variable-name*

If the variable *variable-name* has an empty value, the *text-if-true* is effective;
otherwise, the *text-if-false*, if any, is effective. The rules for expansion and
testing of *variable-name* are identical to the ifdef directive.

Extra spaces are allowed and ignored at the beginning of the conditional directive line,
but a tab is not allowed. (If the line begins with a tab, it will be considered part of a recipe
for a rule.) Aside from this, extra spaces or tabs may be inserted with no effect anywhere
except within the directive name or within an argument. A comment starting with '#' may
appear at the end of the line.

The other two directives that play a part in a conditional are else and endif. Each of
these directives is written as one word, with no arguments. Extra spaces are allowed and
ignored at the beginning of the line, and spaces or tabs at the end. A comment starting
with '#' may appear at the end of the line.

Conditionals affect which lines of the makefile make uses. If the condition is true, make
reads the lines of the *text-if-true* as part of the makefile; if the condition is false, make
ignores those lines completely. It follows that syntactic units of the makefile, such as rules,
may safely be split across the beginning or the end of the conditional.

make evaluates conditionals when it reads a makefile. Consequently, you cannot use
automatic variables in the tests of conditionals because they are not defined until recipes
are run (see Section 10.5.3 [Automatic Variables], page 120).

To prevent intolerable confusion, it is not permitted to start a conditional in one makefile
and end it in another. However, you may write an include directive within a conditional,
provided you do not attempt to terminate the conditional inside the included file.

7.3 Conditionals that Test Flags

You can write a conditional that tests make command flags such as '-t' by using the variable
MAKEFLAGS together with the findstring function (see Section 8.2 [Functions for String

Substitution and Analysis], page 84). This is useful when `touch` is not enough to make a file appear up to date.

The `findstring` function determines whether one string appears as a substring of another. If you want to test for the '-t' flag, use 't' as the first string and the value of `MAKEFLAGS` as the other.

For example, here is how to arrange to use 'ranlib -t' to finish marking an archive file up to date:

```
archive.a: ...
ifneq (,$(findstring t,$(MAKEFLAGS)))
        +touch archive.a
        +ranlib -t archive.a
else
        ranlib archive.a
endif
```

The '+' prefix marks those recipe lines as "recursive" so that they will be executed despite use of the '-t' flag. See Section 5.7 [Recursive Use of make], page 50.

8 Functions for Transforming Text

Functions allow you to do text processing in the makefile to compute the files to operate on or the commands to use in recipes. You use a function in a *function call*, where you give the name of the function and some text (the *arguments*) for the function to operate on. The result of the function's processing is substituted into the makefile at the point of the call, just as a variable might be substituted.

8.1 Function Call Syntax

A function call resembles a variable reference. It can appear anywhere a variable reference can appear, and it is expanded using the same rules as variable references. A function call looks like this:

```
$(function arguments)
```

or like this:

```
${function arguments}
```

Here *function* is a function name; one of a short list of names that are part of `make`. You can also essentially create your own functions by using the `call` built-in function.

The *arguments* are the arguments of the function. They are separated from the function name by one or more spaces or tabs, and if there is more than one argument, then they are separated by commas. Such whitespace and commas are not part of an argument's value. The delimiters which you use to surround the function call, whether parentheses or braces, can appear in an argument only in matching pairs; the other kind of delimiters may appear singly. If the arguments themselves contain other function calls or variable references, it is wisest to use the same kind of delimiters for all the references; write '`$(subst a,b,$(x))`', not '`$(subst a,b,${x})`'. This is because it is clearer, and because only one type of delimiter is matched to find the end of the reference.

The text written for each argument is processed by substitution of variables and function calls to produce the argument value, which is the text on which the function acts. The substitution is done in the order in which the arguments appear.

Commas and unmatched parentheses or braces cannot appear in the text of an argument as written; leading spaces cannot appear in the text of the first argument as written. These characters can be put into the argument value by variable substitution. First define variables `comma` and `space` whose values are isolated comma and space characters, then substitute these variables where such characters are wanted, like this:

```
comma:= ,
empty:=
space:= $(empty) $(empty)
foo:= a b c
bar:= $(subst $(space),$(comma),$(foo))
# bar is now 'a,b,c'.
```

Here the `subst` function replaces each space with a comma, through the value of `foo`, and substitutes the result.

8.2 Functions for String Substitution and Analysis

Here are some functions that operate on strings:

`$(subst from,to,text)`

> Performs a textual replacement on the text *text*: each occurrence of *from* is replaced by *to*. The result is substituted for the function call. For example,
>
> $(subst ee,EE,feet on the street)
>
> substitutes the string 'fEEt on the strEEt'.

`$(patsubst pattern,replacement,text)`

> Finds whitespace-separated words in *text* that match *pattern* and replaces them with *replacement*. Here *pattern* may contain a '%' which acts as a wildcard, matching any number of any characters within a word. If *replacement* also contains a '%', the '%' is replaced by the text that matched the '%' in *pattern*. Only the first '%' in the *pattern* and *replacement* is treated this way; any subsequent '%' is unchanged.
>
> '%' characters in `patsubst` function invocations can be quoted with preceding backslashes ('\'). Backslashes that would otherwise quote '%' characters can be quoted with more backslashes. Backslashes that quote '%' characters or other backslashes are removed from the pattern before it is compared file names or has a stem substituted into it. Backslashes that are not in danger of quoting '%' characters go unmolested. For example, the pattern `the\%weird\\%pattern\\` has 'the%weird\' preceding the operative '%' character, and 'pattern\\' following it. The final two backslashes are left alone because they cannot affect any '%' character.
>
> Whitespace between words is folded into single space characters; leading and trailing whitespace is discarded.
>
> For example,
>
> $(patsubst %.c,%.o,x.c.c bar.c)
>
> produces the value 'x.c.o bar.o'.
>
> Substitution references (see Section 6.3.1 [Substitution References], page 62) are a simpler way to get the effect of the `patsubst` function:
>
> $(var:pattern=replacement)
>
> is equivalent to
>
> $(patsubst pattern,replacement,$(var))
>
> The second shorthand simplifies one of the most common uses of `patsubst`: replacing the suffix at the end of file names.
>
> $(var:suffix=replacement)
>
> is equivalent to
>
> $(patsubst %suffix,%replacement,$(var))
>
> For example, you might have a list of object files:
>
>   objects = foo.o bar.o baz.o
>
> To get the list of corresponding source files, you could simply write:

```
$(objects:.o=.c)
```
instead of using the general form:
```
$(patsubst %.o,%.c,$(objects))
```

$(strip *string*)

> Removes leading and trailing whitespace from *string* and replaces each internal sequence of one or more whitespace characters with a single space. Thus, '$(strip a b c)' results in 'a b c'.
>
> The function strip can be very useful when used in conjunction with conditionals. When comparing something with the empty string '' using ifeq or ifneq, you usually want a string of just whitespace to match the empty string (see Chapter 7 [Conditionals], page 77).
>
> Thus, the following may fail to have the desired results:
>
> ```
> .PHONY: all
> ifneq   "$(needs_made)" ""
> all: $(needs_made)
> else
> all:;@echo 'Nothing to make!'
> endif
> ```
>
> Replacing the variable reference '$(needs_made)' with the function call '$(strip $(needs_made))' in the ifneq directive would make it more robust.

$(findstring *find*,*in*)

> Searches *in* for an occurrence of *find*. If it occurs, the value is *find*; otherwise, the value is empty. You can use this function in a conditional to test for the presence of a specific substring in a given string. Thus, the two examples,
>
> ```
> $(findstring a,a b c)
> $(findstring a,b c)
> ```
>
> produce the values 'a' and '' (the empty string), respectively. See Section 7.3 [Testing Flags], page 80, for a practical application of findstring.

$(filter *pattern...*,*text*)

> Returns all whitespace-separated words in *text* that *do* match any of the *pattern* words, removing any words that *do not* match. The patterns are written using '%', just like the patterns used in the patsubst function above.
>
> The filter function can be used to separate out different types of strings (such as file names) in a variable. For example:
>
> ```
> sources := foo.c bar.c baz.s ugh.h
> foo: $(sources)
>         cc $(filter %.c %.s,$(sources)) -o foo
> ```
>
> says that foo depends of foo.c, bar.c, baz.s and ugh.h but only foo.c, bar.c and baz.s should be specified in the command to the compiler.

$(filter-out *pattern...*,*text*)

> Returns all whitespace-separated words in *text* that *do not* match any of the *pattern* words, removing the words that *do* match one or more. This is the exact opposite of the filter function.

For example, given:

```
objects=main1.o foo.o main2.o bar.o
mains=main1.o main2.o
```

the following generates a list which contains all the object files not in 'mains':

```
$(filter-out $(mains),$(objects))
```

$(sort *list*)

Sorts the words of *list* in lexical order, removing duplicate words. The output is a list of words separated by single spaces. Thus,

```
$(sort foo bar lose)
```

returns the value 'bar foo lose'.

Incidentally, since sort removes duplicate words, you can use it for this purpose even if you don't care about the sort order.

$(word *n*,*text*)

Returns the *n*th word of *text*. The legitimate values of *n* start from 1. If *n* is bigger than the number of words in *text*, the value is empty. For example,

```
$(word 2, foo bar baz)
```

returns 'bar'.

$(wordlist *s*,*e*,*text*)

Returns the list of words in *text* starting with word *s* and ending with word *e* (inclusive). The legitimate values of *s* start from 1; *e* may start from 0. If *s* is bigger than the number of words in *text*, the value is empty. If *e* is bigger than the number of words in *text*, words up to the end of *text* are returned. If *s* is greater than *e*, nothing is returned. For example,

```
$(wordlist 2, 3, foo bar baz)
```

returns 'bar baz'.

$(words *text*)

Returns the number of words in *text*. Thus, the last word of *text* is $(word $(words *text*),*text*).

$(firstword *names*...)

The argument *names* is regarded as a series of names, separated by whitespace. The value is the first name in the series. The rest of the names are ignored.

For example,

```
$(firstword foo bar)
```

produces the result 'foo'. Although $(firstword *text*) is the same as $(word 1,*text*), the firstword function is retained for its simplicity.

$(lastword *names*...)

The argument *names* is regarded as a series of names, separated by whitespace. The value is the last name in the series.

For example,

```
$(lastword foo bar)
```

produces the result 'bar'. Although $(lastword *text*) is the same as $(word $(words *text*),*text*), the lastword function was added for its simplicity and better performance.

Here is a realistic example of the use of subst and patsubst. Suppose that a makefile uses the VPATH variable to specify a list of directories that make should search for prerequisite files (see Section 4.4.1 [VPATH Search Path for All Prerequisites], page 25). This example shows how to tell the C compiler to search for header files in the same list of directories.

The value of VPATH is a list of directories separated by colons, such as 'src:../headers'. First, the subst function is used to change the colons to spaces:

```
$(subst :, ,$(VPATH))
```

This produces 'src ../headers'. Then patsubst is used to turn each directory name into a '-I' flag. These can be added to the value of the variable CFLAGS, which is passed automatically to the C compiler, like this:

```
override CFLAGS += $(patsubst %,-I%,$(subst :, ,$(VPATH)))
```

The effect is to append the text '-Isrc -I../headers' to the previously given value of CFLAGS. The override directive is used so that the new value is assigned even if the previous value of CFLAGS was specified with a command argument (see Section 6.7 [The override Directive], page 68).

8.3 Functions for File Names

Several of the built-in expansion functions relate specifically to taking apart file names or lists of file names.

Each of the following functions performs a specific transformation on a file name. The argument of the function is regarded as a series of file names, separated by whitespace. (Leading and trailing whitespace is ignored.) Each file name in the series is transformed in the same way and the results are concatenated with single spaces between them.

$(dir *names*...)

> Extracts the directory-part of each file name in *names*. The directory-part of the file name is everything up through (and including) the last slash in it. If the file name contains no slash, the directory part is the string './'. For example,

> > $(dir src/foo.c hacks)

> produces the result 'src/ ./'.

$(notdir *names*...)

> Extracts all but the directory-part of each file name in *names*. If the file name contains no slash, it is left unchanged. Otherwise, everything through the last slash is removed from it.

> A file name that ends with a slash becomes an empty string. This is unfortunate, because it means that the result does not always have the same number of whitespace-separated file names as the argument had; but we do not see any other valid alternative.

> For example,

> > $(notdir src/foo.c hacks)

> produces the result 'foo.c hacks'.

`$(suffix names...)`

> Extracts the suffix of each file name in *names*. If the file name contains a period, the suffix is everything starting with the last period. Otherwise, the suffix is the empty string. This frequently means that the result will be empty when *names* is not, and if *names* contains multiple file names, the result may contain fewer file names.
>
> For example,
>
> ```
> $(suffix src/foo.c src-1.0/bar.c hacks)
> ```
>
> produces the result '`.c .c`'.

`$(basename names...)`

> Extracts all but the suffix of each file name in *names*. If the file name contains a period, the basename is everything starting up to (and not including) the last period. Periods in the directory part are ignored. If there is no period, the basename is the entire file name. For example,
>
> ```
> $(basename src/foo.c src-1.0/bar hacks)
> ```
>
> produces the result '`src/foo src-1.0/bar hacks`'.

`$(addsuffix suffix,names...)`

> The argument *names* is regarded as a series of names, separated by whitespace; *suffix* is used as a unit. The value of *suffix* is appended to the end of each individual name and the resulting larger names are concatenated with single spaces between them. For example,
>
> ```
> $(addsuffix .c,foo bar)
> ```
>
> produces the result '`foo.c bar.c`'.

`$(addprefix prefix,names...)`

> The argument *names* is regarded as a series of names, separated by whitespace; *prefix* is used as a unit. The value of *prefix* is prepended to the front of each individual name and the resulting larger names are concatenated with single spaces between them. For example,
>
> ```
> $(addprefix src/,foo bar)
> ```
>
> produces the result '`src/foo src/bar`'.

`$(join list1,list2)`

> Concatenates the two arguments word by word: the two first words (one from each argument) concatenated form the first word of the result, the two second words form the second word of the result, and so on. So the *n*th word of the result comes from the *n*th word of each argument. If one argument has more words that the other, the extra words are copied unchanged into the result.
>
> For example, '`$(join a b,.c .o)`' produces '`a.c b.o`'.
>
> Whitespace between the words in the lists is not preserved; it is replaced with a single space.
>
> This function can merge the results of the `dir` and `notdir` functions, to produce the original list of files which was given to those two functions.

`$(wildcard pattern)`

> The argument *pattern* is a file name pattern, typically containing wildcard
> characters (as in shell file name patterns). The result of `wildcard` is a
> space-separated list of the names of existing files that match the pattern. See
> Section 4.3 [Using Wildcard Characters in File Names], page 23.

`$(realpath names...)`

> For each file name in *names* return the canonical absolute name. A canonical
> name does not contain any `.` or `..` components, nor any repeated path separa-
> tors (`/`) or symlinks. In case of a failure the empty string is returned. Consult
> the `realpath(3)` documentation for a list of possible failure causes.

`$(abspath names...)`

> For each file name in *names* return an absolute name that does not contain
> any `.` or `..` components, nor any repeated path separators (`/`). Note that, in
> contrast to `realpath` function, `abspath` does not resolve symlinks and does not
> require the file names to refer to an existing file or directory. Use the `wildcard`
> function to test for existence.

8.4 Functions for Conditionals

There are three functions that provide conditional expansion. A key aspect of these functions is that not all of the arguments are expanded initially. Only those arguments which
need to be expanded, will be expanded.

`$(if condition,then-part[,else-part])`

> The `if` function provides support for conditional expansion in a functional
> context (as opposed to the GNU `make` makefile conditionals such as `ifeq` (see
> Section 7.2 [Syntax of Conditionals], page 78).
>
> The first argument, *condition*, first has all preceding and trailing whitespace
> stripped, then is expanded. If it expands to any non-empty string, then the con-
> dition is considered to be true. If it expands to an empty string, the condition
> is considered to be false.
>
> If the condition is true then the second argument, *then-part*, is evaluated and
> this is used as the result of the evaluation of the entire `if` function.
>
> If the condition is false then the third argument, *else-part*, is evaluated and this
> is the result of the `if` function. If there is no third argument, the `if` function
> evaluates to nothing (the empty string).
>
> Note that only one of the *then-part* or the *else-part* will be evaluated, never
> both. Thus, either can contain side-effects (such as `shell` function calls, etc.)

`$(or condition1[,condition2[,condition3...]])`

> The `or` function provides a "short-circuiting" OR operation. Each argument
> is expanded, in order. If an argument expands to a non-empty string the
> processing stops and the result of the expansion is that string. If, after all
> arguments are expanded, all of them are false (empty), then the result of the
> expansion is the empty string.

`$(and condition1[,condition2[,condition3...]])`

>   The **and** function provides a "short-circuiting" AND operation. Each argument is expanded, in order. If an argument expands to an empty string the processing stops and the result of the expansion is the empty string. If all arguments expand to a non-empty string then the result of the expansion is the expansion of the last argument.

8.5 The `foreach` Function

The `foreach` function is very different from other functions. It causes one piece of text to be used repeatedly, each time with a different substitution performed on it. It resembles the `for` command in the shell `sh` and the `foreach` command in the C-shell `csh`.

The syntax of the `foreach` function is:

`$(foreach var,list,text)`

The first two arguments, *var* and *list*, are expanded before anything else is done; note that the last argument, *text*, is **not** expanded at the same time. Then for each word of the expanded value of *list*, the variable named by the expanded value of *var* is set to that word, and *text* is expanded. Presumably *text* contains references to that variable, so its expansion will be different each time.

The result is that *text* is expanded as many times as there are whitespace-separated words in *list*. The multiple expansions of *text* are concatenated, with spaces between them, to make the result of `foreach`.

This simple example sets the variable 'files' to the list of all files in the directories in the list 'dirs':

```
dirs := a b c d
files := $(foreach dir,$(dirs),$(wildcard $(dir)/*))
```

Here *text* is '`$(wildcard $(dir)/*)`'. The first repetition finds the value 'a' for `dir`, so it produces the same result as '`$(wildcard a/*)`'; the second repetition produces the result of '`$(wildcard b/*)`'; and the third, that of '`$(wildcard c/*)`'.

This example has the same result (except for setting 'dirs') as the following example:

```
files := $(wildcard a/* b/* c/* d/*)
```

When *text* is complicated, you can improve readability by giving it a name, with an additional variable:

```
find_files = $(wildcard $(dir)/*)
dirs := a b c d
files := $(foreach dir,$(dirs),$(find_files))
```

Here we use the variable `find_files` this way. We use plain '=' to define a recursively-expanding variable, so that its value contains an actual function call to be re-expanded under the control of `foreach`; a simply-expanded variable would not do, since `wildcard` would be called only once at the time of defining `find_files`.

The `foreach` function has no permanent effect on the variable *var*; its value and flavor after the `foreach` function call are the same as they were beforehand. The other values which are taken from *list* are in effect only temporarily, during the execution of `foreach`. The variable *var* is a simply-expanded variable during the execution of `foreach`. If *var* was undefined before the `foreach` function call, it is undefined after the call. See Section 6.2 [The Two Flavors of Variables], page 60.

You must take care when using complex variable expressions that result in variable names because many strange things are valid variable names, but are probably not what you intended. For example,

```
files := $(foreach Esta-escrito-en-espanol!,b c ch,$(find_files))
```

might be useful if the value of `find_files` references the variable whose name is 'Esta-escrito-en-espanol!' (es un nombre bastante largo, no?), but it is more likely to be a mistake.

8.6 The `file` Function

The `file` function allows the makefile to write to a file. Two modes of writing are supported: overwrite, where the text is written to the beginning of the file and any existing content is lost, and append, where the text is written to the end of the file, preserving the existing content. In all cases the file is created if it does not exist.

The syntax of the `file` function is:

```
$(file op filename[,text])
```

The operator *op* can be either > which indicates overwrite mode, or >> which indicates append mode. The *filename* indicates the file to be written to. There may optionally be whitespace between the operator and the file name.

When the `file` function is expanded all its arguments are expanded first, then the file indicated by *filename* will be opened in the mode described by *op*. Finally *text* will be written to the file. If *text* does not already end in a newline, even if empty, a final newline will be written. If the *text* argument is not given, nothing will be written. The result of evaluating the `file` function is always the empty string.

It is a fatal error if the file cannot be opened for writing, or if the write operation fails.

For example, the `file` function can be useful if your build system has a limited command line size and your recipe runs a command that can accept arguments from a file as well. Many commands use the convention that an argument prefixed with an @ specifies a file containing more arguments. Then you might write your recipe in this way:

```
program: $(OBJECTS)
        $(file >$@.in,$^)
        $(CMD) $(CMDFLAGS) @$@.in
        @rm $@.in
```

If the command required each argument to be on a separate line of the input file, you might write your recipe like this:

```
program: $(OBJECTS)
        $(file >$@.in) $(foreach O,$^,$(file >>$@.in,$O))
        $(CMD) $(CMDFLAGS) @$@.in
        @rm $@.in
```

8.7 The `call` Function

The `call` function is unique in that it can be used to create new parameterized functions. You can write a complex expression as the value of a variable, then use `call` to expand it with different values.

The syntax of the `call` function is:

```
$(call variable,param,param,...)
```

When `make` expands this function, it assigns each *param* to temporary variables `$(1)`, `$(2)`, etc. The variable `$(0)` will contain *variable*. There is no maximum number of parameter arguments. There is no minimum, either, but it doesn't make sense to use `call` with no parameters.

Then *variable* is expanded as a `make` variable in the context of these temporary assignments. Thus, any reference to `$(1)` in the value of *variable* will resolve to the first *param* in the invocation of `call`.

Note that *variable* is the *name* of a variable, not a *reference* to that variable. Therefore you would not normally use a '`$`' or parentheses when writing it. (You can, however, use a variable reference in the name if you want the name not to be a constant.)

If *variable* is the name of a built-in function, the built-in function is always invoked (even if a `make` variable by that name also exists).

The `call` function expands the *param* arguments before assigning them to temporary variables. This means that *variable* values containing references to built-in functions that have special expansion rules, like `foreach` or `if`, may not work as you expect.

Some examples may make this clearer.

This macro simply reverses its arguments:

```
reverse = $(2) $(1)

foo = $(call reverse,a,b)
```

Here *foo* will contain 'b a'.

This one is slightly more interesting: it defines a macro to search for the first instance of a program in `PATH`:

```
pathsearch = $(firstword $(wildcard $(addsuffix /$(1),$(subst :, ,$(PATH)))))

LS := $(call pathsearch,ls)
```

Now the variable LS contains `/bin/ls` or similar.

The `call` function can be nested. Each recursive invocation gets its own local values for `$(1)`, etc. that mask the values of higher-level `call`. For example, here is an implementation of a *map* function:

```
map = $(foreach a,$(2),$(call $(1),$(a)))
```

Now you can *map* a function that normally takes only one argument, such as `origin`, to multiple values in one step:

```
o = $(call map,origin,o map MAKE)
```

and end up with *o* containing something like 'file file default'.

A final caution: be careful when adding whitespace to the arguments to `call`. As with other functions, any whitespace contained in the second and subsequent arguments is kept; this can cause strange effects. It's generally safest to remove all extraneous whitespace when providing parameters to `call`.

8.8 The value Function

The value function provides a way for you to use the value of a variable *without* having it expanded. Please note that this does not undo expansions which have already occurred; for example if you create a simply expanded variable its value is expanded during the definition; in that case the value function will return the same result as using the variable directly.

The syntax of the value function is:

```
$(value variable)
```

Note that *variable* is the *name* of a variable, not a *reference* to that variable. Therefore you would not normally use a '$' or parentheses when writing it. (You can, however, use a variable reference in the name if you want the name not to be a constant.)

The result of this function is a string containing the value of *variable*, without any expansion occurring. For example, in this makefile:

```
FOO = $PATH

all:
        @echo $(FOO)
        @echo $(value FOO)
```

The first output line would be ATH, since the "$P" would be expanded as a make variable, while the second output line would be the current value of your $PATH environment variable, since the value function avoided the expansion.

The value function is most often used in conjunction with the eval function (see Section 8.9 [Eval Function], page 93).

8.9 The eval Function

The eval function is very special: it allows you to define new makefile constructs that are not constant; which are the result of evaluating other variables and functions. The argument to the eval function is expanded, then the results of that expansion are parsed as makefile syntax. The expanded results can define new make variables, targets, implicit or explicit rules, etc.

The result of the eval function is always the empty string; thus, it can be placed virtually anywhere in a makefile without causing syntax errors.

It's important to realize that the eval argument is expanded *twice*; first by the eval function, then the results of that expansion are expanded again when they are parsed as makefile syntax. This means you may need to provide extra levels of escaping for "$" characters when using eval. The value function (see Section 8.8 [Value Function], page 93) can sometimes be useful in these situations, to circumvent unwanted expansions.

Here is an example of how eval can be used; this example combines a number of concepts and other functions. Although it might seem overly complex to use eval in this example, rather than just writing out the rules, consider two things: first, the template definition (in PROGRAM_template) could need to be much more complex than it is here; and second, you might put the complex, "generic" part of this example into another makefile, then include it in all the individual makefiles. Now your individual makefiles are quite straightforward.

```
PROGRAMS    = server client

server_OBJS = server.o server_priv.o server_access.o
server_LIBS = priv protocol

client_OBJS = client.o client_api.o client_mem.o
client_LIBS = protocol

# Everything after this is generic

.PHONY: all
all: $(PROGRAMS)

define PROGRAM_template =
 $(1): $$($(1)_OBJS) $$($(1)_LIBS:%=-l%)
 ALL_OBJS    += $$($(1)_OBJS)
endef

$(foreach prog,$(PROGRAMS),$(eval $(call PROGRAM_template,$(prog))))

$(PROGRAMS):
        $(LINK.o) $^ $(LDLIBS) -o $@

clean:
        rm -f $(ALL_OBJS) $(PROGRAMS)
```

8.10 The origin Function

The origin function is unlike most other functions in that it does not operate on the values of variables; it tells you something *about* a variable. Specifically, it tells you where it came from.

The syntax of the origin function is:

    $(origin variable)

Note that *variable* is the *name* of a variable to inquire about, not a *reference* to that variable. Therefore you would not normally use a '$' or parentheses when writing it. (You can, however, use a variable reference in the name if you want the name not to be a constant.)

The result of this function is a string telling you how the variable *variable* was defined:

'undefined'

> if *variable* was never defined.

'default'

> if *variable* has a default definition, as is usual with CC and so on. See Section 10.3 [Variables Used by Implicit Rules], page 115. Note that if you have redefined a default variable, the origin function will return the origin of the later definition.

'environment'
> if *variable* was inherited from the environment provided to make.

'environment override'
> if *variable* was inherited from the environment provided to make, and is overriding a setting for *variable* in the makefile as a result of the '-e' option (see Section 9.7 [Summary of Options], page 104).

'file'
> if *variable* was defined in a makefile.

'command line'
> if *variable* was defined on the command line.

'override'
> if *variable* was defined with an override directive in a makefile (see Section 6.7 [The override Directive], page 68).

'automatic'
> if *variable* is an automatic variable defined for the execution of the recipe for each rule (see Section 10.5.3 [Automatic Variables], page 120).

This information is primarily useful (other than for your curiosity) to determine if you want to believe the value of a variable. For example, suppose you have a makefile foo that includes another makefile bar. You want a variable bletch to be defined in bar if you run the command 'make -f bar', even if the environment contains a definition of bletch. However, if foo defined bletch before including bar, you do not want to override that definition. This could be done by using an override directive in foo, giving that definition precedence over the later definition in bar; unfortunately, the override directive would also override any command line definitions. So, bar could include:

```
ifdef bletch
ifeq "$(origin bletch)" "environment"
bletch = barf, gag, etc.
endif
endif
```

If bletch has been defined from the environment, this will redefine it.

If you want to override a previous definition of bletch if it came from the environment, even under '-e', you could instead write:

```
ifneq "$(findstring environment,$(origin bletch))" ""
bletch = barf, gag, etc.
endif
```

Here the redefinition takes place if '$(origin bletch)' returns either 'environment' or 'environment override'. See Section 8.2 [Functions for String Substitution and Analysis], page 84.

8.11 The flavor Function

The flavor function, like the origin function, does not operate on the values of variables but rather it tells you something *about* a variable. Specifically, it tells you the flavor of a variable (see Section 6.2 [The Two Flavors of Variables], page 60).

The syntax of the `flavor` function is:

    $(flavor variable)

Note that *variable* is the *name* of a variable to inquire about, not a *reference* to that variable. Therefore you would not normally use a '$' or parentheses when writing it. (You can, however, use a variable reference in the name if you want the name not to be a constant.)

The result of this function is a string that identifies the flavor of the variable *variable*:

'undefined'

> if *variable* was never defined.

'recursive'

> if *variable* is a recursively expanded variable.

'simple'

> if *variable* is a simply expanded variable.

8.12 Functions That Control Make

These functions control the way make runs. Generally, they are used to provide information to the user of the makefile or to cause make to stop if some sort of environmental error is detected.

`$(error text...)`

> Generates a fatal error where the message is *text*. Note that the error is generated whenever this function is evaluated. So, if you put it inside a recipe or on the right side of a recursive variable assignment, it won't be evaluated until later. The *text* will be expanded before the error is generated.
>
> For example,
>
>   ifdef ERROR1
> $(error error is $(ERROR1))
>   endif
>
> will generate a fatal error during the read of the makefile if the make variable ERROR1 is defined. Or,
>
>   ERR = $(error found an error!)
>
>   .PHONY: err
>   err: ; $(ERR)
>
> will generate a fatal error while make is running, if the err target is invoked.

`$(warning text...)`

> This function works similarly to the error function, above, except that make doesn't exit. Instead, *text* is expanded and the resulting message is displayed, but processing of the makefile continues.
>
> The result of the expansion of this function is the empty string.

`$(info text...)`

> This function does nothing more than print its (expanded) argument(s) to standard output. No makefile name or line number is added. The result of the expansion of this function is the empty string.

8.13 The `shell` Function

The `shell` function is unlike any other function other than the `wildcard` function (see Section 4.3.3 [The Function `wildcard`], page 24) in that it communicates with the world outside of `make`.

The `shell` function performs the same function that backquotes ('`') perform in most shells: it does *command expansion*. This means that it takes as an argument a shell command and evaluates to the output of the command. The only processing `make` does on the result is to convert each newline (or carriage-return / newline pair) to a single space. If there is a trailing (carriage-return and) newline it will simply be removed.

The commands run by calls to the `shell` function are run when the function calls are expanded (see Section 3.7 [How `make` Reads a Makefile], page 16). Because this function involves spawning a new shell, you should carefully consider the performance implications of using the `shell` function within recursively expanded variables vs. simply expanded variables (see Section 6.2 [The Two Flavors of Variables], page 60).

Here are some examples of the use of the `shell` function:

```
contents := $(shell cat foo)
```

sets `contents` to the contents of the file `foo`, with a space (rather than a newline) separating each line.

```
files := $(shell echo *.c)
```

sets `files` to the expansion of '`*.c`'. Unless `make` is using a very strange shell, this has the same result as '`$(wildcard *.c)`' (as long as at least one '`.c`' file exists).

8.14 The `guile` Function

If GNU `make` is built with support for GNU Guile as an embedded extension language then the `guile` function will be available. The `guile` function takes one argument which is first expanded by `make` in the normal fashion, then passed to the GNU Guile evaluator. The result of the evaluator is converted into a string and used as the expansion of the `guile` function in the makefile. See Section 12.1 [GNU Guile Integration], page 133 for details on writing extensions to `make` in Guile.

You can determine whether GNU Guile support is available by checking the `.FEATURES` variable for the word *guile*.

9 How to Run make

A makefile that says how to recompile a program can be used in more than one way. The simplest use is to recompile every file that is out of date. Usually, makefiles are written so that if you run make with no arguments, it does just that.

But you might want to update only some of the files; you might want to use a different compiler or different compiler options; you might want just to find out which files are out of date without changing them.

By giving arguments when you run make, you can do any of these things and many others.

The exit status of make is always one of three values:

0   The exit status is zero if make is successful.

2   The exit status is two if make encounters any errors. It will print messages describing the particular errors.

1   The exit status is one if you use the '-q' flag and make determines that some target is not already up to date. See Section 9.3 [Instead of Executing Recipes], page 101.

9.1 Arguments to Specify the Makefile

The way to specify the name of the makefile is with the '-f' or '--file' option ('--makefile' also works). For example, '-f altmake' says to use the file altmake as the makefile.

If you use the '-f' flag several times and follow each '-f' with an argument, all the specified files are used jointly as makefiles.

If you do not use the '-f' or '--file' flag, the default is to try GNUmakefile, makefile, and Makefile, in that order, and use the first of these three which exists or can be made (see Chapter 3 [Writing Makefiles], page 11).

9.2 Arguments to Specify the Goals

The *goals* are the targets that make should strive ultimately to update. Other targets are updated as well if they appear as prerequisites of goals, or prerequisites of prerequisites of goals, etc.

By default, the goal is the first target in the makefile (not counting targets that start with a period). Therefore, makefiles are usually written so that the first target is for compiling the entire program or programs they describe. If the first rule in the makefile has several targets, only the first target in the rule becomes the default goal, not the whole list. You can manage the selection of the default goal from within your makefile using the .DEFAULT_GOAL variable (see Section 6.14 [Other Special Variables], page 73).

You can also specify a different goal or goals with command line arguments to make. Use the name of the goal as an argument. If you specify several goals, make processes each of them in turn, in the order you name them.

Any target in the makefile may be specified as a goal (unless it starts with '-' or contains an '=', in which case it will be parsed as a switch or variable definition, respectively). Even targets not in the makefile may be specified, if `make` can find implicit rules that say how to make them.

`Make` will set the special variable `MAKECMDGOALS` to the list of goals you specified on the command line. If no goals were given on the command line, this variable is empty. Note that this variable should be used only in special circumstances.

An example of appropriate use is to avoid including `.d` files during `clean` rules (see Section 4.13 [Automatic Prerequisites], page 38), so `make` won't create them only to immediately remove them again:

```
sources = foo.c bar.c

ifneq ($(MAKECMDGOALS),clean)
include $(sources:.c=.d)
endif
```

One use of specifying a goal is if you want to compile only a part of the program, or only one of several programs. Specify as a goal each file that you wish to remake. For example, consider a directory containing several programs, with a makefile that starts like this:

```
.PHONY: all
all: size nm ld ar as
```

If you are working on the program `size`, you might want to say 'make `size`' so that only the files of that program are recompiled.

Another use of specifying a goal is to make files that are not normally made. For example, there may be a file of debugging output, or a version of the program that is compiled specially for testing, which has a rule in the makefile but is not a prerequisite of the default goal.

Another use of specifying a goal is to run the recipe associated with a phony target (see Section 4.5 [Phony Targets], page 29) or empty target (see Section 4.7 [Empty Target Files to Record Events], page 31). Many makefiles contain a phony target named `clean` which deletes everything except source files. Naturally, this is done only if you request it explicitly with 'make `clean`'. Following is a list of typical phony and empty target names. See Section 15.6 [Standard Targets], page 157, for a detailed list of all the standard target names which GNU software packages use.

`all`   Make all the top-level targets the makefile knows about.

`clean`   Delete all files that are normally created by running `make`.

`mostlyclean`

                Like 'clean', but may refrain from deleting a few files that people normally don't want to recompile. For example, the 'mostlyclean' target for GCC does not delete `libgcc.a`, because recompiling it is rarely necessary and takes a lot of time.

`distclean`
`realclean`
`clobber`   Any of these targets might be defined to delete *more* files than 'clean' does. For example, this would delete configuration files or links that you would normally create as preparation for compilation, even if the makefile itself cannot create these files.

install   Copy the executable file into a directory that users typically search for commands; copy any auxiliary files that the executable uses into the directories where it will look for them.

print   Print listings of the source files that have changed.

tar   Create a tar file of the source files.

shar   Create a shell archive (shar file) of the source files.

dist   Create a distribution file of the source files. This might be a tar file, or a shar file, or a compressed version of one of the above, or even more than one of the above.

TAGS   Update a tags table for this program.

check

test   Perform self tests on the program this makefile builds.

9.3 Instead of Executing Recipes

The makefile tells make how to tell whether a target is up to date, and how to update each target. But updating the targets is not always what you want. Certain options specify other activities for make.

'-n'
'--just-print'
'--dry-run'
'--recon'

        "No-op". Causes make to print the recipes that are needed to make the targets up to date, but not actually execute them. Note that some recipes are still executed, even with this flag (see Section 5.7.1 [How the MAKE Variable Works], page 51). Also any recipes needed to update included makefiles are still executed (see Section 3.5 [How Makefiles Are Remade], page 14).

'-t'
'--touch'

        "Touch". Marks targets as up to date without actually changing them. In other words, make pretends to update the targets but does not really change their contents; instead only their modified times are updated.

'-q'
'--question'

        "Question". Silently check whether the targets are up to date, but do not execute recipes; the exit code shows whether any updates are needed.

'-W file'
'--what-if=file'
'--assume-new=file'
'--new-file=file'

        "What if". Each '-W' flag is followed by a file name. The given files' modification times are recorded by make as being the present time, although the actual modification times remain the same. You can use the '-W' flag in conjunction with the '-n' flag to see what would happen if you were to modify specific files.

With the '-n' flag, make prints the recipe that it would normally execute but usually does not execute it.

With the '-t' flag, make ignores the recipes in the rules and uses (in effect) the command touch for each target that needs to be remade. The touch command is also printed, unless '-s' or .SILENT is used. For speed, make does not actually invoke the program touch. It does the work directly.

With the '-q' flag, make prints nothing and executes no recipes, but the exit status code it returns is zero if and only if the targets to be considered are already up to date. If the exit status is one, then some updating needs to be done. If make encounters an error, the exit status is two, so you can distinguish an error from a target that is not up to date.

It is an error to use more than one of these three flags in the same invocation of make.

The '-n', '-t', and '-q' options do not affect recipe lines that begin with '+' characters or contain the strings '$(MAKE)' or '${MAKE}'. Note that only the line containing the '+' character or the strings '$(MAKE)' or '${MAKE}' is run regardless of these options. Other lines in the same rule are not run unless they too begin with '+' or contain '$(MAKE)' or '${MAKE}' (See Section 5.7.1 [How the MAKE Variable Works], page 51.)

The '-t' flag prevents phony targets (see Section 4.5 [Phony Targets], page 29) from being updated, unless there are recipe lines beginning with '+' or containing '$(MAKE)' or '${MAKE}'.

The '-W' flag provides two features:

- If you also use the '-n' or '-q' flag, you can see what make would do if you were to modify some files.

- Without the '-n' or '-q' flag, when make is actually executing recipes, the '-W' flag can direct make to act as if some files had been modified, without actually running the recipes for those files.

Note that the options '-p' and '-v' allow you to obtain other information about make or about the makefiles in use (see Section 9.7 [Summary of Options], page 104).

9.4 Avoiding Recompilation of Some Files

Sometimes you may have changed a source file but you do not want to recompile all the files that depend on it. For example, suppose you add a macro or a declaration to a header file that many other files depend on. Being conservative, make assumes that any change in the header file requires recompilation of all dependent files, but you know that they do not need to be recompiled and you would rather not waste the time waiting for them to compile.

If you anticipate the problem before changing the header file, you can use the '-t' flag. This flag tells make not to run the recipes in the rules, but rather to mark the target up to date by changing its last-modification date. You would follow this procedure:

1. Use the command 'make' to recompile the source files that really need recompilation, ensuring that the object files are up-to-date before you begin.

2. Make the changes in the header files.

3. Use the command 'make -t' to mark all the object files as up to date. The next time you run make, the changes in the header files will not cause any recompilation.

If you have already changed the header file at a time when some files do need recompilation, it is too late to do this. Instead, you can use the '-o *file*' flag, which marks a specified file as "old" (see Section 9.7 [Summary of Options], page 104). This means that the file itself will not be remade, and nothing else will be remade on its account. Follow this procedure:

1. Recompile the source files that need compilation for reasons independent of the particular header file, with 'make -o *headerfile*'. If several header files are involved, use a separate '-o' option for each header file.

2. Touch all the object files with 'make -t'.

9.5 Overriding Variables

An argument that contains '=' specifies the value of a variable: '*v*=*x*' sets the value of the variable *v* to *x*. If you specify a value in this way, all ordinary assignments of the same variable in the makefile are ignored; we say they have been *overridden* by the command line argument.

The most common way to use this facility is to pass extra flags to compilers. For example, in a properly written makefile, the variable CFLAGS is included in each recipe that runs the C compiler, so a file foo.c would be compiled something like this:

```
cc -c $(CFLAGS) foo.c
```

Thus, whatever value you set for CFLAGS affects each compilation that occurs. The makefile probably specifies the usual value for CFLAGS, like this:

```
CFLAGS=-g
```

Each time you run make, you can override this value if you wish. For example, if you say 'make CFLAGS='-g -O'', each C compilation will be done with 'cc -c -g -O'. (This also illustrates how you can use quoting in the shell to enclose spaces and other special characters in the value of a variable when you override it.)

The variable CFLAGS is only one of many standard variables that exist just so that you can change them this way. See Section 10.3 [Variables Used by Implicit Rules], page 115, for a complete list.

You can also program the makefile to look at additional variables of your own, giving the user the ability to control other aspects of how the makefile works by changing the variables.

When you override a variable with a command line argument, you can define either a recursively-expanded variable or a simply-expanded variable. The examples shown above make a recursively-expanded variable; to make a simply-expanded variable, write ':=' or '::=' instead of '='. But, unless you want to include a variable reference or function call in the *value* that you specify, it makes no difference which kind of variable you create.

There is one way that the makefile can change a variable that you have overridden. This is to use the override directive, which is a line that looks like this: 'override *variable* = *value*' (see Section 6.7 [The override Directive], page 68).

9.6 Testing the Compilation of a Program

Normally, when an error happens in executing a shell command, make gives up immediately, returning a nonzero status. No further recipes are executed for any target. The error implies that the goal cannot be correctly remade, and make reports this as soon as it knows.

When you are compiling a program that you have just changed, this is not what you want. Instead, you would rather that make try compiling every file that can be tried, to show you as many compilation errors as possible.

On these occasions, you should use the '-k' or '--keep-going' flag. This tells make to continue to consider the other prerequisites of the pending targets, remaking them if necessary, before it gives up and returns nonzero status. For example, after an error in compiling one object file, 'make -k' will continue compiling other object files even though it already knows that linking them will be impossible. In addition to continuing after failed shell commands, 'make -k' will continue as much as possible after discovering that it does not know how to make a target or prerequisite file. This will always cause an error message, but without '-k', it is a fatal error (see Section 9.7 [Summary of Options], page 104).

The usual behavior of make assumes that your purpose is to get the goals up to date; once make learns that this is impossible, it might as well report the failure immediately. The '-k' flag says that the real purpose is to test as much as possible of the changes made in the program, perhaps to find several independent problems so that you can correct them all before the next attempt to compile. This is why Emacs' *M-x compile* command passes the '-k' flag by default.

9.7 Summary of Options

Here is a table of all the options make understands:

'-b'

'-m'   These options are ignored for compatibility with other versions of make.

'-B'

'--always-make'
                        Consider all targets out-of-date. GNU make proceeds to consider targets and
                        their prerequisites using the normal algorithms; however, all targets so consid-
                        ered are always remade regardless of the status of their prerequisites. To avoid
                        infinite recursion, if MAKE_RESTARTS (see Section 6.14 [Other Special Variables],
                        page 73) is set to a number greater than 0 this option is disabled when consider-
                        ing whether to remake makefiles (see Section 3.5 [How Makefiles Are Remade],
                        page 14).

'-C dir'

'--directory=dir'
                        Change to directory dir before reading the makefiles. If multiple '-C' options
                        are specified, each is interpreted relative to the previous one: '-C / -C etc' is
                        equivalent to '-C /etc'. This is typically used with recursive invocations of
                        make (see Section 5.7 [Recursive Use of make], page 50).

'-d'

                        Print debugging information in addition to normal processing. The debugging
                        information says which files are being considered for remaking, which file-times

are being compared and with what results, which files actually need to be remade, which implicit rules are considered and which are applied—everything interesting about how make decides what to do. The -d option is equivalent to '--debug=a' (see below).

'--debug[=*options*]'

Print debugging information in addition to normal processing. Various levels and types of output can be chosen. With no arguments, print the "basic" level of debugging. Possible arguments are below; only the first character is considered, and values must be comma- or space-separated.

a (*all*)　　All types of debugging output are enabled. This is equivalent to using '-d'.

b (*basic*)　Basic debugging prints each target that was found to be out-of-date, and whether the build was successful or not.

v (*verbose*)

A level above 'basic'; includes messages about which makefiles were parsed, prerequisites that did not need to be rebuilt, etc. This option also enables 'basic' messages.

i (*implicit*)

Prints messages describing the implicit rule searches for each target. This option also enables 'basic' messages.

j (*jobs*)　　Prints messages giving details on the invocation of specific subcommands.

m (*makefile*)

By default, the above messages are not enabled while trying to remake the makefiles. This option enables messages while rebuilding makefiles, too. Note that the 'all' option does enable this option. This option also enables 'basic' messages.

n (*none*)　　Disable all debugging currently enabled. If additional debugging flags are encountered after this they will still take effect.

'-e'

'--environment-overrides'

Give variables taken from the environment precedence over variables from makefiles. See Section 6.10 [Variables from the Environment], page 70.

'--eval=*string*'

Evaluate *string* as makefile syntax. This is a command-line version of the eval function (see Section 8.9 [Eval Function], page 93). The evaluation is performed after the default rules and variables have been defined, but before any makefiles are read.

'-f *file*'

'--file=*file*'

'--makefile=*file*'

Read the file named *file* as a makefile. See Chapter 3 [Writing Makefiles], page 11.

'-h'

'--help'

        Remind you of the options that `make` understands and then exit.

'-i'

'--ignore-errors'

        Ignore all errors in recipes executed to remake files. See Section 5.5 [Errors in Recipes], page 49.

'-I *dir*'

'--include-dir=*dir*'

        Specifies a directory *dir* to search for included makefiles. See Section 3.3 [Including Other Makefiles], page 13. If several '-I' options are used to specify several directories, the directories are searched in the order specified.

'-j [*jobs*]'

'--jobs[=*jobs*]'

        Specifies the number of recipes (jobs) to run simultaneously. With no argument, `make` runs as many recipes simultaneously as possible. If there is more than one '-j' option, the last one is effective. See Section 5.4 [Parallel Execution], page 47, for more information on how recipes are run. Note that this option is ignored on MS-DOS.

'-k'

'--keep-going'

        Continue as much as possible after an error. While the target that failed, and those that depend on it, cannot be remade, the other prerequisites of these targets can be processed all the same. See Section 9.6 [Testing the Compilation of a Program], page 104.

'-l [*load*]'

'--load-average[=*load*]'

'--max-load[=*load*]'

        Specifies that no new recipes should be started if there are other recipes running and the load average is at least *load* (a floating-point number). With no argument, removes a previous load limit. See Section 5.4 [Parallel Execution], page 47.

'-L'

'--check-symlink-times'

        On systems that support symbolic links, this option causes `make` to consider the timestamps on any symbolic links in addition to the timestamp on the file referenced by those links. When this option is provided, the most recent timestamp among the file and the symbolic links is taken as the modification time for this target file.

'-n'

'--just-print'

'--dry-run'

'--recon'

Print the recipe that would be executed, but do not execute it (except in certain circumstances). See Section 9.3 [Instead of Executing Recipes], page 101.

'-o *file*'
'--old-file=*file*'
'--assume-old=*file*'

Do not remake the file *file* even if it is older than its prerequisites, and do not remake anything on account of changes in *file*. Essentially the file is treated as very old and its rules are ignored. See Section 9.4 [Avoiding Recompilation of Some Files], page 102.

'-O[*type*]'
'--output-sync[=*type*]'

Ensure that the complete output from each recipe is printed in one uninterrupted sequence. This option is only useful when using the --jobs option to run multiple recipes simultaneously (see Section 5.4 [Parallel Execution], page 47) Without this option output will be displayed as it is generated by the recipes.

With no type or the type 'target', output from the entire recipe of each target is grouped together. With the type 'line', output from each line in the recipe is grouped together. With the type 'recurse', the output from an entire recursive make is grouped together. With the type 'none', no output synchronization is performed. See Section 5.4.1 [Output During Parallel Execution], page 47.

'-p'
'--print-data-base'

Print the data base (rules and variable values) that results from reading the makefiles; then execute as usual or as otherwise specified. This also prints the version information given by the '-v' switch (see below). To print the data base without trying to remake any files, use 'make -qp'. To print the data base of predefined rules and variables, use 'make -p -f /dev/null'. The data base output contains file name and line number information for recipe and variable definitions, so it can be a useful debugging tool in complex environments.

'-q'
'--question'

"Question mode". Do not run any recipes, or print anything; just return an exit status that is zero if the specified targets are already up to date, one if any remaking is required, or two if an error is encountered. See Section 9.3 [Instead of Executing Recipes], page 101.

'-r'
'--no-builtin-rules'

Eliminate use of the built-in implicit rules (see Chapter 10 [Using Implicit Rules], page 111). You can still define your own by writing pattern rules (see Section 10.5 [Defining and Redefining Pattern Rules], page 118). The '-r' option also clears out the default list of suffixes for suffix rules (see Section 10.7 [Old-Fashioned Suffix Rules], page 125). But you can still define your own suffixes with a rule for .SUFFIXES, and then define your own suffix rules. Note that only *rules* are affected by the -r option; default variables remain in effect (see Section 10.3 [Variables Used by Implicit Rules], page 115); see the '-R' option below.

'-R'
'--no-builtin-variables'

>Eliminate use of the built-in rule-specific variables (see Section 10.3 [Variables Used by Implicit Rules], page 115). You can still define your own, of course. The '-R' option also automatically enables the '-r' option (see above), since it doesn't make sense to have implicit rules without any definitions for the variables that they use.

'-s'
'--silent'
'--quiet'

>Silent operation; do not print the recipes as they are executed. See Section 5.2 [Recipe Echoing], page 43.

'-S'
'--no-keep-going'
'--stop'

>Cancel the effect of the '-k' option. This is never necessary except in a recursive make where '-k' might be inherited from the top-level make via MAKEFLAGS (see Section 5.7 [Recursive Use of make], page 50) or if you set '-k' in MAKEFLAGS in your environment.

'-t'
'--touch'

>Touch files (mark them up to date without really changing them) instead of running their recipes. This is used to pretend that the recipes were done, in order to fool future invocations of make. See Section 9.3 [Instead of Executing Recipes], page 101.

'--trace' Show tracing information for make execution. Prints the entire recipe to be executed, even for recipes that are normally silent (due to .SILENT or '@'). Also prints the makefile name and line number where the recipe was defined, and information on why the target is being rebuilt.

'-v'
'--version'

>Print the version of the make program plus a copyright, a list of authors, and a notice that there is no warranty; then exit.

'-w'
'--print-directory'

>Print a message containing the working directory both before and after executing the makefile. This may be useful for tracking down errors from complicated nests of recursive make commands. See Section 5.7 [Recursive Use of make], page 50. (In practice, you rarely need to specify this option since 'make' does it for you; see Section 5.7.4 [The '--print-directory' Option], page 55.)

'`--no-print-directory`'

> Disable printing of the working directory under `-w`. This option is useful when `-w` is turned on automatically, but you do not want to see the extra messages. See Section 5.7.4 [The '`--print-directory`' Option], page 55.

'`-W file`'
'`--what-if=file`'
'`--new-file=file`'
'`--assume-new=file`'

> Pretend that the target *file* has just been modified. When used with the '`-n`' flag, this shows you what would happen if you were to modify that file. Without '`-n`', it is almost the same as running a `touch` command on the given file before running `make`, except that the modification time is changed only in the imagination of `make`. See Section 9.3 [Instead of Executing Recipes], page 101.

'`--warn-undefined-variables`'

> Issue a warning message whenever `make` sees a reference to an undefined variable. This can be helpful when you are trying to debug makefiles which use variables in complex ways.

10 Using Implicit Rules

Certain standard ways of remaking target files are used very often. For example, one customary way to make an object file is from a C source file using the C compiler, cc.

Implicit rules tell make how to use customary techniques so that you do not have to specify them in detail when you want to use them. For example, there is an implicit rule for C compilation. File names determine which implicit rules are run. For example, C compilation typically takes a .c file and makes a .o file. So make applies the implicit rule for C compilation when it sees this combination of file name endings.

A chain of implicit rules can apply in sequence; for example, make will remake a .o file from a .y file by way of a .c file. See Section 10.4 [Chains of Implicit Rules], page 117.

The built-in implicit rules use several variables in their recipes so that, by changing the values of the variables, you can change the way the implicit rule works. For example, the variable CFLAGS controls the flags given to the C compiler by the implicit rule for C compilation. See Section 10.3 [Variables Used by Implicit Rules], page 115.

You can define your own implicit rules by writing *pattern rules*. See Section 10.5 [Defining and Redefining Pattern Rules], page 118.

Suffix rules are a more limited way to define implicit rules. Pattern rules are more general and clearer, but suffix rules are retained for compatibility. See Section 10.7 [Old-Fashioned Suffix Rules], page 125.

10.1 Using Implicit Rules

To allow make to find a customary method for updating a target file, all you have to do is refrain from specifying recipes yourself. Either write a rule with no recipe, or don't write a rule at all. Then make will figure out which implicit rule to use based on which kind of source file exists or can be made.

For example, suppose the makefile looks like this:

```
foo : foo.o bar.o
        cc -o foo foo.o bar.o $(CFLAGS) $(LDFLAGS)
```

Because you mention foo.o but do not give a rule for it, make will automatically look for an implicit rule that tells how to update it. This happens whether or not the file foo.o currently exists.

If an implicit rule is found, it can supply both a recipe and one or more prerequisites (the source files). You would want to write a rule for foo.o with no recipe if you need to specify additional prerequisites, such as header files, that the implicit rule cannot supply.

Each implicit rule has a target pattern and prerequisite patterns. There may be many implicit rules with the same target pattern. For example, numerous rules make '.o' files: one, from a '.c' file with the C compiler; another, from a '.p' file with the Pascal compiler; and so on. The rule that actually applies is the one whose prerequisites exist or can be made. So, if you have a file foo.c, make will run the C compiler; otherwise, if you have a file foo.p, make will run the Pascal compiler; and so on.

Of course, when you write the makefile, you know which implicit rule you want make to use, and you know it will choose that one because you know which possible prerequisite files are supposed to exist. See Section 10.2 [Catalogue of Built-In Rules], page 112, for a catalogue of all the predefined implicit rules.

Above, we said an implicit rule applies if the required prerequisites "exist or can be made". A file "can be made" if it is mentioned explicitly in the makefile as a target or a prerequisite, or if an implicit rule can be recursively found for how to make it. When an implicit prerequisite is the result of another implicit rule, we say that *chaining* is occurring. See Section 10.4 [Chains of Implicit Rules], page 117.

In general, make searches for an implicit rule for each target, and for each double-colon rule, that has no recipe. A file that is mentioned only as a prerequisite is considered a target whose rule specifies nothing, so implicit rule search happens for it. See Section 10.8 [Implicit Rule Search Algorithm], page 127, for the details of how the search is done.

Note that explicit prerequisites do not influence implicit rule search. For example, consider this explicit rule:

        foo.o: foo.p

The prerequisite on foo.p does not necessarily mean that make will remake foo.o according to the implicit rule to make an object file, a .o file, from a Pascal source file, a .p file. For example, if foo.c also exists, the implicit rule to make an object file from a C source file is used instead, because it appears before the Pascal rule in the list of predefined implicit rules (see Section 10.2 [Catalogue of Built-In Rules], page 112).

If you do not want an implicit rule to be used for a target that has no recipe, you can give that target an empty recipe by writing a semicolon (see Section 5.9 [Defining Empty Recipes], page 57).

10.2 Catalogue of Built-In Rules

Here is a catalogue of predefined implicit rules which are always available unless the makefile explicitly overrides or cancels them. See Section 10.5.6 [Canceling Implicit Rules], page 124, for information on canceling or overriding an implicit rule. The '-r' or '--no-builtin-rules' option cancels all predefined rules.

This manual only documents the default rules available on POSIX-based operating systems. Other operating systems, such as VMS, Windows, OS/2, etc. may have different sets of default rules. To see the full list of default rules and variables available in your version of GNU make, run 'make -p' in a directory with no makefile.

Not all of these rules will always be defined, even when the '-r' option is not given. Many of the predefined implicit rules are implemented in make as suffix rules, so which ones will be defined depends on the *suffix list* (the list of prerequisites of the special target .SUFFIXES). The default suffix list is: .out, .a, .ln, .o, .c, .cc, .C, .cpp, .p, .f, .F, .m, .r, .y, .l, .ym, .lm, .s, .S, .mod, .sym, .def, .h, .info, .dvi, .tex, .texinfo, .texi, .txinfo, .w, .ch .web, .sh, .elc, .el. All of the implicit rules described below whose prerequisites have one of these suffixes are actually suffix rules. If you modify the suffix list, the only predefined suffix rules in effect will be those named by one or two of the suffixes that are on the list you specify; rules whose suffixes fail to be on the list are disabled. See Section 10.7 [Old-Fashioned Suffix Rules], page 125, for full details on suffix rules.

Compiling C programs

> *n*.o is made automatically from *n*.c with a recipe of the form '$(CC) $(CPPFLAGS) $(CFLAGS) -c'.

Compiling C++ programs

> n.o is made automatically from n.cc, n.cpp, or n.C with a recipe of the form '$(CXX) $(CPPFLAGS) $(CXXFLAGS) -c'. We encourage you to use the suffix '.cc' for C++ source files instead of '.C'.

Compiling Pascal programs

> n.o is made automatically from n.p with the recipe '$(PC) $(PFLAGS) -c'.

Compiling Fortran and Ratfor programs

> n.o is made automatically from n.r, n.F or n.f by running the Fortran compiler. The precise recipe used is as follows:

> '.f'   '$(FC) $(FFLAGS) -c'.

> '.F'   '$(FC) $(FFLAGS) $(CPPFLAGS) -c'.

> '.r'   '$(FC) $(FFLAGS) $(RFLAGS) -c'.

Preprocessing Fortran and Ratfor programs

> n.f is made automatically from n.r or n.F. This rule runs just the preprocessor to convert a Ratfor or preprocessable Fortran program into a strict Fortran program. The precise recipe used is as follows:

> '.F'   '$(FC) $(CPPFLAGS) $(FFLAGS) -F'.

> '.r'   '$(FC) $(FFLAGS) $(RFLAGS) -F'.

Compiling Modula-2 programs

> n.sym is made from n.def with a recipe of the form '$(M2C) $(M2FLAGS) $(DEFFLAGS)'. n.o is made from n.mod; the form is: '$(M2C) $(M2FLAGS) $(MODFLAGS)'.

Assembling and preprocessing assembler programs

> n.o is made automatically from n.s by running the assembler, as. The precise recipe is '$(AS) $(ASFLAGS)'.

> n.s is made automatically from n.S by running the C preprocessor, cpp. The precise recipe is '$(CPP) $(CPPFLAGS)'.

Linking a single object file

> n is made automatically from n.o by running the linker (usually called ld) via the C compiler. The precise recipe used is '$(CC) $(LDFLAGS) n.o $(LOADLIBES) $(LDLIBS)'.

> This rule does the right thing for a simple program with only one source file. It will also do the right thing if there are multiple object files (presumably coming from various other source files), one of which has a name matching that of the executable file. Thus,

> ```
> x: y.o z.o
> ```

> when x.c, y.c and z.c all exist will execute:

```
cc -c x.c -o x.o
cc -c y.c -o y.o
cc -c z.c -o z.o
cc x.o y.o z.o -o x
rm -f x.o
rm -f y.o
rm -f z.o
```

In more complicated cases, such as when there is no object file whose name derives from the executable file name, you must write an explicit recipe for linking.

Each kind of file automatically made into '.o' object files will be automatically linked by using the compiler ('$(CC)', '$(FC)' or '$(PC)'; the C compiler '$(CC)' is used to assemble '.s' files) without the '-c' option. This could be done by using the '.o' object files as intermediates, but it is faster to do the compiling and linking in one step, so that's how it's done.

Yacc for C programs
: *n*.c is made automatically from *n*.y by running Yacc with the recipe '$(YACC) $(YFLAGS)'.

Lex for C programs
: *n*.c is made automatically from *n*.l by running Lex. The actual recipe is '$(LEX) $(LFLAGS)'.

Lex for Ratfor programs
: *n*.r is made automatically from *n*.l by running Lex. The actual recipe is '$(LEX) $(LFLAGS)'.

The convention of using the same suffix '.l' for all Lex files regardless of whether they produce C code or Ratfor code makes it impossible for **make** to determine automatically which of the two languages you are using in any particular case. If **make** is called upon to remake an object file from a '.l' file, it must guess which compiler to use. It will guess the C compiler, because that is more common. If you are using Ratfor, make sure **make** knows this by mentioning *n*.r in the makefile. Or, if you are using Ratfor exclusively, with no C files, remove '.c' from the list of implicit rule suffixes with:

```
.SUFFIXES:
.SUFFIXES: .o .r .f .l ...
```

Making Lint Libraries from C, Yacc, or Lex programs
: *n*.ln is made from *n*.c by running **lint**. The precise recipe is '$(LINT) $(LINTFLAGS) $(CPPFLAGS) -i'. The same recipe is used on the C code produced from *n*.y or *n*.l.

T_EX and Web
: *n*.dvi is made from *n*.tex with the recipe '$(TEX)'. *n*.tex is made from *n*.web with '$(WEAVE)', or from *n*.w (and from *n*.ch if it exists or can be made) with '$(CWEAVE)'. *n*.p is made from *n*.web with '$(TANGLE)' and *n*.c is made from *n*.w (and from *n*.ch if it exists or can be made) with '$(CTANGLE)'.

Texinfo and Info

> *n*.dvi is made from *n*.texinfo, *n*.texi, or *n*.txinfo, with the recipe '$(TEXI2DVI) $(TEXI2DVI_FLAGS)'. *n*.info is made from *n*.texinfo, *n*.texi, or *n*.txinfo, with the recipe '$(MAKEINFO) $(MAKEINFO_FLAGS)'.

RCS

> Any file *n* is extracted if necessary from an RCS file named either *n*,v or RCS/*n*,v. The precise recipe used is '$(CO) $(COFLAGS)'. *n* will not be extracted from RCS if it already exists, even if the RCS file is newer. The rules for RCS are terminal (see Section 10.5.5 [Match-Anything Pattern Rules], page 123), so RCS files cannot be generated from another source; they must actually exist.

SCCS

> Any file *n* is extracted if necessary from an SCCS file named either s.*n* or SCCS/s.*n*. The precise recipe used is '$(GET) $(GFLAGS)'. The rules for SCCS are terminal (see Section 10.5.5 [Match-Anything Pattern Rules], page 123), so SCCS files cannot be generated from another source; they must actually exist.
>
> For the benefit of SCCS, a file *n* is copied from *n*.sh and made executable (by everyone). This is for shell scripts that are checked into SCCS. Since RCS preserves the execution permission of a file, you do not need to use this feature with RCS.
>
> We recommend that you avoid using of SCCS. RCS is widely held to be superior, and is also free. By choosing free software in place of comparable (or inferior) proprietary software, you support the free software movement.

Usually, you want to change only the variables listed in the table above, which are documented in the following section.

However, the recipes in built-in implicit rules actually use variables such as COMPILE.c, LINK.p, and PREPROCESS.S, whose values contain the recipes listed above.

make follows the convention that the rule to compile a .*x* source file uses the variable COMPILE.*x*. Similarly, the rule to produce an executable from a .*x* file uses LINK.*x*; and the rule to preprocess a .*x* file uses PREPROCESS.*x*.

Every rule that produces an object file uses the variable OUTPUT_OPTION. make defines this variable either to contain '-o $@', or to be empty, depending on a compile-time option. You need the '-o' option to ensure that the output goes into the right file when the source file is in a different directory, as when using VPATH (see Section 4.4 [Directory Search], page 25). However, compilers on some systems do not accept a '-o' switch for object files. If you use such a system, and use VPATH, some compilations will put their output in the wrong place. A possible workaround for this problem is to give OUTPUT_OPTION the value '; mv $*.o $@'.

10.3 Variables Used by Implicit Rules

The recipes in built-in implicit rules make liberal use of certain predefined variables. You can alter the values of these variables in the makefile, with arguments to make, or in the environment to alter how the implicit rules work without redefining the rules themselves. You can cancel all variables used by implicit rules with the '-R' or '--no-builtin-variables' option.

For example, the recipe used to compile a C source file actually says '$(CC) -c $(CFLAGS) $(CPPFLAGS)'. The default values of the variables used are 'cc' and nothing, resulting in the command 'cc -c'. By redefining 'CC' to 'ncc', you could cause 'ncc' to be used for all C compilations performed by the implicit rule. By redefining 'CFLAGS' to be '-g', you could pass the '-g' option to each compilation. *All* implicit rules that do C compilation use '$(CC)' to get the program name for the compiler and *all* include '$(CFLAGS)' among the arguments given to the compiler.

The variables used in implicit rules fall into two classes: those that are names of programs (like CC) and those that contain arguments for the programs (like CFLAGS). (The "name of a program" may also contain some command arguments, but it must start with an actual executable program name.) If a variable value contains more than one argument, separate them with spaces.

The following tables describe of some of the more commonly-used predefined variables. This list is not exhaustive, and the default values shown here may not be what make selects for your environment. To see the complete list of predefined variables for your instance of GNU make you can run 'make -p' in a directory with no makefiles.

Here is a table of some of the more common variables used as names of programs in built-in rules:

AR   Archive-maintaining program; default 'ar'.

AS   Program for compiling assembly files; default 'as'.

CC   Program for compiling C programs; default 'cc'.

CXX   Program for compiling C++ programs; default 'g++'.

CPP   Program for running the C preprocessor, with results to standard output; default '$(CC) -E'.

FC   Program for compiling or preprocessing Fortran and Ratfor programs; default 'f77'.

M2C   Program to use to compile Modula-2 source code; default 'm2c'.

PC   Program for compiling Pascal programs; default 'pc'.

CO   Program for extracting a file from RCS; default 'co'.

GET   Program for extracting a file from SCCS; default 'get'.

LEX   Program to use to turn Lex grammars into source code; default 'lex'.

YACC   Program to use to turn Yacc grammars into source code; default 'yacc'.

LINT   Program to use to run lint on source code; default 'lint'.

MAKEINFO Program to convert a Texinfo source file into an Info file; default 'makeinfo'.

TEX   Program to make TeX DVI files from TeX source; default 'tex'.

TEXI2DVI Program to make TeX DVI files from Texinfo source; default 'texi2dvi'.

WEAVE   Program to translate Web into TeX; default 'weave'.

CWEAVE   Program to translate C Web into TeX; default 'cweave'.

TANGLE   Program to translate Web into Pascal; default 'tangle'.

CTANGLE   Program to translate C Web into C; default 'ctangle'.

RM   Command to remove a file; default 'rm -f'.

Here is a table of variables whose values are additional arguments for the programs above. The default values for all of these is the empty string, unless otherwise noted.

ARFLAGS   Flags to give the archive-maintaining program; default 'rv'.

ASFLAGS   Extra flags to give to the assembler (when explicitly invoked on a '.s' or '.S' file).

CFLAGS   Extra flags to give to the C compiler.

CXXFLAGS   Extra flags to give to the C++ compiler.

COFLAGS   Extra flags to give to the RCS co program.

CPPFLAGS   Extra flags to give to the C preprocessor and programs that use it (the C and Fortran compilers).

FFLAGS   Extra flags to give to the Fortran compiler.

GFLAGS   Extra flags to give to the SCCS get program.

LDFLAGS   Extra flags to give to compilers when they are supposed to invoke the linker, 'ld', such as -L. Libraries (-lfoo) should be added to the LDLIBS variable instead.

LDLIBS   Library flags or names given to compilers when they are supposed to invoke the linker, 'ld'. LOADLIBES is a deprecated (but still supported) alternative to LDLIBS. Non-library linker flags, such as -L, should go in the LDFLAGS variable.

LFLAGS   Extra flags to give to Lex.

YFLAGS   Extra flags to give to Yacc.

PFLAGS   Extra flags to give to the Pascal compiler.

RFLAGS   Extra flags to give to the Fortran compiler for Ratfor programs.

LINTFLAGS
            Extra flags to give to lint.

10.4 Chains of Implicit Rules

Sometimes a file can be made by a sequence of implicit rules. For example, a file n.o could be made from n.y by running first Yacc and then cc. Such a sequence is called a *chain*.

If the file n.c exists, or is mentioned in the makefile, no special searching is required: make finds that the object file can be made by C compilation from n.c; later on, when considering how to make n.c, the rule for running Yacc is used. Ultimately both n.c and n.o are updated.

However, even if n.c does not exist and is not mentioned, make knows how to envision it as the missing link between n.o and n.y! In this case, n.c is called an *intermediate file*.

Once make has decided to use the intermediate file, it is entered in the data base as if it had been mentioned in the makefile, along with the implicit rule that says how to create it.

Intermediate files are remade using their rules just like all other files. But intermediate files are treated differently in two ways.

The first difference is what happens if the intermediate file does not exist. If an ordinary file *b* does not exist, and make considers a target that depends on *b*, it invariably creates *b* and then updates the target from *b*. But if *b* is an intermediate file, then make can leave well enough alone. It won't bother updating *b*, or the ultimate target, unless some prerequisite of *b* is newer than that target or there is some other reason to update that target.

The second difference is that if make *does* create *b* in order to update something else, it deletes *b* later on after it is no longer needed. Therefore, an intermediate file which did not exist before make also does not exist after make. make reports the deletion to you by printing a 'rm -f' command showing which file it is deleting.

Ordinarily, a file cannot be intermediate if it is mentioned in the makefile as a target or prerequisite. However, you can explicitly mark a file as intermediate by listing it as a prerequisite of the special target .INTERMEDIATE. This takes effect even if the file is mentioned explicitly in some other way.

You can prevent automatic deletion of an intermediate file by marking it as a *secondary* file. To do this, list it as a prerequisite of the special target .SECONDARY. When a file is secondary, make will not create the file merely because it does not already exist, but make does not automatically delete the file. Marking a file as secondary also marks it as intermediate.

You can list the target pattern of an implicit rule (such as '%.o') as a prerequisite of the special target .PRECIOUS to preserve intermediate files made by implicit rules whose target patterns match that file's name; see Section 5.6 [Interrupts], page 50.

A chain can involve more than two implicit rules. For example, it is possible to make a file foo from RCS/foo.y,v by running RCS, Yacc and cc. Then both foo.y and foo.c are intermediate files that are deleted at the end.

No single implicit rule can appear more than once in a chain. This means that make will not even consider such a ridiculous thing as making foo from foo.o.o by running the linker twice. This constraint has the added benefit of preventing any infinite loop in the search for an implicit rule chain.

There are some special implicit rules to optimize certain cases that would otherwise be handled by rule chains. For example, making foo from foo.c could be handled by compiling and linking with separate chained rules, using foo.o as an intermediate file. But what actually happens is that a special rule for this case does the compilation and linking with a single cc command. The optimized rule is used in preference to the step-by-step chain because it comes earlier in the ordering of rules.

10.5 Defining and Redefining Pattern Rules

You define an implicit rule by writing a *pattern rule*. A pattern rule looks like an ordinary rule, except that its target contains the character '%' (exactly one of them). The target is considered a pattern for matching file names; the '%' can match any nonempty substring, while other characters match only themselves. The prerequisites likewise use '%' to show how their names relate to the target name.

Thus, a pattern rule '%.o : %.c' says how to make any file `stem.o` from another file `stem.c`.

Note that expansion using '%' in pattern rules occurs **after** any variable or function expansions, which take place when the makefile is read. See Chapter 6 [How to Use Variables], page 59, and Chapter 8 [Functions for Transforming Text], page 83.

10.5.1 Introduction to Pattern Rules

A pattern rule contains the character '%' (exactly one of them) in the target; otherwise, it looks exactly like an ordinary rule. The target is a pattern for matching file names; the '%' matches any nonempty substring, while other characters match only themselves.

For example, '%.c' as a pattern matches any file name that ends in '.c'. 's.%.c' as a pattern matches any file name that starts with 's.', ends in '.c' and is at least five characters long. (There must be at least one character to match the '%'.) The substring that the '%' matches is called the *stem*.

'%' in a prerequisite of a pattern rule stands for the same stem that was matched by the '%' in the target. In order for the pattern rule to apply, its target pattern must match the file name under consideration and all of its prerequisites (after pattern substitution) must name files that exist or can be made. These files become prerequisites of the target.

Thus, a rule of the form

```
%.o : %.c ; recipe...
```

specifies how to make a file `n.o`, with another file `n.c` as its prerequisite, provided that `n.c` exists or can be made.

There may also be prerequisites that do not use '%'; such a prerequisite attaches to every file made by this pattern rule. These unvarying prerequisites are useful occasionally.

A pattern rule need not have any prerequisites that contain '%', or in fact any prerequisites at all. Such a rule is effectively a general wildcard. It provides a way to make any file that matches the target pattern. See Section 10.6 [Last Resort], page 125.

More than one pattern rule may match a target. In this case **make** will choose the "best fit" rule. See Section 10.5.4 [How Patterns Match], page 122.

Pattern rules may have more than one target. Unlike normal rules, this does not act as many different rules with the same prerequisites and recipe. If a pattern rule has multiple targets, **make** knows that the rule's recipe is responsible for making all of the targets. The recipe is executed only once to make all the targets. When searching for a pattern rule to match a target, the target patterns of a rule other than the one that matches the target in need of a rule are incidental: **make** worries only about giving a recipe and prerequisites to the file presently in question. However, when this file's recipe is run, the other targets are marked as having been updated themselves.

10.5.2 Pattern Rule Examples

Here are some examples of pattern rules actually predefined in **make**. First, the rule that compiles '.c' files into '.o' files:

```
%.o : %.c
        $(CC) -c $(CFLAGS) $(CPPFLAGS) $< -o $@
```

defines a rule that can make any file `x.o` from `x.c`. The recipe uses the automatic variables '`$@`' and '`$<`' to substitute the names of the target file and the source file in each case where the rule applies (see Section 10.5.3 [Automatic Variables], page 120).

Here is a second built-in rule:

```
% :: RCS/%,v
        $(CO) $(COFLAGS) $<
```

defines a rule that can make any file `x` whatsoever from a corresponding file `x,v` in the sub-directory `RCS`. Since the target is '`%`', this rule will apply to any file whatever, provided the appropriate prerequisite file exists. The double colon makes the rule *terminal*, which means that its prerequisite may not be an intermediate file (see Section 10.5.5 [Match-Anything Pattern Rules], page 123).

This pattern rule has two targets:

```
%.tab.c %.tab.h: %.y
        bison -d $<
```

This tells `make` that the recipe '`bison -d x.y`' will make both `x.tab.c` and `x.tab.h`. If the file `foo` depends on the files `parse.tab.o` and `scan.o` and the file `scan.o` depends on the file `parse.tab.h`, when `parse.y` is changed, the recipe '`bison -d parse.y`' will be executed only once, and the prerequisites of both `parse.tab.o` and `scan.o` will be satisfied. (Presumably the file `parse.tab.o` will be recompiled from `parse.tab.c` and the file `scan.o` from `scan.c`, while `foo` is linked from `parse.tab.o`, `scan.o`, and its other prerequisites, and it will execute happily ever after.)

10.5.3 Automatic Variables

Suppose you are writing a pattern rule to compile a '`.c`' file into a '`.o`' file: how do you write the '`cc`' command so that it operates on the right source file name? You cannot write the name in the recipe, because the name is different each time the implicit rule is applied.

What you do is use a special feature of `make`, the *automatic variables*. These variables have values computed afresh for each rule that is executed, based on the target and prerequisites of the rule. In this example, you would use '`$@`' for the object file name and '`$<`' for the source file name.

It's very important that you recognize the limited scope in which automatic variable values are available: they only have values within the recipe. In particular, you cannot use them anywhere within the target list of a rule; they have no value there and will expand to the empty string. Also, they cannot be accessed directly within the prerequisite list of a rule. A common mistake is attempting to use `$@` within the prerequisites list; this will not work. However, there is a special feature of GNU `make`, secondary expansion (see Section 3.8 [Secondary Expansion], page 18), which will allow automatic variable values to be used in prerequisite lists.

Here is a table of automatic variables:

`$@`   The file name of the target of the rule. If the target is an archive member, then '`$@`' is the name of the archive file. In a pattern rule that has multiple targets (see Section 10.5.1 [Introduction to Pattern Rules], page 119), '`$@`' is the name of whichever target caused the rule's recipe to be run.

$%   The target member name, when the target is an archive member. See
            Chapter 11 [Archives], page 129. For example, if the target is `foo.a(bar.o)`
            then '`$%`' is `bar.o` and '`$@`' is `foo.a`. '`$%`' is empty when the target is not an
            archive member.

$<   The name of the first prerequisite. If the target got its recipe from an implicit
            rule, this will be the first prerequisite added by the implicit rule (see Chapter 10
            [Implicit Rules], page 111).

$?   The names of all the prerequisites that are newer than the target, with spaces
            between them. For prerequisites which are archive members, only the named
            member is used (see Chapter 11 [Archives], page 129).

$^   The names of all the prerequisites, with spaces between them. For prerequisites
            which are archive members, only the named member is used (see Chapter 11
            [Archives], page 129). A target has only one prerequisite on each other file it
            depends on, no matter how many times each file is listed as a prerequisite. So
            if you list a prerequisite more than once for a target, the value of `$^` contains
            just one copy of the name. This list does **not** contain any of the order-only
            prerequisites; for those see the '`$|`' variable, below.

$+   This is like '`$^`', but prerequisites listed more than once are duplicated in the
            order they were listed in the makefile. This is primarily useful for use in linking
            commands where it is meaningful to repeat library file names in a particular
            order.

$| The names of all the order-only prerequisites, with spaces between them.

$*   The stem with which an implicit rule matches (see Section 10.5.4 [How Patterns
            Match], page 122). If the target is `dir/a.foo.b` and the target pattern is `a.%.b`
            then the stem is `dir/foo`. The stem is useful for constructing names of related
            files.

            In a static pattern rule, the stem is part of the file name that matched the '`%`'
            in the target pattern.

            In an explicit rule, there is no stem; so '`$*`' cannot be determined in that way.
            Instead, if the target name ends with a recognized suffix (see Section 10.7 [Old-
            Fashioned Suffix Rules], page 125), '`$*`' is set to the target name minus the
            suffix. For example, if the target name is '`foo.c`', then '`$*`' is set to '`foo`', since
            '`.c`' is a suffix. GNU `make` does this bizarre thing only for compatibility with
            other implementations of `make`. You should generally avoid using '`$*`' except in
            implicit rules or static pattern rules.

            If the target name in an explicit rule does not end with a recognized suffix, '`$*`'
            is set to the empty string for that rule.

'`$?`' is useful even in explicit rules when you wish to operate on only the prerequisites
that have changed. For example, suppose that an archive named `lib` is supposed to contain
copies of several object files. This rule copies just the changed object files into the archive:

```
lib: foo.o bar.o lose.o win.o
        ar r lib $?
```

Of the variables listed above, four have values that are single file names, and three have values that are lists of file names. These seven have variants that get just the file's directory name or just the file name within the directory. The variant variables' names are formed by appending 'D' or 'F', respectively. These variants are semi-obsolete in GNU make since the functions dir and notdir can be used to get a similar effect (see Section 8.3 [Functions for File Names], page 87). Note, however, that the 'D' variants all omit the trailing slash which always appears in the output of the dir function. Here is a table of the variants:

'$(@D)'   The directory part of the file name of the target, with the trailing slash removed. If the value of '$@' is dir/foo.o then '$(@D)' is dir. This value is . if '$@' does not contain a slash.

'$(@F)'   The file-within-directory part of the file name of the target. If the value of '$@' is dir/foo.o then '$(@F)' is foo.o. '$(@F)' is equivalent to '$(notdir $@)'.

'$(*D)'
'$(*F)'   The directory part and the file-within-directory part of the stem; dir and foo in this example.

'$(%D)'
'$(%F)'   The directory part and the file-within-directory part of the target archive member name. This makes sense only for archive member targets of the form archive(member) and is useful only when member may contain a directory name. (See Section 11.1 [Archive Members as Targets], page 129.)

'$(<D)'
'$(<F)'   The directory part and the file-within-directory part of the first prerequisite.

'$(^D)'
'$(^F)'   Lists of the directory parts and the file-within-directory parts of all prerequisites.

'$(+D)'
'$(+F)'   Lists of the directory parts and the file-within-directory parts of all prerequisites, including multiple instances of duplicated prerequisites.

'$(?D)'
'$(?F)'   Lists of the directory parts and the file-within-directory parts of all prerequisites that are newer than the target.

Note that we use a special stylistic convention when we talk about these automatic variables; we write "the value of '$<'", rather than "the variable <" as we would write for ordinary variables such as objects and CFLAGS. We think this convention looks more natural in this special case. Please do not assume it has a deep significance; '$<' refers to the variable named < just as '$(CFLAGS)' refers to the variable named CFLAGS. You could just as well use '$(<)' in place of '$<'.

10.5.4 How Patterns Match

A target pattern is composed of a '%' between a prefix and a suffix, either or both of which may be empty. The pattern matches a file name only if the file name starts with the prefix and ends with the suffix, without overlap. The text between the prefix and the suffix is called the *stem*. Thus, when the pattern '%.o' matches the file name test.o, the stem is 'test'. The pattern rule prerequisites are turned into actual file names by substituting the stem for the character '%'. Thus, if in the same example one of the prerequisites is written as '%.c', it expands to 'test.c'.

When the target pattern does not contain a slash (and it usually does not), directory names in the file names are removed from the file name before it is compared with the target prefix and suffix. After the comparison of the file name to the target pattern, the directory names, along with the slash that ends them, are added on to the prerequisite file names generated from the pattern rule's prerequisite patterns and the file name. The directories are ignored only for the purpose of finding an implicit rule to use, not in the application of that rule. Thus, 'e%t' matches the file name src/eat, with 'src/a' as the stem. When prerequisites are turned into file names, the directories from the stem are added at the front, while the rest of the stem is substituted for the '%'. The stem 'src/a' with a prerequisite pattern 'c%r' gives the file name src/car.

A pattern rule can be used to build a given file only if there is a target pattern that matches the file name, *and* all prerequisites in that rule either exist or can be built. The rules you write take precedence over those that are built in. Note however, that a rule whose prerequisites actually exist or are mentioned always takes priority over a rule with prerequisites that must be made by chaining other implicit rules.

It is possible that more than one pattern rule will meet these criteria. In that case, make will choose the rule with the shortest stem (that is, the pattern that matches most specifically). If more than one pattern rule has the shortest stem, make will choose the first one found in the makefile.

This algorithm results in more specific rules being preferred over more generic ones; for example:

```
%.o: %.c
        $(CC) -c $(CFLAGS) $(CPPFLAGS) $< -o $@

%.o : %.f
        $(COMPILE.F) $(OUTPUT_OPTION) $<

lib/%.o: lib/%.c
        $(CC) -fPIC -c $(CFLAGS) $(CPPFLAGS) $< -o $@
```

Given these rules and asked to build bar.o where both bar.c and bar.f exist, make will choose the first rule and compile bar.c into bar.o. In the same situation where bar.c does not exist, then make will choose the second rule and compile bar.f into bar.o.

If make is asked to build lib/bar.o and both lib/bar.c and lib/bar.f exist, then the third rule will be chosen since the stem for this rule ('bar') is shorter than the stem for the first rule ('lib/bar'). If lib/bar.c does not exist then the third rule is not eligible and the second rule will be used, even though the stem is longer.

10.5.5 Match-Anything Pattern Rules

When a pattern rule's target is just '%', it matches any file name whatever. We call these rules *match-anything* rules. They are very useful, but it can take a lot of time for make to think about them, because it must consider every such rule for each file name listed either as a target or as a prerequisite.

Suppose the makefile mentions `foo.c`. For this target, `make` would have to consider making it by linking an object file `foo.c.o`, or by C compilation-and-linking in one step from `foo.c.c`, or by Pascal compilation-and-linking from `foo.c.p`, and many other possibilities.

We know these possibilities are ridiculous since `foo.c` is a C source file, not an executable. If `make` did consider these possibilities, it would ultimately reject them, because files such as `foo.c.o` and `foo.c.p` would not exist. But these possibilities are so numerous that `make` would run very slowly if it had to consider them.

To gain speed, we have put various constraints on the way `make` considers match-anything rules. There are two different constraints that can be applied, and each time you define a match-anything rule you must choose one or the other for that rule.

One choice is to mark the match-anything rule as *terminal* by defining it with a double colon. When a rule is terminal, it does not apply unless its prerequisites actually exist. Prerequisites that could be made with other implicit rules are not good enough. In other words, no further chaining is allowed beyond a terminal rule.

For example, the built-in implicit rules for extracting sources from RCS and SCCS files are terminal; as a result, if the file `foo.c,v` does not exist, `make` will not even consider trying to make it as an intermediate file from `foo.c,v.o` or from `RCS/SCCS/s.foo.c,v`. RCS and SCCS files are generally ultimate source files, which should not be remade from any other files; therefore, `make` can save time by not looking for ways to remake them.

If you do not mark the match-anything rule as terminal, then it is non-terminal. A non-terminal match-anything rule cannot apply to a file name that indicates a specific type of data. A file name indicates a specific type of data if some non-match-anything implicit rule target matches it.

For example, the file name `foo.c` matches the target for the pattern rule '`%.c : %.y`' (the rule to run Yacc). Regardless of whether this rule is actually applicable (which happens only if there is a file `foo.y`), the fact that its target matches is enough to prevent consideration of any non-terminal match-anything rules for the file `foo.c`. Thus, `make` will not even consider trying to make `foo.c` as an executable file from `foo.c.o`, `foo.c.c`, `foo.c.p`, etc.

The motivation for this constraint is that non-terminal match-anything rules are used for making files containing specific types of data (such as executable files) and a file name with a recognized suffix indicates some other specific type of data (such as a C source file).

Special built-in dummy pattern rules are provided solely to recognize certain file names so that non-terminal match-anything rules will not be considered. These dummy rules have no prerequisites and no recipes, and they are ignored for all other purposes. For example, the built-in implicit rule

```
%.p :
```

exists to make sure that Pascal source files such as `foo.p` match a specific target pattern and thereby prevent time from being wasted looking for `foo.p.o` or `foo.p.c`.

Dummy pattern rules such as the one for '`%.p`' are made for every suffix listed as valid for use in suffix rules (see Section 10.7 [Old-Fashioned Suffix Rules], page 125).

10.5.6 Canceling Implicit Rules

You can override a built-in implicit rule (or one you have defined yourself) by defining a new pattern rule with the same target and prerequisites, but a different recipe. When the new rule is defined, the built-in one is replaced. The new rule's position in the sequence of implicit rules is determined by where you write the new rule.

You can cancel a built-in implicit rule by defining a pattern rule with the same target and prerequisites, but no recipe. For example, the following would cancel the rule that runs the assembler:

```
%.o : %.s
```

10.6 Defining Last-Resort Default Rules

You can define a last-resort implicit rule by writing a terminal match-anything pattern rule with no prerequisites (see Section 10.5.5 [Match-Anything Rules], page 123). This is just like any other pattern rule; the only thing special about it is that it will match any target. So such a rule's recipe is used for all targets and prerequisites that have no recipe of their own and for which no other implicit rule applies.

For example, when testing a makefile, you might not care if the source files contain real data, only that they exist. Then you might do this:

```
%::
        touch $@
```

to cause all the source files needed (as prerequisites) to be created automatically.

You can instead define a recipe to be used for targets for which there are no rules at all, even ones which don't specify recipes. You do this by writing a rule for the target .DEFAULT. Such a rule's recipe is used for all prerequisites which do not appear as targets in any explicit rule, and for which no implicit rule applies. Naturally, there is no .DEFAULT rule unless you write one.

If you use .DEFAULT with no recipe or prerequisites:

```
.DEFAULT:
```

the recipe previously stored for .DEFAULT is cleared. Then make acts as if you had never defined .DEFAULT at all.

If you do not want a target to get the recipe from a match-anything pattern rule or .DEFAULT, but you also do not want any recipe to be run for the target, you can give it an empty recipe (see Section 5.9 [Defining Empty Recipes], page 57).

You can use a last-resort rule to override part of another makefile. See Section 3.6 [Overriding Part of Another Makefile], page 15.

10.7 Old-Fashioned Suffix Rules

Suffix rules are the old-fashioned way of defining implicit rules for make. Suffix rules are obsolete because pattern rules are more general and clearer. They are supported in GNU make for compatibility with old makefiles. They come in two kinds: *double-suffix* and *single-suffix*.

A double-suffix rule is defined by a pair of suffixes: the target suffix and the source suffix. It matches any file whose name ends with the target suffix. The corresponding implicit prerequisite is made by replacing the target suffix with the source suffix in the file name. A two-suffix rule whose target and source suffixes are '.o' and '.c' is equivalent to the pattern rule '%.o : %.c'.

A single-suffix rule is defined by a single suffix, which is the source suffix. It matches any file name, and the corresponding implicit prerequisite name is made by appending the source suffix. A single-suffix rule whose source suffix is '.c' is equivalent to the pattern rule '% : %.c'.

Suffix rule definitions are recognized by comparing each rule's target against a defined list of known suffixes. When make sees a rule whose target is a known suffix, this rule is considered a single-suffix rule. When make sees a rule whose target is two known suffixes concatenated, this rule is taken as a double-suffix rule.

For example, '.c' and '.o' are both on the default list of known suffixes. Therefore, if you define a rule whose target is '.c.o', make takes it to be a double-suffix rule with source suffix '.c' and target suffix '.o'. Here is the old-fashioned way to define the rule for compiling a C source file:

```
.c.o:
        $(CC) -c $(CFLAGS) $(CPPFLAGS) -o $@ $<
```

Suffix rules cannot have any prerequisites of their own. If they have any, they are treated as normal files with funny names, not as suffix rules. Thus, the rule:

```
.c.o: foo.h
        $(CC) -c $(CFLAGS) $(CPPFLAGS) -o $@ $<
```

tells how to make the file .c.o from the prerequisite file foo.h, and is not at all like the pattern rule:

```
%.o: %.c foo.h
        $(CC) -c $(CFLAGS) $(CPPFLAGS) -o $@ $<
```

which tells how to make '.o' files from '.c' files, and makes all '.o' files using this pattern rule also depend on foo.h.

Suffix rules with no recipe are also meaningless. They do not remove previous rules as do pattern rules with no recipe (see Section 10.5.6 [Canceling Implicit Rules], page 124). They simply enter the suffix or pair of suffixes concatenated as a target in the data base.

The known suffixes are simply the names of the prerequisites of the special target .SUFFIXES. You can add your own suffixes by writing a rule for .SUFFIXES that adds more prerequisites, as in:

```
.SUFFIXES: .hack .win
```

which adds '.hack' and '.win' to the end of the list of suffixes.

If you wish to eliminate the default known suffixes instead of just adding to them, write a rule for .SUFFIXES with no prerequisites. By special dispensation, this eliminates all existing prerequisites of .SUFFIXES. You can then write another rule to add the suffixes you want. For example,

```
.SUFFIXES:              # Delete the default suffixes
.SUFFIXES: .c .o .h     # Define our suffix list
```

The '-r' or '--no-builtin-rules' flag causes the default list of suffixes to be empty.

The variable SUFFIXES is defined to the default list of suffixes before make reads any makefiles. You can change the list of suffixes with a rule for the special target .SUFFIXES, but that does not alter this variable.

10.8 Implicit Rule Search Algorithm

Here is the procedure make uses for searching for an implicit rule for a target t. This procedure is followed for each double-colon rule with no recipe, for each target of ordinary rules none of which have a recipe, and for each prerequisite that is not the target of any rule. It is also followed recursively for prerequisites that come from implicit rules, in the search for a chain of rules.

Suffix rules are not mentioned in this algorithm because suffix rules are converted to equivalent pattern rules once the makefiles have been read in.

For an archive member target of the form 'archive(member)', the following algorithm is run twice, first using the entire target name t, and second using '(member)' as the target t if the first run found no rule.

1. Split t into a directory part, called d, and the rest, called n. For example, if t is 'src/foo.o', then d is 'src/' and n is 'foo.o'.

2. Make a list of all the pattern rules one of whose targets matches t or n. If the target pattern contains a slash, it is matched against t; otherwise, against n.

3. If any rule in that list is *not* a match-anything rule, then remove all non-terminal match-anything rules from the list.

4. Remove from the list all rules with no recipe.

5. For each pattern rule in the list:

   a. Find the stem s, which is the nonempty part of t or n matched by the '%' in the target pattern.

   b. Compute the prerequisite names by substituting s for '%'; if the target pattern does not contain a slash, append d to the front of each prerequisite name.

   c. Test whether all the prerequisites exist or ought to exist. (If a file name is mentioned in the makefile as a target or as an explicit prerequisite, then we say it ought to exist.)

      If all prerequisites exist or ought to exist, or there are no prerequisites, then this rule applies.

6. If no pattern rule has been found so far, try harder. For each pattern rule in the list:

   a. If the rule is terminal, ignore it and go on to the next rule.

   b. Compute the prerequisite names as before.

   c. Test whether all the prerequisites exist or ought to exist.

   d. For each prerequisite that does not exist, follow this algorithm recursively to see if the prerequisite can be made by an implicit rule.

   e. If all prerequisites exist, ought to exist, or can be made by implicit rules, then this rule applies.

7. If no implicit rule applies, the rule for .DEFAULT, if any, applies. In that case, give t the same recipe that .DEFAULT has. Otherwise, there is no recipe for t.

Once a rule that applies has been found, for each target pattern of the rule other than the one that matched t or n, the '%' in the pattern is replaced with s and the resultant file name is stored until the recipe to remake the target file t is executed. After the recipe is executed, each of these stored file names are entered into the data base and marked as having been updated and having the same update status as the file t.

When the recipe of a pattern rule is executed for t, the automatic variables are set corresponding to the target and prerequisites. See Section 10.5.3 [Automatic Variables], page 120.

11 Using make to Update Archive Files

Archive files are files containing named sub-files called *members*; they are maintained with the program ar and their main use is as subroutine libraries for linking.

11.1 Archive Members as Targets

An individual member of an archive file can be used as a target or prerequisite in make. You specify the member named *member* in archive file *archive* as follows:

    archive(member)

This construct is available only in targets and prerequisites, not in recipes! Most programs that you might use in recipes do not support this syntax and cannot act directly on archive members. Only ar and other programs specifically designed to operate on archives can do so. Therefore, valid recipes to update an archive member target probably must use ar. For example, this rule says to create a member hack.o in archive foolib by copying the file hack.o:

    foolib(hack.o) : hack.o
            ar cr foolib hack.o

In fact, nearly all archive member targets are updated in just this way and there is an implicit rule to do it for you. **Please note:** The 'c' flag to ar is required if the archive file does not already exist.

To specify several members in the same archive, you can write all the member names together between the parentheses. For example:

    foolib(hack.o kludge.o)

is equivalent to:

    foolib(hack.o) foolib(kludge.o)

You can also use shell-style wildcards in an archive member reference. See Section 4.3 [Using Wildcard Characters in File Names], page 23. For example, 'foolib(*.o)' expands to all existing members of the foolib archive whose names end in '.o'; perhaps 'foolib(hack.o) foolib(kludge.o)'.

11.2 Implicit Rule for Archive Member Targets

Recall that a target that looks like a(m) stands for the member named *m* in the archive file *a*.

When make looks for an implicit rule for such a target, as a special feature it considers implicit rules that match (m), as well as those that match the actual target a(m).

This causes one special rule whose target is (%) to match. This rule updates the target a(m) by copying the file *m* into the archive. For example, it will update the archive member target foo.a(bar.o) by copying the *file* bar.o into the archive foo.a as a *member* named bar.o.

When this rule is chained with others, the result is very powerful. Thus, 'make "foo.a(bar.o)"' (the quotes are needed to protect the '(' and ')' from being interpreted specially by the shell) in the presence of a file bar.c is enough to cause the following recipe to be run, even without a makefile:

```
cc -c bar.c -o bar.o
ar r foo.a bar.o
rm -f bar.o
```

Here make has envisioned the file bar.o as an intermediate file. See Section 10.4 [Chains of Implicit Rules], page 117.

Implicit rules such as this one are written using the automatic variable '$%'. See Section 10.5.3 [Automatic Variables], page 120.

An archive member name in an archive cannot contain a directory name, but it may be useful in a makefile to pretend that it does. If you write an archive member target foo.a(dir/file.o), make will perform automatic updating with this recipe:

```
ar r foo.a dir/file.o
```

which has the effect of copying the file dir/file.o into a member named file.o. In connection with such usage, the automatic variables %D and %F may be useful.

11.2.1 Updating Archive Symbol Directories

An archive file that is used as a library usually contains a special member named __.SYMDEF that contains a directory of the external symbol names defined by all the other members. After you update any other members, you need to update __.SYMDEF so that it will summarize the other members properly. This is done by running the ranlib program:

```
ranlib archivefile
```

Normally you would put this command in the rule for the archive file, and make all the members of the archive file prerequisites of that rule. For example,

```
libfoo.a: libfoo.a(x.o) libfoo.a(y.o) ...
        ranlib libfoo.a
```

The effect of this is to update archive members x.o, y.o, etc., and then update the symbol directory member __.SYMDEF by running ranlib. The rules for updating the members are not shown here; most likely you can omit them and use the implicit rule which copies files into the archive, as described in the preceding section.

This is not necessary when using the GNU ar program, which updates the __.SYMDEF member automatically.

11.3 Dangers When Using Archives

It is important to be careful when using parallel execution (the -j switch; see Section 5.4 [Parallel Execution], page 47) and archives. If multiple ar commands run at the same time on the same archive file, they will not know about each other and can corrupt the file.

Possibly a future version of make will provide a mechanism to circumvent this problem by serializing all recipes that operate on the same archive file. But for the time being, you must either write your makefiles to avoid this problem in some other way, or not use -j.

11.4 Suffix Rules for Archive Files

You can write a special kind of suffix rule for dealing with archive files. See Section 10.7 [Suffix Rules], page 125, for a full explanation of suffix rules. Archive suffix rules are obsolete in GNU make, because pattern rules for archives are a more general mechanism (see Section 11.2 [Archive Update], page 129). But they are retained for compatibility with other makes.

To write a suffix rule for archives, you simply write a suffix rule using the target suffix '.a' (the usual suffix for archive files). For example, here is the old-fashioned suffix rule to update a library archive from C source files:

```
.c.a:
        $(CC) $(CFLAGS) $(CPPFLAGS) -c $< -o $*.o
        $(AR) r $@ $*.o
        $(RM) $*.o
```

This works just as if you had written the pattern rule:

```
(%.o): %.c
        $(CC) $(CFLAGS) $(CPPFLAGS) -c $< -o $*.o
        $(AR) r $@ $*.o
        $(RM) $*.o
```

In fact, this is just what make does when it sees a suffix rule with '.a' as the target suffix. Any double-suffix rule '.x.a' is converted to a pattern rule with the target pattern '(%.o)' and a prerequisite pattern of '%.x'.

Since you might want to use '.a' as the suffix for some other kind of file, make also converts archive suffix rules to pattern rules in the normal way (see Section 10.7 [Suffix Rules], page 125). Thus a double-suffix rule '.x.a' produces two pattern rules: '(%.o): %.x' and '%.a: %.x'.

12 Extending GNU make

GNU make provides many advanced capabilities, including many useful functions. However, it does not contain a complete programming language and so it has limitations. Sometimes these limitations can be overcome through use of the shell function to invoke a separate program, although this can be inefficient.

In cases where the built-in capabilities of GNU make are insufficient to your requirements there are two options for extending make. On systems where it's provided, you can utilize GNU Guile as an embedded scripting language (see Section 12.1 [GNU Guile Integration], page 133). On systems which support dynamically loadable objects, you can write your own extension in any language (which can be compiled into such an object) and load it to provide extended capabilities (see Section 12.2.1 [The load Directive], page 136).

12.1 GNU Guile Integration

GNU make may be built with support for GNU Guile as an embedded extension language. Guile implements the Scheme language. A review of GNU Guile and the Scheme language and its features is beyond the scope of this manual: see the documentation for GNU Guile and Scheme.

You can determine if make contains support for Guile by examining the .FEATURES variable; it will contain the word *guile* if Guile support is available.

The Guile integration provides one new make function: guile. The guile function takes one argument which is first expanded by make in the normal fashion, then passed to the GNU Guile evaluator. The result of the evaluator is converted into a string and used as the expansion of the guile function in the makefile.

In addition, GNU make exposes Guile procedures for use in Guile scripts.

12.1.1 Conversion of Guile Types

There is only one "data type" in make: a string. GNU Guile, on the other hand, provides a rich variety of different data types. An important aspect of the interface between make and GNU Guile is the conversion of Guile data types into make strings.

This conversion is relevant in two places: when a makefile invokes the guile function to evaluate a Guile expression, the result of that evaluation must be converted into a make string so it can be further evaluated by make. And secondly, when a Guile script invokes one of the procedures exported by make the argument provided to the procedure must be converted into a string.

The conversion of Guile types into make strings is as below:

#f   False is converted into the empty string: in make conditionals the empty string
            is considered false.

#t   True is converted to the string '#t': in make conditionals any non-empty string
            is considered true.

symbol

number   A symbol or number is converted into the string representation of that symbol
            or number.

character
>   A printable character is converted to the same character.

string   A string containing only printable characters is converted to the same string.

list   A list is converted recursively according to the above rules. This implies that any structured list will be flattened (that is, a result of ''(a b (c d) e)' will be converted to the make string 'a b c d e').

other   Any other Guile type results in an error. In future versions of make, other Guile types may be converted.

The translation of '#f' (to the empty string) and '#t' (to the non-empty string '#t') is designed to allow you to use Guile boolean results directly as make boolean conditions. For example:

```
$(if $(guile (access? "myfile" R_OK)),$(info myfile exists))
```

As a consequence of these conversion rules you must consider the result of your Guile script, as that result will be converted into a string and parsed by make. If there is no natural result for the script (that is, the script exists solely for its side-effects), you should add '#f' as the final expression in order to avoid syntax errors in your makefile.

12.1.2 Interfaces from Guile to make

In addition to the guile function available in makefiles, make exposes some procedures for use in your Guile scripts. At startup make creates a new Guile module, gnu make, and exports these procedures as public interfaces from that module:

gmk-expand
>   This procedure takes a single argument which is converted into a string. The string is expanded by make using normal make expansion rules. The result of the expansion is converted into a Guile string and provided as the result of the procedure.

gmk-eval   This procedure takes a single argument which is converted into a string. The string is evaluated by make as if it were a makefile. This is the same capability available via the eval function (see Section 8.9 [Eval Function], page 93). The result of the gmk-eval procedure is always the empty string.

>   Note that gmk-eval is not quite the same as using gmk-expand with the eval function: in the latter case the evaluated string will be expanded *twice*; first by gmk-expand, then again by the eval function.

12.1.3 Example Using Guile in make

Here is a very simple example using GNU Guile to manage writing to a file. These Guile procedures simply open a file, allow writing to the file (one string per line), and close the file. Note that because we cannot store complex values such as Guile ports in make variables, we'll keep the port as a global variable in the Guile interpreter.

You can create Guile functions easily using define/endef to create a Guile script, then use the guile function to internalize it:

```
define GUILEIO
;; A simple Guile IO library for GNU make

(define MKPORT #f)

(define (mkopen name mode)
  (set! MKPORT (open-file name mode))
  #f)

(define (mkwrite s)
  (display s MKPORT)
  (newline MKPORT)
  #f)

(define (mkclose)
  (close-port MKPORT)
  #f)

#f
endef


# Internalize the Guile IO functions
$(guile $(GUILEIO))
```

If you have a significant amount of Guile support code, you might consider keeping it in a different file (e.g., `guileio.scm`) and then loading it in your makefile using the `guile` function:

```
$(guile (load "guileio.scm"))
```

An advantage to this method is that when editing `guileio.scm`, your editor will understand that this file contains Scheme syntax rather than makefile syntax.

Now you can use these Guile functions to create files. Suppose you need to operate on a very large list, which cannot fit on the command line, but the utility you're using accepts the list as input as well:

```
prog: $(PREREQS)
        @$(guile (mkopen "tmp.out" "w")) \
         $(foreach X,$^,$(guile (mkwrite "$(X)"))) \
         $(guile (mkclose))
        $(LINK) < tmp.out
```

A more comprehensive suite of file manipulation procedures is possible of course. You could, for example, maintain multiple output files at the same time by choosing a symbol for each one and using it as the key to a hash table, where the value is a port, then returning the symbol to be stored in a `make` variable.

12.2 Loading Dynamic Objects

> **Warning:** The `load` directive and extension capability is considered a "technology preview" in this release of GNU make. We encourage you to experiment with this feature and we appreciate any feedback on it. However we cannot guarantee to maintain backward-compatibility in the next release. Consider using GNU Guile instead for extending GNU make (see Section 8.14 [The `guile` Function], page 97).

Many operating systems provide a facility for dynamically loading compiled objects. If your system provides this facility, GNU `make` can make use of it to load dynamic objects at runtime, providing new capabilities which may then be invoked by your makefile.

The `load` directive is used to load a dynamic object. Once the object is loaded, a "setup" function will be invoked to allow the object to initialize itself and register new facilities with GNU `make`. A dynamic object might include new `make` functions, for example, and the "setup" function would register them with GNU `make`'s function handling system.

12.2.1 The `load` Directive

Objects are loaded into GNU `make` by placing the `load` directive into your makefile. The syntax of the `load` directive is as follows:

```
load object-file ...
```

or:

```
load object-file(symbol-name) ...
```

The file *object-file* is dynamically loaded by GNU `make`. If *object-file* does not include a directory path then it is first looked for in the current directory. If it is not found there, or a directory path is included, then system-specific paths will be searched. If the load fails for any reason, `make` will print a message and exit.

If the load succeeds `make` will invoke an initializing function.

If *symbol-name* is provided, it will be used as the name of the initializing function.

If no *symbol-name* is provided, the initializing function name is created by taking the base file name of *object-file*, up to the first character which is not a valid symbol name character (alphanumerics and underscores are valid symbol name characters). To this prefix will be appended the suffix `_gmk_setup`.

More than one object file may be loaded with a single `load` directive, and both forms of `load` arguments may be used in the same directive.

The initializing function will be provided the file name and line number of the invocation of the `load` operation. It should return a value of type `int`, which must be 0 on failure and non-0 on success. If the return value is `-1`, then GNU make will *not* attempt to rebuild the object file (see Section 12.2.2 [How Loaded Objects Are Remade], page 137).

For example:

```
load ../mk_funcs.so
```

will load the dynamic object `../mk_funcs.so`. After the object is loaded, `make` will invoke the function (assumed to be defined by the shared object) `mk_funcs_gmk_setup`.

On the other hand:

```
load ../mk_funcs.so(init_mk_func)
```

will load the dynamic object `../mk_funcs.so`. After the object is loaded, `make` will invoke the function `init_mk_func`.

Regardless of how many times an object file appears in a `load` directive, it will only be loaded (and its setup function will only be invoked) once.

After an object has been successfully loaded, its file name is appended to the `.LOADED` variable.

If you would prefer that failure to load a dynamic object not be reported as an error, you can use the `-load` directive instead of `load`. GNU make will not fail and no message will be generated if an object fails to load. The failed object is not added to the `.LOADED` variable, which can then be consulted to determine if the load was successful.

12.2.2 How Loaded Objects Are Remade

Loaded objects undergo the same re-make procedure as makefiles (see Section 3.5 [How Makefiles Are Remade], page 14). If any loaded object is recreated, then make will start from scratch and re-read all the makefiles, and reload the object files again. It is not necessary for the loaded object to do anything special to support this.

It's up to the makefile author to provide the rules needed for rebuilding the loaded object.

12.2.3 Loaded Object Interface

> **Warning:** For this feature to be useful your extensions will need to invoke various functions internal to GNU make. The programming interfaces provided in this release should not be considered stable: functions may be added, removed, or change calling signatures or implementations in future versions of GNU make.

To be useful, loaded objects must be able to interact with GNU make. This interaction includes both interfaces the loaded object provides to makefiles and also interfaces make provides to the loaded object to manipulate make's operation.

The interface between loaded objects and make is defined by the `gnumake.h` C header file. All loaded objects written in C should include this header file. Any loaded object not written in C will need to implement the interface defined in this header file.

Typically, a loaded object will register one or more new GNU make functions using the `gmk_add_function` routine from within its setup function. The implementations of these make functions may make use of the `gmk_expand` and `gmk_eval` routines to perform their tasks, then optionally return a string as the result of the function expansion.

Loaded Object Licensing

Every dynamic extension should define the global symbol `plugin_is_GPL_compatible` to assert that it has been licensed under a GPL-compatible license. If this symbol does not exist, make emits a fatal error and exits when it tries to load your extension.

The declared type of the symbol should be `int`. It does not need to be in any allocated section, though. The code merely asserts that the symbol exists in the global scope. Something like this is enough:

```
int plugin_is_GPL_compatible;
```

Data Structures

gmk_floc   This structure represents a filename/location pair. It is provided when defining
items, so GNU make can inform the user later where the definition occurred if
necessary.

Registering Functions

There is currently one way for makefiles to invoke operations provided by the loaded object:
through the make function call interface. A loaded object can register one or more new
functions which may then be invoked from within the makefile in the same way as any
other function.

Use gmk_add_function to create a new make function. Its arguments are as follows:

name   The function name. This is what the makefile should use to invoke the function.
The name must be between 1 and 255 characters long and it may only contain
alphanumeric, period ('.'), dash ('-'), and underscore ('_') characters. It may
not begin with a period.

func_ptr   A pointer to a function that make will invoke when it expands the function in
a makefile. This function must be defined by the loaded object.

min_args   The minimum number of arguments the function will accept. Must be between
0 and 255. GNU make will check this and fail before invoking func_ptr if the
function was invoked with too few arguments.

max_args   The maximum number of arguments the function will accept. Must be between
0 and 255. GNU make will check this and fail before invoking func_ptr if the
function was invoked with too few arguments. If the value is 0, then any number
of arguments is accepted. If the value is greater than 0, then it must be greater
than or equal to min_args.

flags   Flags that specify how this function will operate; the desired flags should be
OR'd together. If the GMK_FUNC_NOEXPAND flag is given then the function arguments will not be expanded before the function is called; otherwise they will
be expanded first.

Registered Function Interface

A function registered with make must match the gmk_func_ptr type. It will be invoked
with three parameters: name (the name of the function), argc (the number of arguments
to the function), and argv (an array of pointers to arguments to the function). The last
pointer (that is, argv[argc]) will be null (0).

The return value of the function is the result of expanding the function. If the function
expands to nothing the return value may be null. Otherwise, it must be a pointer to a
string created with gmk_alloc. Once the function returns, make owns this string and will
free it when appropriate; it cannot be accessed by the loaded object.

GNU make Facilities

There are some facilities exported by GNU make for use by loaded objects. Typically these
would be run from within the setup function and/or the functions registered via gmk_add_
function, to retrieve or modify the data make works with.

`gmk_expand`

> This function takes a string and expands it using **make** expansion rules. The result of the expansion is returned in a nil-terminated string buffer. The caller is responsible for calling `gmk_free` with a pointer to the returned buffer when done.

`gmk_eval`   This function takes a buffer and evaluates it as a segment of makefile syntax. This function can be used to define new variables, new rules, etc. It is equivalent to using the **eval make** function.

Note that there is a difference between `gmk_eval` and calling `gmk_expand` with a string using the **eval** function: in the latter case the string will be expanded *twice*; once by `gmk_expand` and then again by the **eval** function. Using `gmk_eval` the buffer is only expanded once, at most (as it's read by the **make** parser).

Memory Management

Some systems allow for different memory management schemes. Thus you should never pass memory that you've allocated directly to any **make** function, nor should you attempt to directly free any memory returned to you by any **make** function. Instead, use the `gmk_alloc` and `gmk_free` functions.

In particular, the string returned to **make** by a function registered using `gmk_add_function` *must* be allocated using `gmk_alloc`, and the string returned from the **make** `gmk_expand` function *must* be freed (when no longer needed) using `gmk_free`.

`gmk_alloc`

> Return a pointer to a newly-allocated buffer. This function will always return a valid pointer; if not enough memory is available **make** will exit.

`gmk_free`   Free a buffer returned to you by **make**. Once the `gmk_free` function returns the string will no longer be valid.

12.2.4 Example Loaded Object

Let's suppose we wanted to write a new GNU **make** function that would create a temporary file and return its name. We would like our function to take a prefix as an argument. First we can write the function in a file `mk_temp.c`:

```
#include <stdlib.h>
#include <stdlib.h>
#include <stdio.h>
#include <string.h>
#include <unistd.h>
#include <errno.h>

#include <gnumake.h>

int plugin_is_GPL_compatible;

char *
gen_tmpfile(const char *nm, int argc, char **argv)
{
  int fd;

  /* Compute the size of the filename and allocate space for it.  */
  int len = strlen (argv[0]) + 6 + 1;
  char *buf = gmk_alloc (len);

  strcpy (buf, argv[0]);
  strcat (buf, "XXXXXX");

  fd = mkstemp(buf);
  if (fd >= 0)
    {
      /* Don't leak the file descriptor.  */
      close (fd);
      return buf;
    }

  /* Failure.  */
  fprintf (stderr, "mkstemp(%s) failed: %s\n", buf, strerror (errno));
  gmk_free (buf);
  return NULL;
}

int
mk_temp_gmk_setup ()
{
  /* Register the function with make name "mk-temp".  */
  gmk_add_function ("mk-temp", gen_tmpfile, 1, 1, 1);
  return 1;
}
```

Next, we will write a makefile that can build this shared object, load it, and use it:

```
all:
        @echo Temporary file: $(mk-temp tmpfile.)

load mk_temp.so

mk_temp.so: mk_temp.c
        $(CC) -shared -fPIC -o $ $<
```

On MS-Windows, due to peculiarities of how shared objects are produced, the compiler needs to scan the *import library* produced when building make, typically called libgnumake-*version*.dll.a, where *version* is the version of the load object API. So the recipe to produce a shared object will look on Windows like this (assuming the API version is 1):

```
mk_temp.dll: mk_temp.c
        $(CC) -shared -o $ $< -lgnumake-1
```

Now when you run make you'll see something like:

```
$ make
cc -shared -fPIC -o mk_temp.so mk_temp.c
Temporary filename: tmpfile.A7JEwd
```

13 Features of GNU make

Here is a summary of the features of GNU make, for comparison with and credit to other versions of make. We consider the features of make in 4.2 BSD systems as a baseline. If you are concerned with writing portable makefiles, you should not use the features of make listed here, nor the ones in Chapter 14 [Missing], page 147.

Many features come from the version of make in System V.

- The VPATH variable and its special meaning. See Section 4.4 [Searching Directories for Prerequisites], page 25. This feature exists in System V make, but is undocumented. It is documented in 4.3 BSD make (which says it mimics System V's VPATH feature).

- Included makefiles. See Section 3.3 [Including Other Makefiles], page 13. Allowing multiple files to be included with a single directive is a GNU extension.

- Variables are read from and communicated via the environment. See Section 6.10 [Variables from the Environment], page 70.

- Options passed through the variable MAKEFLAGS to recursive invocations of make. See Section 5.7.3 [Communicating Options to a Sub-make], page 54.

- The automatic variable $% is set to the member name in an archive reference. See Section 10.5.3 [Automatic Variables], page 120.

- The automatic variables $@, $*, $<, $%, and $? have corresponding forms like $(@F) and $(@D). We have generalized this to $^ as an obvious extension. See Section 10.5.3 [Automatic Variables], page 120.

- Substitution variable references. See Section 6.1 [Basics of Variable References], page 59.

- The command line options '-b' and '-m', accepted and ignored. In System V make, these options actually do something.

- Execution of recursive commands to run make via the variable MAKE even if '-n', '-q' or '-t' is specified. See Section 5.7 [Recursive Use of make], page 50.

- Support for suffix '.a' in suffix rules. See Section 11.4 [Archive Suffix Rules], page 130. This feature is obsolete in GNU make, because the general feature of rule chaining (see Section 10.4 [Chains of Implicit Rules], page 117) allows one pattern rule for installing members in an archive (see Section 11.2 [Archive Update], page 129) to be sufficient.

- The arrangement of lines and backslash/newline combinations in recipes is retained when the recipes are printed, so they appear as they do in the makefile, except for the stripping of initial whitespace.

The following features were inspired by various other versions of make. In some cases it is unclear exactly which versions inspired which others.

- Pattern rules using '%'. This has been implemented in several versions of make. We're not sure who invented it first, but it's been spread around a bit. See Section 10.5 [Defining and Redefining Pattern Rules], page 118.

- Rule chaining and implicit intermediate files. This was implemented by Stu Feldman in his version of make for AT&T Eighth Edition Research Unix, and later by Andrew Hume of AT&T Bell Labs in his mk program (where he terms it "transitive closure"). We do not really know if we got this from either of them or thought it up ourselves at the same time. See Section 10.4 [Chains of Implicit Rules], page 117.

- The automatic variable $ contaning a list of all prerequisites of the current target. We did not invent this, but we have no idea who did. See Section 10.5.3 [Automatic Variables], page 120. The automatic variable $+ is a simple extension of $.

- The "what if" flag ('-W' in GNU make) was (as far as we know) invented by Andrew Hume in mk. See Section 9.3 [Instead of Executing Recipes], page 101.

- The concept of doing several things at once (parallelism) exists in many incarnations of make and similar programs, though not in the System V or BSD implementations. See Section 5.3 [Recipe Execution], page 44.

- A number of different build tools that support parallelism also support collecting output and displaying as a single block. See Section 5.4.1 [Output During Parallel Execution], page 47.

- Modified variable references using pattern substitution come from SunOS 4. See Section 6.1 [Basics of Variable References], page 59. This functionality was provided in GNU make by the patsubst function before the alternate syntax was implemented for compatibility with SunOS 4. It is not altogether clear who inspired whom, since GNU make had patsubst before SunOS 4 was released.

- The special significance of '+' characters preceding recipe lines (see Section 9.3 [Instead of Executing Recipes], page 101) is mandated by *IEEE Standard 1003.2-1992* (POSIX.2).

- The '+=' syntax to append to the value of a variable comes from SunOS 4 make. See Section 6.6 [Appending More Text to Variables], page 66.

- The syntax 'archive(mem1 mem2...)' to list multiple members in a single archive file comes from SunOS 4 make. See Section 11.1 [Archive Members], page 129.

- The -include directive to include makefiles with no error for a nonexistent file comes from SunOS 4 make. (But note that SunOS 4 make does not allow multiple makefiles to be specified in one -include directive.) The same feature appears with the name sinclude in SGI make and perhaps others.

- The != shell assignment operator exists in many BSD of make and is purposefully implemented here to behave identically to those implementations.

- Various build management tools are implemented using scripting languages such as Perl or Python and thus provide a natural embedded scripting language, similar to GNU make's integration of GNU Guile.

The remaining features are inventions new in GNU make:

- Use the '-v' or '--version' option to print version and copyright information.

- Use the '-h' or '--help' option to summarize the options to make.

- Simply-expanded variables. See Section 6.2 [The Two Flavors of Variables], page 60.

- Pass command line variable assignments automatically through the variable MAKE to recursive make invocations. See Section 5.7 [Recursive Use of make], page 50.

- Use the '-C' or '--directory' command option to change directory. See Section 9.7 [Summary of Options], page 104.

- Make verbatim variable definitions with define. See Section 6.8 [Defining Multi-Line Variables], page 69.

- Declare phony targets with the special target `.PHONY`.

  Andrew Hume of AT&T Bell Labs implemented a similar feature with a different syntax in his `mk` program. This seems to be a case of parallel discovery. See Section 4.5 [Phony Targets], page 29.

- Manipulate text by calling functions. See Chapter 8 [Functions for Transforming Text], page 83.

- Use the '`-o`' or '`--old-file`' option to pretend a file's modification-time is old. See Section 9.4 [Avoiding Recompilation of Some Files], page 102.

- Conditional execution.

  This feature has been implemented numerous times in various versions of `make`; it seems a natural extension derived from the features of the C preprocessor and similar macro languages and is not a revolutionary concept. See Chapter 7 [Conditional Parts of Makefiles], page 77.

- Specify a search path for included makefiles. See Section 3.3 [Including Other Makefiles], page 13.

- Specify extra makefiles to read with an environment variable. See Section 3.4 [The Variable `MAKEFILES`], page 14.

- Strip leading sequences of '`./`' from file names, so that `./file` and `file` are considered to be the same file.

- Use a special search method for library prerequisites written in the form '`-lname`'. See Section 4.4.6 [Directory Search for Link Libraries], page 28.

- Allow suffixes for suffix rules (see Section 10.7 [Old-Fashioned Suffix Rules], page 125) to contain any characters. In other versions of `make`, they must begin with '`.`' and not contain any '`/`' characters.

- Keep track of the current level of `make` recursion using the variable `MAKELEVEL`. See Section 5.7 [Recursive Use of `make`], page 50.

- Provide any goals given on the command line in the variable `MAKECMDGOALS`. See Section 9.2 [Arguments to Specify the Goals], page 99.

- Specify static pattern rules. See Section 4.11 [Static Pattern Rules], page 36.

- Provide selective `vpath` search. See Section 4.4 [Searching Directories for Prerequisites], page 25.

- Provide computed variable references. See Section 6.1 [Basics of Variable References], page 59.

- Update makefiles. See Section 3.5 [How Makefiles Are Remade], page 14. System V `make` has a very, very limited form of this functionality in that it will check out SCCS files for makefiles.

- Various new built-in implicit rules. See Section 10.2 [Catalogue of Built-In Rules], page 112.

- Load dynamic objects which can modify the behavior of `make`. See Section 12.2 [Loading Dynamic Objects], page 135.

14 Incompatibilities and Missing Features

The `make` programs in various other systems support a few features that are not implemented in GNU `make`. The POSIX.2 standard (*IEEE Standard 1003.2-1992*) which specifies `make` does not require any of these features.

- A target of the form '`file((entry))`' stands for a member of archive file *file*. The member is chosen, not by name, but by being an object file which defines the linker symbol *entry*.

  This feature was not put into GNU `make` because of the non-modularity of putting knowledge into `make` of the internal format of archive file symbol tables. See Section 11.2.1 [Updating Archive Symbol Directories], page 130.

- Suffixes (used in suffix rules) that end with the character '`~`' have a special meaning to System V `make`; they refer to the SCCS file that corresponds to the file one would get without the '`~`'. For example, the suffix rule '`.c~.o`' would make the file `n.o` from the SCCS file `s.n.c`. For complete coverage, a whole series of such suffix rules is required. See Section 10.7 [Old-Fashioned Suffix Rules], page 125.

  In GNU `make`, this entire series of cases is handled by two pattern rules for extraction from SCCS, in combination with the general feature of rule chaining. See Section 10.4 [Chains of Implicit Rules], page 117.

- In System V and 4.3 BSD `make`, files found by `VPATH` search (see Section 4.4 [Searching Directories for Prerequisites], page 25) have their names changed inside recipes. We feel it is much cleaner to always use automatic variables and thus make this feature obsolete.

- In some Unix `makes`, the automatic variable `$*` appearing in the prerequisites of a rule has the amazingly strange "feature" of expanding to the full name of the *target of that rule*. We cannot imagine what went on in the minds of Unix `make` developers to do this; it is utterly inconsistent with the normal definition of `$*`.

- In some Unix `makes`, implicit rule search (see Chapter 10 [Using Implicit Rules], page 111) is apparently done for *all* targets, not just those without recipes. This means you can do:

  ```
  foo.o:
          cc -c foo.c
  ```

  and Unix `make` will intuit that `foo.o` depends on `foo.c`.

  We feel that such usage is broken. The prerequisite properties of `make` are well-defined (for GNU `make`, at least), and doing such a thing simply does not fit the model.

- GNU `make` does not include any built-in implicit rules for compiling or preprocessing EFL programs. If we hear of anyone who is using EFL, we will gladly add them.

- It appears that in SVR4 `make`, a suffix rule can be specified with no recipe, and it is treated as if it had an empty recipe (see Section 5.9 [Empty Recipes], page 57). For example:

  ```
  .c.a:
  ```

  will override the built-in `.c.a` suffix rule.

We feel that it is cleaner for a rule without a recipe to always simply add to the prerequisite list for the target. The above example can be easily rewritten to get the desired behavior in GNU make:

```
.c.a: ;
```

- Some versions of make invoke the shell with the '-e' flag, except under '-k' (see Section 9.6 [Testing the Compilation of a Program], page 104). The '-e' flag tells the shell to exit as soon as any program it runs returns a nonzero status. We feel it is cleaner to write each line of the recipe to stand on its own and not require this special treatment.

15 Makefile Conventions

This chapter describes conventions for writing the Makefiles for GNU programs. Using Automake will help you write a Makefile that follows these conventions. For more information on portable Makefiles, see POSIX and Section "Portable Make" in *Autoconf*.

15.1 General Conventions for Makefiles

Every Makefile should contain this line:

```
SHELL = /bin/sh
```

to avoid trouble on systems where the `SHELL` variable might be inherited from the environment. (This is never a problem with GNU `make`.)

Different `make` programs have incompatible suffix lists and implicit rules, and this sometimes creates confusion or misbehavior. So it is a good idea to set the suffix list explicitly using only the suffixes you need in the particular Makefile, like this:

```
.SUFFIXES:
.SUFFIXES: .c .o
```

The first line clears out the suffix list, the second introduces all suffixes which may be subject to implicit rules in this Makefile.

Don't assume that `.` is in the path for command execution. When you need to run programs that are a part of your package during the make, please make sure that it uses `./` if the program is built as part of the make or `$(srcdir)/` if the file is an unchanging part of the source code. Without one of these prefixes, the current search path is used.

The distinction between `./` (the *build directory*) and `$(srcdir)/` (the *source directory*) is important because users can build in a separate directory using the '`--srcdir`' option to `configure`. A rule of the form:

```
foo.1 : foo.man sedscript
        sed -f sedscript foo.man > foo.1
```

will fail when the build directory is not the source directory, because `foo.man` and `sedscript` are in the source directory.

When using GNU `make`, relying on '`VPATH`' to find the source file will work in the case where there is a single dependency file, since the `make` automatic variable '`$<`' will represent the source file wherever it is. (Many versions of `make` set '`$<`' only in implicit rules.) A Makefile target like

```
foo.o : bar.c
        $(CC) -I. -I$(srcdir) $(CFLAGS) -c bar.c -o foo.o
```

should instead be written as

```
foo.o : bar.c
        $(CC) -I. -I$(srcdir) $(CFLAGS) -c $< -o $@
```

in order to allow '`VPATH`' to work correctly. When the target has multiple dependencies, using an explicit '`$(srcdir)`' is the easiest way to make the rule work well. For example, the target above for `foo.1` is best written as:

```
foo.1 : foo.man sedscript
        sed -f $(srcdir)/sedscript $(srcdir)/foo.man > $@
```

GNU distributions usually contain some files which are not source files—for example, Info files, and the output from Autoconf, Automake, Bison or Flex. Since these files normally appear in the source directory, they should always appear in the source directory, not in the build directory. So Makefile rules to update them should put the updated files in the source directory.

However, if a file does not appear in the distribution, then the Makefile should not put it in the source directory, because building a program in ordinary circumstances should not modify the source directory in any way.

Try to make the build and installation targets, at least (and all their subtargets) work correctly with a parallel make.

15.2 Utilities in Makefiles

Write the Makefile commands (and any shell scripts, such as `configure`) to run under `sh` (both the traditional Bourne shell and the POSIX shell), not `csh`. Don't use any special features of `ksh` or `bash`, or POSIX features not widely supported in traditional Bourne `sh`.

The `configure` script and the Makefile rules for building and installation should not use any utilities directly except these:

```
awk cat cmp cp diff echo egrep expr false grep install-info ln ls
mkdir mv printf pwd rm rmdir sed sleep sort tar test touch tr true
```

Compression programs such as `gzip` can be used in the `dist` rule.

Generally, stick to the widely-supported (usually POSIX-specified) options and features of these programs. For example, don't use 'mkdir -p', convenient as it may be, because a few systems don't support it at all and with others, it is not safe for parallel execution. For a list of known incompatibilities, see Section "Portable Shell" in *Autoconf*.

It is a good idea to avoid creating symbolic links in makefiles, since a few file systems don't support them.

The Makefile rules for building and installation can also use compilers and related programs, but should do so via `make` variables so that the user can substitute alternatives. Here are some of the programs we mean:

```
ar bison cc flex install ld ldconfig lex
make makeinfo ranlib texi2dvi yacc
```

Use the following `make` variables to run those programs:

```
$(AR) $(BISON) $(CC) $(FLEX) $(INSTALL) $(LD) $(LDCONFIG) $(LEX)
$(MAKE) $(MAKEINFO) $(RANLIB) $(TEXI2DVI) $(YACC)
```

When you use `ranlib` or `ldconfig`, you should make sure nothing bad happens if the system does not have the program in question. Arrange to ignore an error from that command, and print a message before the command to tell the user that failure of this command does not mean a problem. (The Autoconf 'AC_PROG_RANLIB' macro can help with this.)

If you use symbolic links, you should implement a fallback for systems that don't have symbolic links.

Additional utilities that can be used via Make variables are:

```
chgrp chmod chown mknod
```

It is ok to use other utilities in Makefile portions (or scripts) intended only for particular systems where you know those utilities exist.

15.3 Variables for Specifying Commands

Makefiles should provide variables for overriding certain commands, options, and so on.

In particular, you should run most utility programs via variables. Thus, if you use Bison, have a variable named BISON whose default value is set with 'BISON = bison', and refer to it with $(BISON) whenever you need to use Bison.

File management utilities such as ln, rm, mv, and so on, need not be referred to through variables in this way, since users don't need to replace them with other programs.

Each program-name variable should come with an options variable that is used to supply options to the program. Append 'FLAGS' to the program-name variable name to get the options variable name—for example, BISONFLAGS. (The names CFLAGS for the C compiler, YFLAGS for yacc, and LFLAGS for lex, are exceptions to this rule, but we keep them because they are standard.) Use CPPFLAGS in any compilation command that runs the preprocessor, and use LDFLAGS in any compilation command that does linking as well as in any direct use of ld.

If there are C compiler options that *must* be used for proper compilation of certain files, do not include them in CFLAGS. Users expect to be able to specify CFLAGS freely themselves. Instead, arrange to pass the necessary options to the C compiler independently of CFLAGS, by writing them explicitly in the compilation commands or by defining an implicit rule, like this:

```
CFLAGS = -g
ALL_CFLAGS = -I. $(CFLAGS)
.c.o:
        $(CC) -c $(CPPFLAGS) $(ALL_CFLAGS) $<
```

Do include the '-g' option in CFLAGS, because that is not *required* for proper compilation. You can consider it a default that is only recommended. If the package is set up so that it is compiled with GCC by default, then you might as well include '-O' in the default value of CFLAGS as well.

Put CFLAGS last in the compilation command, after other variables containing compiler options, so the user can use CFLAGS to override the others.

CFLAGS should be used in every invocation of the C compiler, both those which do compilation and those which do linking.

Every Makefile should define the variable INSTALL, which is the basic command for installing a file into the system.

Every Makefile should also define the variables INSTALL_PROGRAM and INSTALL_DATA. (The default for INSTALL_PROGRAM should be $(INSTALL); the default for INSTALL_DATA should be ${INSTALL} -m 644.) Then it should use those variables as the commands for actual installation, for executables and non-executables respectively. Minimal use of these variables is as follows:

```
$(INSTALL_PROGRAM) foo $(bindir)/foo
$(INSTALL_DATA) libfoo.a $(libdir)/libfoo.a
```

However, it is preferable to support a DESTDIR prefix on the target files, as explained in the next section.

It is acceptable, but not required, to install multiple files in one command, with the final argument being a directory, as in:

```
$(INSTALL_PROGRAM) foo bar baz $(bindir)
```

15.4 DESTDIR: Support for Staged Installs

DESTDIR is a variable prepended to each installed target file, like this:

```
$(INSTALL_PROGRAM) foo $(DESTDIR)$(bindir)/foo
$(INSTALL_DATA) libfoo.a $(DESTDIR)$(libdir)/libfoo.a
```

The DESTDIR variable is specified by the user on the make command line as an absolute file name. For example:

```
make DESTDIR=/tmp/stage install
```

DESTDIR should be supported only in the install* and uninstall* targets, as those are the only targets where it is useful.

If your installation step would normally install /usr/local/bin/foo and /usr/local/lib/libfoo.a, then an installation invoked as in the example above would install /tmp/stage/usr/local/bin/foo and /tmp/stage/usr/local/lib/libfoo.a instead.

Prepending the variable DESTDIR to each target in this way provides for *staged installs*, where the installed files are not placed directly into their expected location but are instead copied into a temporary location (DESTDIR). However, installed files maintain their relative directory structure and any embedded file names will not be modified.

You should not set the value of DESTDIR in your Makefile at all; then the files are installed into their expected locations by default. Also, specifying DESTDIR should not change the operation of the software in any way, so its value should not be included in any file contents.

DESTDIR support is commonly used in package creation. It is also helpful to users who want to understand what a given package will install where, and to allow users who don't normally have permissions to install into protected areas to build and install before gaining those permissions. Finally, it can be useful with tools such as stow, where code is installed in one place but made to appear to be installed somewhere else using symbolic links or special mount operations. So, we strongly recommend GNU packages support DESTDIR, though it is not an absolute requirement.

15.5 Variables for Installation Directories

Installation directories should always be named by variables, so it is easy to install in a nonstandard place. The standard names for these variables and the values they should have in GNU packages are described below. They are based on a standard file system layout; variants of it are used in GNU/Linux and other modern operating systems.

Installers are expected to override these values when calling make (e.g., *make prefix=/usr install* or configure (e.g., *configure --prefix=/usr*). GNU packages should not try to guess which value should be appropriate for these variables on the system they are being installed onto: use the default settings specified here so that all GNU packages behave identically, allowing the installer to achieve any desired layout.

All installation directories, and their parent directories, should be created (if necessary) before they are installed into.

These first two variables set the root for the installation. All the other installation directories should be subdirectories of one of these two, and nothing should be directly installed into these two directories.

prefix A prefix used in constructing the default values of the variables listed below. The default value of `prefix` should be /usr/local. When building the complete GNU system, the prefix will be empty and /usr will be a symbolic link to /. (If you are using Autoconf, write it as '@prefix@'.)

     Running 'make install' with a different value of `prefix` from the one used to build the program should *not* recompile the program.

exec_prefix

     A prefix used in constructing the default values of some of the variables listed below. The default value of `exec_prefix` should be $(prefix). (If you are using Autoconf, write it as '@exec_prefix@'.)

     Generally, $(exec_prefix) is used for directories that contain machine-specific files (such as executables and subroutine libraries), while $(prefix) is used directly for other directories.

     Running 'make install' with a different value of `exec_prefix` from the one used to build the program should *not* recompile the program.

  Executable programs are installed in one of the following directories.

bindir The directory for installing executable programs that users can run. This should normally be /usr/local/bin, but write it as $(exec_prefix)/bin. (If you are using Autoconf, write it as '@bindir@'.)

sbindir The directory for installing executable programs that can be run from the shell, but are only generally useful to system administrators. This should normally be /usr/local/sbin, but write it as $(exec_prefix)/sbin. (If you are using Autoconf, write it as '@sbindir@'.)

libexecdir

     The directory for installing executable programs to be run by other programs rather than by users. This directory should normally be /usr/local/libexec, but write it as $(exec_prefix)/libexec. (If you are using Autoconf, write it as '@libexecdir@'.)

     The definition of 'libexecdir' is the same for all packages, so you should install your data in a subdirectory thereof. Most packages install their data under $(libexecdir)/*package-name*/, possibly within additional subdirectories thereof, such as $(libexecdir)/*package-name/machine/version*.

  Data files used by the program during its execution are divided into categories in two ways.

- Some files are normally modified by programs; others are never normally modified (though users may edit some of these).

- Some files are architecture-independent and can be shared by all machines at a site; some are architecture-dependent and can be shared only by machines of the same kind and operating system; others may never be shared between two machines.

  This makes for six different possibilities. However, we want to discourage the use of architecture-dependent files, aside from object files and libraries. It is much cleaner to make other data files architecture-independent, and it is generally not hard.

Here are the variables Makefiles should use to specify directories to put these various kinds of files in:

'datarootdir'
>	The root of the directory tree for read-only architecture-independent data files. This should normally be /usr/local/share, but write it as $(prefix)/share. (If you are using Autoconf, write it as '@datarootdir@'.) 'datadir''s default value is based on this variable; so are 'infodir', 'mandir', and others.

'datadir'	The directory for installing idiosyncratic read-only architecture-independent data files for this program. This is usually the same place as 'datarootdir', but we use the two separate variables so that you can move these program-specific files without altering the location for Info files, man pages, etc.

>	This should normally be /usr/local/share, but write it as $(datarootdir). (If you are using Autoconf, write it as '@datadir@'.)

>	The definition of 'datadir' is the same for all packages, so you should install your data in a subdirectory thereof. Most packages install their data under $(datadir)/package-name/.

'sysconfdir'
>	The directory for installing read-only data files that pertain to a single machine–that is to say, files for configuring a host. Mailer and network configuration files, /etc/passwd, and so forth belong here. All the files in this directory should be ordinary ASCII text files. This directory should normally be /usr/local/etc, but write it as $(prefix)/etc. (If you are using Autoconf, write it as '@sysconfdir@'.)

>	Do not install executables here in this directory (they probably belong in $(libexecdir) or $(sbindir)). Also do not install files that are modified in the normal course of their use (programs whose purpose is to change the configuration of the system excluded). Those probably belong in $(localstatedir).

'sharedstatedir'
>	The directory for installing architecture-independent data files which the programs modify while they run. This should normally be /usr/local/com, but write it as $(prefix)/com. (If you are using Autoconf, write it as '@sharedstatedir@'.)

'localstatedir'
>	The directory for installing data files which the programs modify while they run, and that pertain to one specific machine. Users should never need to modify files in this directory to configure the package's operation; put such configuration information in separate files that go in $(datadir) or $(sysconfdir). $(localstatedir) should normally be /usr/local/var, but write it as $(prefix)/var. (If you are using Autoconf, write it as '@localstatedir@'.)

'runstatedir'
>	The directory for installing data files which the programs modify while they run, that pertain to one specific machine, and which need not persist longer than the execution of the program—which is generally long-lived, for example, until

the next reboot. PID files for system daemons are a typical use. In addition, this directory should not be cleaned except perhaps at reboot, while the general /tmp (TMPDIR) may be cleaned arbitrarily. This should normally be /var/run, but write it as $(localstatedir)/run. Having it as a separate variable allows the use of /run if desired, for example. (If you are using Autoconf 2.70 or later, write it as '@runstatedir@'.)

These variables specify the directory for installing certain specific types of files, if your program has them. Every GNU package should have Info files, so every program needs 'infodir', but not all need 'libdir' or 'lispdir'.

'includedir'

> The directory for installing header files to be included by user programs with the C '#include' preprocessor directive. This should normally be /usr/local/include, but write it as $(prefix)/include. (If you are using Autoconf, write it as '@includedir@'.)
>
> Most compilers other than GCC do not look for header files in directory /usr/local/include. So installing the header files this way is only useful with GCC. Sometimes this is not a problem because some libraries are only really intended to work with GCC. But some libraries are intended to work with other compilers. They should install their header files in two places, one specified by includedir and one specified by oldincludedir.

'oldincludedir'

> The directory for installing '#include' header files for use with compilers other than GCC. This should normally be /usr/include. (If you are using Autoconf, you can write it as '@oldincludedir@'.)
>
> The Makefile commands should check whether the value of oldincludedir is empty. If it is, they should not try to use it; they should cancel the second installation of the header files.
>
> A package should not replace an existing header in this directory unless the header came from the same package. Thus, if your Foo package provides a header file foo.h, then it should install the header file in the oldincludedir directory if either (1) there is no foo.h there or (2) the foo.h that exists came from the Foo package.
>
> To tell whether foo.h came from the Foo package, put a magic string in the file—part of a comment—and grep for that string.

'docdir'   The directory for installing documentation files (other than Info) for this package. By default, it should be /usr/local/share/doc/*yourpkg*, but it should be written as $(datarootdir)/doc/*yourpkg*. (If you are using Autoconf, write it as '@docdir@'.) The *yourpkg* subdirectory, which may include a version number, prevents collisions among files with common names, such as README.

'infodir'   The directory for installing the Info files for this package. By default, it should be /usr/local/share/info, but it should be written as $(datarootdir)/info. (If you are using Autoconf, write it as '@infodir@'.) infodir is separate from docdir for compatibility with existing practice.

'htmldir'
'dvidir'
'pdfdir'
'psdir'   Directories for installing documentation files in the particular format. They
              should all be set to $(docdir) by default. (If you are using Autoconf,
              write them as '@htmldir@', '@dvidir@', etc.) Packages which supply several
              translations of their documentation should install them in '$(htmldir)/'*ll*,
              '$(pdfdir)/'*ll*, etc. where *ll* is a locale abbreviation such as 'en' or 'pt_BR'.

'libdir'   The directory for object files and libraries of object code. Do not install ex-
              ecutables here, they probably ought to go in $(libexecdir) instead. The
              value of libdir should normally be /usr/local/lib, but write it as $(exec_
              prefix)/lib. (If you are using Autoconf, write it as '@libdir@'.)

'lispdir'   The directory for installing any Emacs Lisp files in this package. By default,
              it should be /usr/local/share/emacs/site-lisp, but it should be written as
              $(datarootdir)/emacs/site-lisp.

              If you are using Autoconf, write the default as '@lispdir@'. In order to make
              '@lispdir@' work, you need the following lines in your configure.ac file:

                  lispdir='${datarootdir}/emacs/site-lisp'
                  AC_SUBST(lispdir)

'localedir'
              The directory for installing locale-specific message catalogs for this package.
              By default, it should be /usr/local/share/locale, but it should be
              written as $(datarootdir)/locale. (If you are using Autoconf, write it as
              '@localedir@'.) This directory usually has a subdirectory per locale.

        Unix-style man pages are installed in one of the following:

'mandir'   The top-level directory for installing the man pages (if any) for this pack-
              age. It will normally be /usr/local/share/man, but you should write it as
              $(datarootdir)/man. (If you are using Autoconf, write it as '@mandir@'.)

'man1dir'   The directory for installing section 1 man pages. Write it as $(mandir)/man1.

'man2dir'   The directory for installing section 2 man pages. Write it as $(mandir)/man2

'...'

              **Don't make the primary documentation for any GNU software be a man page.
              Write a manual in Texinfo instead. Man pages are just for the sake of people
              running GNU software on Unix, which is a secondary application only.**

'manext'   The file name extension for the installed man page. This should contain a
              period followed by the appropriate digit; it should normally be '.1'.

'man1ext'   The file name extension for installed section 1 man pages.

'man2ext'   The file name extension for installed section 2 man pages.

'...'   Use these names instead of 'manext' if the package needs to install man pages
              in more than one section of the manual.

        And finally, you should set the following variable:

'srcdir'   The directory for the sources being compiled. The value of this variable is
            normally inserted by the `configure` shell script. (If you are using Autoconf,
            use 'srcdir = @srcdir@'.)

For example:

```
# Common prefix for installation directories.
# NOTE: This directory must exist when you start the install.
prefix = /usr/local
datarootdir = $(prefix)/share
datadir = $(datarootdir)
exec_prefix = $(prefix)
# Where to put the executable for the command 'gcc'.
bindir = $(exec_prefix)/bin
# Where to put the directories used by the compiler.
libexecdir = $(exec_prefix)/libexec
# Where to put the Info files.
infodir = $(datarootdir)/info
```

If your program installs a large number of files into one of the standard user-specified
directories, it might be useful to group them into a subdirectory particular to that program.
If you do this, you should write the `install` rule to create these subdirectories.

Do not expect the user to include the subdirectory name in the value of any of the
variables listed above. The idea of having a uniform set of variable names for installation
directories is to enable the user to specify the exact same values for several different GNU
packages. In order for this to be useful, all the packages must be designed so that they will
work sensibly when the user does so.

At times, not all of these variables may be implemented in the current release of Autoconf
and/or Automake; but as of Autoconf 2.60, we believe all of them are. When any are
missing, the descriptions here serve as specifications for what Autoconf will implement. As
a programmer, you can either use a development version of Autoconf or avoid using these
variables until a stable release is made which supports them.

15.6 Standard Targets for Users

All GNU programs should have the following targets in their Makefiles:

'all'   Compile the entire program. This should be the default target. This target need
            not rebuild any documentation files; Info files should normally be included in
            the distribution, and DVI (and other documentation format) files should be
            made only when explicitly asked for.

            By default, the Make rules should compile and link with '-g', so that executable
            programs have debugging symbols. Otherwise, you are essentially helpless in
            the face of a crash, and it is often far from easy to reproduce with a fresh build.

'install'   Compile the program and copy the executables, libraries, and so on to the file
            names where they should reside for actual use. If there is a simple test to verify
            that a program is properly installed, this target should run that test.

            Do not strip executables when installing them. This helps eventual debugging
            that may be needed later, and nowadays disk space is cheap and dynamic loaders
            typically ensure debug sections are not loaded during normal execution. Users
            that need stripped binaries may invoke the `install-strip` target to do that.

If possible, write the `install` target rule so that it does not modify anything in the directory where the program was built, provided 'make all' has just been done. This is convenient for building the program under one user name and installing it under another.

The commands should create all the directories in which files are to be installed, if they don't already exist. This includes the directories specified as the values of the variables `prefix` and `exec_prefix`, as well as all subdirectories that are needed. One way to do this is by means of an `installdirs` target as described below.

Use '-' before any command for installing a man page, so that `make` will ignore any errors. This is in case there are systems that don't have the Unix man page documentation system installed.

The way to install Info files is to copy them into `$(infodir)` with `$(INSTALL_DATA)` (see Section 15.3 [Command Variables], page 151), and then run the `install-info` program if it is present. `install-info` is a program that edits the Info `dir` file to add or update the menu entry for the given Info file; it is part of the Texinfo package.

Here is a sample rule to install an Info file that also tries to handle some additional situations, such as `install-info` not being present.

```
do-install-info: foo.info installdirs
        $(NORMAL_INSTALL)
# Prefer an info file in . to one in srcdir.
        if test -f foo.info; then d=.; \
         else d="$(srcdir)"; fi; \
        $(INSTALL_DATA) $$d/foo.info \
          "$(DESTDIR)$(infodir)/foo.info"
# Run install-info only if it exists.
# Use 'if' instead of just prepending '-' to the
# line so we notice real errors from install-info.
# Use '$(SHELL) -c' because some shells do not
# fail gracefully when there is an unknown command.
        $(POST_INSTALL)
        if $(SHELL) -c 'install-info --version' \
           >/dev/null 2>&1; then \
         install-info --dir-file="$(DESTDIR)$(infodir)/dir" \
                      "$(DESTDIR)$(infodir)/foo.info"; \
        else true; fi
```

When writing the `install` target, you must classify all the commands into three categories: normal ones, *pre-installation* commands and *post-installation* commands. See Section 15.7 [Install Command Categories], page 162.

'install-html'
'install-dvi'
'install-pdf'
'install-ps'

These targets install documentation in formats other than Info; they're intended to be called explicitly by the person installing the package, if that format is desired. GNU prefers Info files, so these must be installed by the `install` target.

When you have many documentation files to install, we recommend that you avoid collisions and clutter by arranging for these targets to install in subdirectories of the appropriate installation directory, such as htmldir. As one example, if your package has multiple manuals, and you wish to install HTML documentation with many files (such as the "split" mode output by makeinfo --html), you'll certainly want to use subdirectories, or two nodes with the same name in different manuals will overwrite each other.

Please make these install-*format* targets invoke the commands for the *format* target, for example, by making *format* a dependency.

'uninstall'

Delete all the installed files—the copies that the 'install' and 'install-*' targets create.

This rule should not modify the directories where compilation is done, only the directories where files are installed.

The uninstallation commands are divided into three categories, just like the installation commands. See Section 15.7 [Install Command Categories], page 162.

'install-strip'

Like install, but strip the executable files while installing them. In simple cases, this target can use the install target in a simple way:

```
install-strip:
        $(MAKE) INSTALL_PROGRAM='$(INSTALL_PROGRAM) -s' \
                install
```

But if the package installs scripts as well as real executables, the install-strip target can't just refer to the install target; it has to strip the executables but not the scripts.

install-strip should not strip the executables in the build directory which are being copied for installation. It should only strip the copies that are installed.

Normally we do not recommend stripping an executable unless you are sure the program has no bugs. However, it can be reasonable to install a stripped executable for actual execution while saving the unstripped executable elsewhere in case there is a bug.

'clean'   Delete all files in the current directory that are normally created by building the program. Also delete files in other directories if they are created by this makefile. However, don't delete the files that record the configuration. Also preserve files that could be made by building, but normally aren't because the distribution comes with them. There is no need to delete parent directories that were created with 'mkdir -p', since they could have existed anyway.

Delete .dvi files here if they are not part of the distribution.

'distclean'

Delete all files in the current directory (or created by this makefile) that are created by configuring or building the program. If you have unpacked the source and built the program without creating any other files, 'make distclean' should leave only the files that were in the distribution. However, there is no need to delete parent directories that were created with 'mkdir -p', since they could have existed anyway.

'mostlyclean'
> Like 'clean', but may refrain from deleting a few files that people normally don't want to recompile. For example, the 'mostlyclean' target for GCC does not delete libgcc.a, because recompiling it is rarely necessary and takes a lot of time.

'maintainer-clean'
> Delete almost everything that can be reconstructed with this Makefile. This typically includes everything deleted by distclean, plus more: C source files produced by Bison, tags tables, Info files, and so on.
>
> The reason we say "almost everything" is that running the command 'make maintainer-clean' should not delete configure even if configure can be remade using a rule in the Makefile. More generally, 'make maintainer-clean' should not delete anything that needs to exist in order to run configure and then begin to build the program. Also, there is no need to delete parent directories that were created with 'mkdir -p', since they could have existed anyway. These are the only exceptions; maintainer-clean should delete everything else that can be rebuilt.
>
> The 'maintainer-clean' target is intended to be used by a maintainer of the package, not by ordinary users. You may need special tools to reconstruct some of the files that 'make maintainer-clean' deletes. Since these files are normally included in the distribution, we don't take care to make them easy to reconstruct. If you find you need to unpack the full distribution again, don't blame us.
>
> To help make users aware of this, the commands for the special maintainer-clean target should start with these two:
>
> ```
> @echo 'This command is intended for maintainers to use; it'
> @echo 'deletes files that may need special tools to rebuild.'
> ```

'TAGS'   Update a tags table for this program.

'info'   Generate any Info files needed. The best way to write the rules is as follows:

> ```
> info: foo.info
>
> foo.info: foo.texi chap1.texi chap2.texi
>         $(MAKEINFO) $(srcdir)/foo.texi
> ```

> You must define the variable MAKEINFO in the Makefile. It should run the makeinfo program, which is part of the Texinfo distribution.
>
> Normally a GNU distribution comes with Info files, and that means the Info files are present in the source directory. Therefore, the Make rule for an info file should update it in the source directory. When users build the package, ordinarily Make will not update the Info files because they will already be up to date.

'dvi'
'html'
'pdf'
'ps'   Generate documentation files in the given format. These targets should always exist, but any or all can be a no-op if the given output format cannot be

generated. These targets should not be dependencies of the `all` target; the user must manually invoke them.

Here's an example rule for generating DVI files from Texinfo:

```
dvi: foo.dvi

foo.dvi: foo.texi chap1.texi chap2.texi
        $(TEXI2DVI) $(srcdir)/foo.texi
```

You must define the variable `TEXI2DVI` in the Makefile. It should run the program `texi2dvi`, which is part of the Texinfo distribution. (`texi2dvi` uses TEX to do the real work of formatting. TEX is not distributed with Texinfo.) Alternatively, write only the dependencies, and allow GNU `make` to provide the command.

Here's another example, this one for generating HTML from Texinfo:

```
html: foo.html

foo.html: foo.texi chap1.texi chap2.texi
        $(TEXI2HTML) $(srcdir)/foo.texi
```

Again, you would define the variable `TEXI2HTML` in the Makefile; for example, it might run `makeinfo --no-split --html` (`makeinfo` is part of the Texinfo distribution).

'dist'   Create a distribution tar file for this program. The tar file should be set up so that the file names in the tar file start with a subdirectory name which is the name of the package it is a distribution for. This name can include the version number.

For example, the distribution tar file of GCC version 1.40 unpacks into a subdirectory named `gcc-1.40`.

The easiest way to do this is to create a subdirectory appropriately named, use `ln` or `cp` to install the proper files in it, and then `tar` that subdirectory.

Compress the tar file with `gzip`. For example, the actual distribution file for GCC version 1.40 is called `gcc-1.40.tar.gz`. It is ok to support other free compression formats as well.

The `dist` target should explicitly depend on all non-source files that are in the distribution, to make sure they are up to date in the distribution. See Section "Making Releases" in *GNU Coding Standards*.

'check'   Perform self-tests (if any). The user must build the program before running the tests, but need not install the program; you should write the self-tests so that they work when the program is built but not installed.

The following targets are suggested as conventional names, for programs in which they are useful.

installcheck
              Perform installation tests (if any). The user must build and install the program before running the tests. You should not assume that `$(bindir)` is in the search path.

`installdirs`

It's useful to add a target named 'installdirs' to create the directories where files are installed, and their parent directories. There is a script called `mkinstalldirs` which is convenient for this; you can find it in the Gnulib package. You can use a rule like this:

```
# Make sure all installation directories (e.g. $(bindir))
# actually exist by making them if necessary.
installdirs: mkinstalldirs
        $(srcdir)/mkinstalldirs $(bindir) $(datadir) \
                                $(libdir) $(infodir) \
                                $(mandir)
```

or, if you wish to support `DESTDIR` (strongly encouraged),

```
# Make sure all installation directories (e.g. $(bindir))
# actually exist by making them if necessary.
installdirs: mkinstalldirs
        $(srcdir)/mkinstalldirs \
            $(DESTDIR)$(bindir) $(DESTDIR)$(datadir) \
            $(DESTDIR)$(libdir) $(DESTDIR)$(infodir) \
            $(DESTDIR)$(mandir)
```

This rule should not modify the directories where compilation is done. It should do nothing but create installation directories.

15.7 Install Command Categories

When writing the `install` target, you must classify all the commands into three categories: normal ones, *pre-installation* commands and *post-installation* commands.

Normal commands move files into their proper places, and set their modes. They may not alter any files except the ones that come entirely from the package they belong to.

Pre-installation and post-installation commands may alter other files; in particular, they can edit global configuration files or data bases.

Pre-installation commands are typically executed before the normal commands, and post-installation commands are typically run after the normal commands.

The most common use for a post-installation command is to run `install-info`. This cannot be done with a normal command, since it alters a file (the Info directory) which does not come entirely and solely from the package being installed. It is a post-installation command because it needs to be done after the normal command which installs the package's Info files.

Most programs don't need any pre-installation commands, but we have the feature just in case it is needed.

To classify the commands in the `install` rule into these three categories, insert *category lines* among them. A category line specifies the category for the commands that follow.

A category line consists of a tab and a reference to a special Make variable, plus an optional comment at the end. There are three variables you can use, one for each category; the variable name specifies the category. Category lines are no-ops in ordinary execution because these three Make variables are normally undefined (and you *should not* define them in the makefile).

Here are the three possible category lines, each with a comment that explains what it means:

```
$(PRE_INSTALL)      # Pre-install commands follow.
$(POST_INSTALL)     # Post-install commands follow.
$(NORMAL_INSTALL)   # Normal commands follow.
```

If you don't use a category line at the beginning of the install rule, all the commands are classified as normal until the first category line. If you don't use any category lines, all the commands are classified as normal.

These are the category lines for uninstall:

```
$(PRE_UNINSTALL)      # Pre-uninstall commands follow.
$(POST_UNINSTALL)     # Post-uninstall commands follow.
$(NORMAL_UNINSTALL)   # Normal commands follow.
```

Typically, a pre-uninstall command would be used for deleting entries from the Info directory.

If the install or uninstall target has any dependencies which act as subroutines of installation, then you should start *each* dependency's commands with a category line, and start the main target's commands with a category line also. This way, you can ensure that each command is placed in the right category regardless of which of the dependencies actually run.

Pre-installation and post-installation commands should not run any programs except for these:

```
[ basename bash cat chgrp chmod chown cmp cp dd diff echo
egrep expand expr false fgrep find getopt grep gunzip gzip
hostname install install-info kill ldconfig ln ls md5sum
mkdir mkfifo mknod mv printenv pwd rm rmdir sed sort tee
test touch true uname xargs yes
```

The reason for distinguishing the commands in this way is for the sake of making binary packages. Typically a binary package contains all the executables and other files that need to be installed, and has its own method of installing them—so it does not need to run the normal installation commands. But installing the binary package does need to execute the pre-installation and post-installation commands.

Programs to build binary packages work by extracting the pre-installation and post-installation commands. Here is one way of extracting the pre-installation commands (the -s option to make is needed to silence messages about entering subdirectories):

```
make -s -n install -o all \
      PRE_INSTALL=pre-install \
      POST_INSTALL=post-install \
      NORMAL_INSTALL=normal-install \
   | gawk -f pre-install.awk
```

where the file pre-install.awk could contain this:

```
$0 ~ /^(normal-install|post-install)[ \t]*$/ {on = 0}
on {print $0}
$0 ~ /^pre-install[ \t]*$/ {on = 1}
```

Appendix A Quick Reference

This appendix summarizes the directives, text manipulation functions, and special variables which GNU `make` understands. See Section 4.8 [Special Targets], page 32, Section 10.2 [Catalogue of Built-In Rules], page 112, and Section 9.7 [Summary of Options], page 104, for other summaries.

Here is a summary of the directives GNU `make` recognizes:

```
define variable
define variable =
define variable :=
define variable ::=
define variable +=
define variable ?=
endef
```
        Define multi-line variables.
        See Section 6.8 [Multi-Line], page 69.

```
undefine variable
```
        Undefining variables.
        See Section 6.9 [Undefine Directive], page 69.

```
ifdef variable
ifndef variable
ifeq (a,b)
ifeq "a" "b"
ifeq 'a' 'b'
ifneq (a,b)
ifneq "a" "b"
ifneq 'a' 'b'
else
endif
```
        Conditionally evaluate part of the makefile.
        See Chapter 7 [Conditionals], page 77.

```
include file
-include file
sinclude file
```
        Include another makefile.
        See Section 3.3 [Including Other Makefiles], page 13.

```
override variable-assignment
```
        Define a variable, overriding any previous definition, even one from the command line.
        See Section 6.7 [The `override` Directive], page 68.

`export`   Tell `make` to export all variables to child processes by default.
        See Section 5.7.2 [Communicating Variables to a Sub-make], page 52.

`export` *variable*
`export` *variable-assignment*
`unexport` *variable*

> Tell `make` whether or not to export a particular variable to child processes.
> See Section 5.7.2 [Communicating Variables to a Sub-make], page 52.

`private` *variable-assignment*

> Do not allow this variable assignment to be inherited by prerequisites.
> See Section 6.13 [Suppressing Inheritance], page 72.

`vpath` *pattern path*

> Specify a search path for files matching a '%' pattern.
> See Section 4.4.2 [The `vpath` Directive], page 26.

`vpath` *pattern*

> Remove all search paths previously specified for *pattern*.

`vpath`

> Remove all search paths previously specified in any `vpath` directive.

Here is a summary of the built-in functions (see Chapter 8 [Functions], page 83):

`$(subst` *from*`,`*to*`,`*text*`)`

> Replace *from* with *to* in *text*.
> See Section 8.2 [Functions for String Substitution and Analysis], page 84.

`$(patsubst` *pattern*`,`*replacement*`,`*text*`)`

> Replace words matching *pattern* with *replacement* in *text*.
> See Section 8.2 [Functions for String Substitution and Analysis], page 84.

`$(strip` *string*`)`

> Remove excess whitespace characters from *string*.
> See Section 8.2 [Functions for String Substitution and Analysis], page 84.

`$(findstring` *find*`,`*text*`)`

> Locate *find* in *text*.
> See Section 8.2 [Functions for String Substitution and Analysis], page 84.

`$(filter` *pattern*`...,`*text*`)`

> Select words in *text* that match one of the *pattern* words.
> See Section 8.2 [Functions for String Substitution and Analysis], page 84.

`$(filter-out` *pattern*`...,`*text*`)`

> Select words in *text* that *do not* match any of the *pattern* words.
> See Section 8.2 [Functions for String Substitution and Analysis], page 84.

`$(sort` *list*`)`

> Sort the words in *list* lexicographically, removing duplicates.
> See Section 8.2 [Functions for String Substitution and Analysis], page 84.

`$(word` *n*`,`*text*`)`

> Extract the *n*th word (one-origin) of *text*.
> See Section 8.2 [Functions for String Substitution and Analysis], page 84.

`$(words` *text*`)`

> Count the number of words in *text*.
> See Section 8.2 [Functions for String Substitution and Analysis], page 84.

`$(wordlist s,e,text)`
> Returns the list of words in *text* from *s* to *e*.
> See Section 8.2 [Functions for String Substitution and Analysis], page 84.

`$(firstword names...)`
> Extract the first word of *names*.
> See Section 8.2 [Functions for String Substitution and Analysis], page 84.

`$(lastword names...)`
> Extract the last word of *names*.
> See Section 8.2 [Functions for String Substitution and Analysis], page 84.

`$(dir names...)`
> Extract the directory part of each file name.
> See Section 8.3 [Functions for File Names], page 87.

`$(notdir names...)`
> Extract the non-directory part of each file name.
> See Section 8.3 [Functions for File Names], page 87.

`$(suffix names...)`
> Extract the suffix (the last '.' and following characters) of each file name.
> See Section 8.3 [Functions for File Names], page 87.

`$(basename names...)`
> Extract the base name (name without suffix) of each file name.
> See Section 8.3 [Functions for File Names], page 87.

`$(addsuffix suffix,names...)`
> Append *suffix* to each word in *names*.
> See Section 8.3 [Functions for File Names], page 87.

`$(addprefix prefix,names...)`
> Prepend *prefix* to each word in *names*.
> See Section 8.3 [Functions for File Names], page 87.

`$(join list1,list2)`
> Join two parallel lists of words.
> See Section 8.3 [Functions for File Names], page 87.

`$(wildcard pattern...)`
> Find file names matching a shell file name pattern (*not* a '%' pattern).
> See Section 4.3.3 [The Function `wildcard`], page 24.

`$(realpath names...)`
> For each file name in *names*, expand to an absolute name that does not contain
> any ., .., nor symlinks.
> See Section 8.3 [Functions for File Names], page 87.

`$(abspath names...)`
> For each file name in *names*, expand to an absolute name that does not contain
> any . or .. components, but preserves symlinks.
> See Section 8.3 [Functions for File Names], page 87.

`$(error text...)`

> When this function is evaluated, **make** generates a fatal error with the message *text*.
>
> See Section 8.12 [Functions That Control Make], page 96.

`$(warning text...)`

> When this function is evaluated, **make** generates a warning with the message *text*.
>
> See Section 8.12 [Functions That Control Make], page 96.

`$(shell command)`

> Execute a shell command and return its output.
>
> See Section 8.13 [The **shell** Function], page 97.

`$(origin variable)`

> Return a string describing how the **make** variable *variable* was defined.
>
> See Section 8.10 [The **origin** Function], page 94.

`$(flavor variable)`

> Return a string describing the flavor of the **make** variable *variable*.
>
> See Section 8.11 [The **flavor** Function], page 95.

`$(foreach var,words,text)`

> Evaluate *text* with *var* bound to each word in *words*, and concatenate the results.
>
> See Section 8.5 [The **foreach** Function], page 90.

`$(if condition,then-part[,else-part])`

> Evaluate the condition *condition*; if it's non-empty substitute the expansion of the *then-part* otherwise substitute the expansion of the *else-part*.
>
> See Section 8.4 [Functions for Conditionals], page 89.

`$(or condition1[,condition2[,condition3...]])`

> Evaluate each condition *conditionN* one at a time; substitute the first non-empty expansion. If all expansions are empty, substitute the empty string.
>
> See Section 8.4 [Functions for Conditionals], page 89.

`$(and condition1[,condition2[,condition3...]])`

> Evaluate each condition *conditionN* one at a time; if any expansion results in the empty string substitute the empty string. If all expansions result in a non-empty string, substitute the expansion of the last *condition*.
>
> See Section 8.4 [Functions for Conditionals], page 89.

`$(call var,param,...)`

> Evaluate the variable *var* replacing any references to `$(1)`, `$(2)` with the first, second, etc. *param* values.
>
> See Section 8.7 [The **call** Function], page 92.

`$(eval text)`

> Evaluate *text* then read the results as makefile commands. Expands to the empty string.
>
> See Section 8.9 [The **eval** Function], page 93.

`$(file op filename,text)`

> Expand the arguments, then open the file *filename* using mode *op* and write *text* to that file.
>
> See Section 8.6 [The `file` Function], page 91.

`$(value var)`

> Evaluates to the contents of the variable *var*, with no expansion performed on it.
>
> See Section 8.8 [The `value` Function], page 93.

Here is a summary of the automatic variables. See Section 10.5.3 [Automatic Variables], page 120, for full information.

`$@`	The file name of the target.
`$%`	The target member name, when the target is an archive member.
`$<`	The name of the first prerequisite.
`$?`	The names of all the prerequisites that are newer than the target, with spaces between them. For prerequisites which are archive members, only the named member is used (see Chapter 11 [Archives], page 129).
`$^`	
`$+`	The names of all the prerequisites, with spaces between them. For prerequisites which are archive members, only the named member is used (see Chapter 11 [Archives], page 129). The value of `$^` omits duplicate prerequisites, while `$+` retains them and preserves their order.
`$*`	The stem with which an implicit rule matches (see Section 10.5.4 [How Patterns Match], page 122).
`$(@D)`	
`$(@F)`	The directory part and the file-within-directory part of `$@`.
`$(*D)`	
`$(*F)`	The directory part and the file-within-directory part of `$*`.
`$(%D)`	
`$(%F)`	The directory part and the file-within-directory part of `$%`.
`$(<D)`	
`$(<F)`	The directory part and the file-within-directory part of `$<`.
`$(^D)`	
`$(^F)`	The directory part and the file-within-directory part of `$^`.
`$(+D)`	
`$(+F)`	The directory part and the file-within-directory part of `$+`.
`$(?D)`	
`$(?F)`	The directory part and the file-within-directory part of `$?`.

These variables are used specially by GNU `make`:

MAKEFILES

Makefiles to be read on every invocation of make.
See Section 3.4 [The Variable MAKEFILES], page 14.

VPATH

Directory search path for files not found in the current directory.
See Section 4.4.1 [VPATH Search Path for All Prerequisites], page 25.

SHELL

The name of the system default command interpreter, usually /bin/sh. You can set SHELL in the makefile to change the shell used to run recipes. See Section 5.3 [Recipe Execution], page 44. The SHELL variable is handled specially when importing from and exporting to the environment. See Section 5.3.2 [Choosing the Shell], page 45.

MAKESHELL

On MS-DOS only, the name of the command interpreter that is to be used by make. This value takes precedence over the value of SHELL. See Section 5.3 [MAKESHELL variable], page 44.

MAKE

The name with which make was invoked. Using this variable in recipes has special meaning. See Section 5.7.1 [How the MAKE Variable Works], page 51.

MAKE_VERSION

The built-in variable 'MAKE_VERSION' expands to the version number of the GNU make program.

MAKE_HOST

The built-in variable 'MAKE_HOST' expands to a string representing the host that GNU make was built to run on.

MAKELEVEL

The number of levels of recursion (sub-makes).
See Section 5.7.2 [Variables/Recursion], page 52.

MAKEFLAGS

The flags given to make. You can set this in the environment or a makefile to set flags.
See Section 5.7.3 [Communicating Options to a Sub-make], page 54.

It is *never* appropriate to use MAKEFLAGS directly in a recipe line: its contents may not be quoted correctly for use in the shell. Always allow recursive make's to obtain these values through the environment from its parent.

GNUMAKEFLAGS

Other flags parsed by make. You can set this in the environment or a makefile to set make command-line flags. GNU make never sets this variable itself. This variable is only needed if you'd like to set GNU make-specific flags in a POSIX-compliant makefile. This variable will be seen by GNU make and ignored by other make implementations. It's not needed if you only use GNU make; just use MAKEFLAGS directly. See Section 5.7.3 [Communicating Options to a Sub-make], page 54.

MAKECMDGOALS

> The targets given to **make** on the command line. Setting this variable has no effect on the operation of **make**.
> See Section 9.2 [Arguments to Specify the Goals], page 99.

CURDIR

> Set to the pathname of the current working directory (after all -C options are processed, if any). Setting this variable has no effect on the operation of **make**.
> See Section 5.7 [Recursive Use of **make**], page 50.

SUFFIXES

> The default list of suffixes before **make** reads any makefiles.

.LIBPATTERNS

> Defines the naming of the libraries **make** searches for, and their order.
> See Section 4.4.6 [Directory Search for Link Libraries], page 28.

Appendix B Errors Generated by Make

Here is a list of the more common errors you might see generated by make, and some information about what they mean and how to fix them.

Sometimes make errors are not fatal, especially in the presence of a - prefix on a recipe line, or the -k command line option. Errors that are fatal are prefixed with the string ***.

Error messages are all either prefixed with the name of the program (usually 'make'), or, if the error is found in a makefile, the name of the file and line number containing the problem.

In the table below, these common prefixes are left off.

'[*foo*] Error *NN*'
'[*foo*] *signal description*'

> These errors are not really make errors at all. They mean that a program that make invoked as part of a recipe returned a non-0 error code ('Error *NN*'), which make interprets as failure, or it exited in some other abnormal fashion (with a signal of some type). See Section 5.5 [Errors in Recipes], page 49.
>
> If no *** is attached to the message, then the sub-process failed but the rule in the makefile was prefixed with the - special character, so make ignored the error.

'missing separator. Stop.'
'missing separator (did you mean TAB instead of 8 spaces?). Stop.'

> This means that make could not understand much of anything about the makefile line it just read. GNU make looks for various separators (:, =, recipe prefix characters, etc.) to indicate what kind of line it's parsing. This message means it couldn't find a valid one.
>
> One of the most common reasons for this message is that you (or perhaps your oh-so-helpful editor, as is the case with many MS-Windows editors) have attempted to indent your recipe lines with spaces instead of a tab character. In this case, make will use the second form of the error above. Remember that every line in the recipe must begin with a tab character (unless you set .RECIPEPREFIX; see Section 6.14 [Special Variables], page 73). Eight spaces do not count. See Section 4.1 [Rule Syntax], page 21.

'recipe commences before first target. Stop.'
'missing rule before recipe. Stop.'

> This means the first thing in the makefile seems to be part of a recipe: it begins with a recipe prefix character and doesn't appear to be a legal make directive (such as a variable assignment). Recipes must always be associated with a target.
>
> The second form is generated if the line has a semicolon as the first non-whitespace character; make interprets this to mean you left out the "target: prerequisite" section of a rule. See Section 4.1 [Rule Syntax], page 21.

'No rule to make target '*xxx*'.'
'No rule to make target '*xxx*', needed by '*yyy*'.'
> This means that make decided it needed to build a target, but then couldn't find any instructions in the makefile on how to do that, either explicit or implicit (including in the default rules database).
>
> If you want that file to be built, you will need to add a rule to your makefile describing how that target can be built. Other possible sources of this problem are typos in the makefile (if that file name is wrong) or a corrupted source tree (if that file is not supposed to be built, but rather only a prerequisite).

'No targets specified and no makefile found. Stop.'
'No targets. Stop.'
> The former means that you didn't provide any targets to be built on the command line, and make couldn't find any makefiles to read in. The latter means that some makefile was found, but it didn't contain any default goal and none was given on the command line. GNU make has nothing to do in these situations. See Section 9.1 [Arguments to Specify the Makefile], page 99.

'Makefile '*xxx*' was not found.'
'Included makefile '*xxx*' was not found.'
> A makefile specified on the command line (first form) or included (second form) was not found.

'warning: overriding recipe for target '*xxx*''
'warning: ignoring old recipe for target '*xxx*''
> GNU make allows only one recipe to be specified per target (except for double-colon rules). If you give a recipe for a target which already has been defined to have one, this warning is issued and the second recipe will overwrite the first. See Section 4.10 [Multiple Rules for One Target], page 35.

'Circular *xxx* <- *yyy* dependency dropped.'
> This means that make detected a loop in the dependency graph: after tracing the prerequisite *yyy* of target *xxx*, and its prerequisites, etc., one of them depended on *xxx* again.

'Recursive variable '*xxx*' references itself (eventually). Stop.'
> This means you've defined a normal (recursive) make variable *xxx* that, when it's expanded, will refer to itself (*xxx*). This is not allowed; either use simply-expanded variables (':=' or '::=') or use the append operator ('+='). See Chapter 6 [How to Use Variables], page 59.

'Unterminated variable reference. Stop.'
> This means you forgot to provide the proper closing parenthesis or brace in your variable or function reference.

'insufficient arguments to function '*xxx*'. Stop.'
> This means you haven't provided the requisite number of arguments for this function. See the documentation of the function for a description of its arguments. See Chapter 8 [Functions for Transforming Text], page 83.

'missing target pattern. Stop.'
'multiple target patterns. Stop.'
'target pattern contains no '%'. Stop.'
'mixed implicit and static pattern rules. Stop.'

> These are generated for malformed static pattern rules. The first means there's no pattern in the target section of the rule; the second means there are multiple patterns in the target section; the third means the target doesn't contain a pattern character (%); and the fourth means that all three parts of the static pattern rule contain pattern characters (%)–only the first two parts should. If you see these errors and you aren't trying to create a static pattern rule, check the value of any variables in your target and prerequisite lists to be sure they do not contain colons. See Section 4.11.1 [Syntax of Static Pattern Rules], page 36.

'warning: -jN forced in submake: disabling jobserver mode.'

> This warning and the next are generated if **make** detects error conditions related to parallel processing on systems where sub-**makes** can communicate (see Section 5.7.3 [Communicating Options to a Sub-make], page 54). This warning is generated if a recursive invocation of a **make** process is forced to have '-jN' in its argument list (where N is greater than one). This could happen, for example, if you set the MAKE environment variable to 'make -j2'. In this case, the sub-**make** doesn't communicate with other **make** processes and will simply pretend it has two jobs of its own.

'warning: jobserver unavailable: using -j1. Add '+' to parent make rule.'

> In order for **make** processes to communicate, the parent will pass information to the child. Since this could result in problems if the child process isn't actually a **make**, the parent will only do this if it thinks the child is a **make**. The parent uses the normal algorithms to determine this (see Section 5.7.1 [How the MAKE Variable Works], page 51). If the makefile is constructed such that the parent doesn't know the child is a **make** process, then the child will receive only part of the information necessary. In this case, the child will generate this warning message and proceed with its build in a sequential manner.

Appendix C Complex Makefile Example

Here is the makefile for the GNU `tar` program. This is a moderately complex makefile. The first line uses a `#!` setting to allow the makefile to be executed directly.

Because it is the first target, the default goal is 'all'. An interesting feature of this makefile is that `testpad.h` is a source file automatically created by the `testpad` program, itself compiled from `testpad.c`.

If you type 'make' or 'make all', then `make` creates the `tar` executable, the `rmt` daemon that provides remote tape access, and the `tar.info` Info file.

If you type 'make install', then `make` not only creates `tar`, `rmt`, and `tar.info`, but also installs them.

If you type 'make clean', then `make` removes the '.o' files, and the `tar`, `rmt`, `testpad`, `testpad.h`, and `core` files.

If you type 'make distclean', then `make` not only removes the same files as does 'make clean' but also the `TAGS`, `Makefile`, and `config.status` files. (Although it is not evident, this makefile (and `config.status`) is generated by the user with the `configure` program, which is provided in the `tar` distribution, but is not shown here.)

If you type 'make realclean', then `make` removes the same files as does 'make distclean' and also removes the Info files generated from `tar.texinfo`.

In addition, there are targets `shar` and `dist` that create distribution kits.

```
#!/usr/bin/make -f
# Generated automatically from Makefile.in by configure.
# Un*x Makefile for GNU tar program.
# Copyright (C) 1991 Free Software Foundation, Inc.

# This program is free software; you can redistribute
# it and/or modify it under the terms of the GNU
# General Public License ...
...
...

SHELL = /bin/sh

#### Start of system configuration section. ####

srcdir = .

# If you use gcc, you should either run the
# fixincludes script that comes with it or else use
# gcc with the -traditional option.  Otherwise ioctl
# calls will be compiled incorrectly on some systems.
CC = gcc -O
YACC = bison -y
INSTALL = /usr/local/bin/install -c
INSTALLDATA = /usr/local/bin/install -c -m 644
```

```
# Things you might add to DEFS:
# -DSTDC_HEADERS        If you have ANSI C headers and
#                       libraries.
# -DPOSIX               If you have POSIX.1 headers and
#                       libraries.
# -DBSD42               If you have sys/dir.h (unless
#                       you use -DPOSIX), sys/file.h,
#                       and st_blocks in 'struct stat'.
# -DUSG                 If you have System V/ANSI C
#                       string and memory functions
#                       and headers, sys/sysmacros.h,
#                       fcntl.h, getcwd, no valloc,
#                       and ndir.h (unless
#                       you use -DDIRENT).
# -DNO_MEMORY_H         If USG or STDC_HEADERS but do not
#                       include memory.h.
# -DDIRENT              If USG and you have dirent.h
#                       instead of ndir.h.
# -DSIGTYPE=int         If your signal handlers
#                       return int, not void.
# -DNO_MTIO             If you lack sys/mtio.h
#                       (magtape ioctls).
# -DNO_REMOTE           If you do not have a remote shell
#                       or rexec.
# -DUSE_REXEC           To use rexec for remote tape
#                       operations instead of
#                       forking rsh or remsh.
# -DVPRINTF_MISSING     If you lack vprintf function
#                       (but have _doprnt).
# -DDOPRNT_MISSING      If you lack _doprnt function.
#                       Also need to define
#                       -DVPRINTF_MISSING.
# -DFTIME_MISSING       If you lack ftime system call.
# -DSTRSTR_MISSING      If you lack strstr function.
# -DVALLOC_MISSING      If you lack valloc function.
# -DMKDIR_MISSING       If you lack mkdir and
#                       rmdir system calls.
# -DRENAME_MISSING      If you lack rename system call.
# -DFTRUNCATE_MISSING   If you lack ftruncate
#                       system call.
# -DV7                  On Version 7 Unix (not
#                       tested in a long time).
# -DEMUL_OPEN3          If you lack a 3-argument version
#                       of open, and want to emulate it
#                       with system calls you do have.
# -DNO_OPEN3            If you lack the 3-argument open
```

```
#                       and want to disable the tar -k
#                       option instead of emulating open.
# -DXENIX                If you have sys/inode.h
#                       and need it 94 to be included.

DEFS =  -DSIGTYPE=int -DDIRENT -DSTRSTR_MISSING \
        -DVPRINTF_MISSING -DBSD42
# Set this to rtapelib.o unless you defined NO_REMOTE,
# in which case make it empty.
RTAPELIB = rtapelib.o
LIBS =
DEF_AR_FILE = /dev/rmt8
DEFBLOCKING = 20


CDEBUG = -g
CFLAGS = $(CDEBUG) -I. -I$(srcdir) $(DEFS) \
        -DDEF_AR_FILE=\"$(DEF_AR_FILE)\" \
        -DDEFBLOCKING=$(DEFBLOCKING)
LDFLAGS = -g


prefix = /usr/local
# Prefix for each installed program,
# normally empty or 'g'.
binprefix =

# The directory to install tar in.
bindir = $(prefix)/bin

# The directory to install the info files in.
infodir = $(prefix)/info

#### End of system configuration section. ####

SRCS_C  = tar.c create.c extract.c buffer.c   \
          getoldopt.c update.c gnu.c mangle.c \
          version.c list.c names.c diffarch.c \
          port.c wildmat.c getopt.c getopt1.c \
          regex.c
SRCS_Y  = getdate.y
SRCS    = $(SRCS_C) $(SRCS_Y)
OBJS    = $(SRCS_C:.c=.o) $(SRCS_Y:.y=.o) $(RTAPELIB)
```

```
AUX =    README COPYING ChangeLog Makefile.in  \
         makefile.pc configure configure.in \
         tar.texinfo tar.info* texinfo.tex \
         tar.h port.h open3.h getopt.h regex.h \
         rmt.h rmt.c rtapelib.c alloca.c \
         msd_dir.h msd_dir.c tcexparg.c \
         level-0 level-1 backup-specs testpad.c

.PHONY: all
all:     tar rmt tar.info

tar:     $(OBJS)
         $(CC) $(LDFLAGS) -o $@ $(OBJS) $(LIBS)

rmt:     rmt.c
         $(CC) $(CFLAGS) $(LDFLAGS) -o $@ rmt.c

tar.info: tar.texinfo
         makeinfo tar.texinfo

.PHONY: install
install: all
         $(INSTALL) tar $(bindir)/$(binprefix)tar
         -test ! -f rmt || $(INSTALL) rmt /etc/rmt
         $(INSTALLDATA) $(srcdir)/tar.info* $(infodir)

$(OBJS): tar.h port.h testpad.h
regex.o buffer.o tar.o: regex.h
# getdate.y has 8 shift/reduce conflicts.

testpad.h: testpad
         ./testpad

testpad: testpad.o
         $(CC) -o $@ testpad.o

TAGS:    $(SRCS)
         etags $(SRCS)

.PHONY: clean
clean:
         rm -f *.o tar rmt testpad testpad.h core

.PHONY: distclean
distclean: clean
         rm -f TAGS Makefile config.status
```

```
.PHONY: realclean
realclean: distclean
        rm -f tar.info*

.PHONY: shar
shar: $(SRCS) $(AUX)
        shar $(SRCS) $(AUX) | compress \
          > tar-`sed -e '/version_string/!d' \
                  -e 's/[^0-9.]*\([0-9.]*\).*/\1/' \
                  -e q
                  version.c`.shar.Z

.PHONY: dist
dist: $(SRCS) $(AUX)
        echo tar-`sed \
            -e '/version_string/!d' \
            -e 's/[^0-9.]*\([0-9.]*\).*/\1/' \
            -e q
            version.c` > .fname
        -rm -rf `cat .fname`
        mkdir `cat .fname`
        ln $(SRCS) $(AUX) `cat .fname`
        tar chZf `cat .fname`.tar.Z `cat .fname`
        -rm -rf `cat .fname` .fname

tar.zoo: $(SRCS) $(AUX)
        -rm -rf tmp.dir
        -mkdir tmp.dir
        -rm tar.zoo
        for X in $(SRCS) $(AUX) ; do \
            echo $$X ; \
            sed 's/$$/^M/' $$X \
            > tmp.dir/$$X ; done
        cd tmp.dir ; zoo aM ../tar.zoo *
        -rm -rf tmp.dir
```

C.1 GNU Free Documentation License

Version 1.3, 3 November 2008

Copyright © 2000, 2001, 2002, 2007, 2008 Free Software Foundation, Inc.
`http://fsf.org/`

Everyone is permitted to copy and distribute verbatim copies
of this license document, but changing it is not allowed.

0. PREAMBLE

The purpose of this License is to make a manual, textbook, or other functional and
useful document *free* in the sense of freedom: to assure everyone the effective freedom

to copy and redistribute it, with or without modifying it, either commercially or non-commercially. Secondarily, this License preserves for the author and publisher a way to get credit for their work, while not being considered responsible for modifications made by others.

This License is a kind of "copyleft", which means that derivative works of the document must themselves be free in the same sense. It complements the GNU General Public License, which is a copyleft license designed for free software.

We have designed this License in order to use it for manuals for free software, because free software needs free documentation: a free program should come with manuals providing the same freedoms that the software does. But this License is not limited to software manuals; it can be used for any textual work, regardless of subject matter or whether it is published as a printed book. We recommend this License principally for works whose purpose is instruction or reference.

1. APPLICABILITY AND DEFINITIONS

This License applies to any manual or other work, in any medium, that contains a notice placed by the copyright holder saying it can be distributed under the terms of this License. Such a notice grants a world-wide, royalty-free license, unlimited in duration, to use that work under the conditions stated herein. The "Document", below, refers to any such manual or work. Any member of the public is a licensee, and is addressed as "you". You accept the license if you copy, modify or distribute the work in a way requiring permission under copyright law.

A "Modified Version" of the Document means any work containing the Document or a portion of it, either copied verbatim, or with modifications and/or translated into another language.

A "Secondary Section" is a named appendix or a front-matter section of the Document that deals exclusively with the relationship of the publishers or authors of the Document to the Document's overall subject (or to related matters) and contains nothing that could fall directly within that overall subject. (Thus, if the Document is in part a textbook of mathematics, a Secondary Section may not explain any mathematics.) The relationship could be a matter of historical connection with the subject or with related matters, or of legal, commercial, philosophical, ethical or political position regarding them.

The "Invariant Sections" are certain Secondary Sections whose titles are designated, as being those of Invariant Sections, in the notice that says that the Document is released under this License. If a section does not fit the above definition of Secondary then it is not allowed to be designated as Invariant. The Document may contain zero Invariant Sections. If the Document does not identify any Invariant Sections then there are none.

The "Cover Texts" are certain short passages of text that are listed, as Front-Cover Texts or Back-Cover Texts, in the notice that says that the Document is released under this License. A Front-Cover Text may be at most 5 words, and a Back-Cover Text may be at most 25 words.

A "Transparent" copy of the Document means a machine-readable copy, represented in a format whose specification is available to the general public, that is suitable for revising the document straightforwardly with generic text editors or (for images composed of pixels) generic paint programs or (for drawings) some widely available drawing editor, and that is suitable for input to text formatters or for automatic translation to a variety of formats suitable for input to text formatters. A copy made in an otherwise Transparent file format whose markup, or absence of markup, has been arranged to thwart or discourage subsequent modification by readers is not Transparent. An image format is not Transparent if used for any substantial amount of text. A copy that is not "Transparent" is called "Opaque".

Examples of suitable formats for Transparent copies include plain ASCII without markup, Texinfo input format, LaTeX input format, SGML or XML using a publicly available DTD, and standard-conforming simple HTML, PostScript or PDF designed for human modification. Examples of transparent image formats include PNG, XCF and JPG. Opaque formats include proprietary formats that can be read and edited only by proprietary word processors, SGML or XML for which the DTD and/or processing tools are not generally available, and the machine-generated HTML, PostScript or PDF produced by some word processors for output purposes only.

The "Title Page" means, for a printed book, the title page itself, plus such following pages as are needed to hold, legibly, the material this License requires to appear in the title page. For works in formats which do not have any title page as such, "Title Page" means the text near the most prominent appearance of the work's title, preceding the beginning of the body of the text.

The "publisher" means any person or entity that distributes copies of the Document to the public.

A section "Entitled XYZ" means a named subunit of the Document whose title either is precisely XYZ or contains XYZ in parentheses following text that translates XYZ in another language. (Here XYZ stands for a specific section name mentioned below, such as "Acknowledgements", "Dedications", "Endorsements", or "History".) To "Preserve the Title" of such a section when you modify the Document means that it remains a section "Entitled XYZ" according to this definition.

The Document may include Warranty Disclaimers next to the notice which states that this License applies to the Document. These Warranty Disclaimers are considered to be included by reference in this License, but only as regards disclaiming warranties: any other implication that these Warranty Disclaimers may have is void and has no effect on the meaning of this License.

2. VERBATIM COPYING

You may copy and distribute the Document in any medium, either commercially or noncommercially, provided that this License, the copyright notices, and the license notice saying this License applies to the Document are reproduced in all copies, and that you add no other conditions whatsoever to those of this License. You may not use technical measures to obstruct or control the reading or further copying of the copies you make or distribute. However, you may accept compensation in exchange for copies. If you distribute a large enough number of copies you must also follow the conditions in section 3.

You may also lend copies, under the same conditions stated above, and you may publicly display copies.

3. COPYING IN QUANTITY

If you publish printed copies (or copies in media that commonly have printed covers) of the Document, numbering more than 100, and the Document's license notice requires Cover Texts, you must enclose the copies in covers that carry, clearly and legibly, all these Cover Texts: Front-Cover Texts on the front cover, and Back-Cover Texts on the back cover. Both covers must also clearly and legibly identify you as the publisher of these copies. The front cover must present the full title with all words of the title equally prominent and visible. You may add other material on the covers in addition. Copying with changes limited to the covers, as long as they preserve the title of the Document and satisfy these conditions, can be treated as verbatim copying in other respects.

If the required texts for either cover are too voluminous to fit legibly, you should put the first ones listed (as many as fit reasonably) on the actual cover, and continue the rest onto adjacent pages.

If you publish or distribute Opaque copies of the Document numbering more than 100, you must either include a machine-readable Transparent copy along with each Opaque copy, or state in or with each Opaque copy a computer-network location from which the general network-using public has access to download using public-standard network protocols a complete Transparent copy of the Document, free of added material. If you use the latter option, you must take reasonably prudent steps, when you begin distribution of Opaque copies in quantity, to ensure that this Transparent copy will remain thus accessible at the stated location until at least one year after the last time you distribute an Opaque copy (directly or through your agents or retailers) of that edition to the public.

It is requested, but not required, that you contact the authors of the Document well before redistributing any large number of copies, to give them a chance to provide you with an updated version of the Document.

4. MODIFICATIONS

You may copy and distribute a Modified Version of the Document under the conditions of sections 2 and 3 above, provided that you release the Modified Version under precisely this License, with the Modified Version filling the role of the Document, thus licensing distribution and modification of the Modified Version to whoever possesses a copy of it. In addition, you must do these things in the Modified Version:

A. Use in the Title Page (and on the covers, if any) a title distinct from that of the Document, and from those of previous versions (which should, if there were any, be listed in the History section of the Document). You may use the same title as a previous version if the original publisher of that version gives permission.

B. List on the Title Page, as authors, one or more persons or entities responsible for authorship of the modifications in the Modified Version, together with at least five of the principal authors of the Document (all of its principal authors, if it has fewer than five), unless they release you from this requirement.

C. State on the Title page the name of the publisher of the Modified Version, as the publisher.

D. Preserve all the copyright notices of the Document.

E. Add an appropriate copyright notice for your modifications adjacent to the other copyright notices.

F. Include, immediately after the copyright notices, a license notice giving the public permission to use the Modified Version under the terms of this License, in the form shown in the Addendum below.

G. Preserve in that license notice the full lists of Invariant Sections and required Cover Texts given in the Document's license notice.

H. Include an unaltered copy of this License.

I. Preserve the section Entitled "History", Preserve its Title, and add to it an item stating at least the title, year, new authors, and publisher of the Modified Version as given on the Title Page. If there is no section Entitled "History" in the Document, create one stating the title, year, authors, and publisher of the Document as given on its Title Page, then add an item describing the Modified Version as stated in the previous sentence.

J. Preserve the network location, if any, given in the Document for public access to a Transparent copy of the Document, and likewise the network locations given in the Document for previous versions it was based on. These may be placed in the "History" section. You may omit a network location for a work that was published at least four years before the Document itself, or if the original publisher of the version it refers to gives permission.

K. For any section Entitled "Acknowledgements" or "Dedications", Preserve the Title of the section, and preserve in the section all the substance and tone of each of the contributor acknowledgements and/or dedications given therein.

L. Preserve all the Invariant Sections of the Document, unaltered in their text and in their titles. Section numbers or the equivalent are not considered part of the section titles.

M. Delete any section Entitled "Endorsements". Such a section may not be included in the Modified Version.

N. Do not retitle any existing section to be Entitled "Endorsements" or to conflict in title with any Invariant Section.

O. Preserve any Warranty Disclaimers.

If the Modified Version includes new front-matter sections or appendices that qualify as Secondary Sections and contain no material copied from the Document, you may at your option designate some or all of these sections as invariant. To do this, add their titles to the list of Invariant Sections in the Modified Version's license notice. These titles must be distinct from any other section titles.

You may add a section Entitled "Endorsements", provided it contains nothing but endorsements of your Modified Version by various parties—for example, statements of peer review or that the text has been approved by an organization as the authoritative definition of a standard.

You may add a passage of up to five words as a Front-Cover Text, and a passage of up to 25 words as a Back-Cover Text, to the end of the list of Cover Texts in the Modified Version. Only one passage of Front-Cover Text and one of Back-Cover Text may be added by (or through arrangements made by) any one entity. If the Document already includes a cover text for the same cover, previously added by you or by arrangement made by the same entity you are acting on behalf of, you may not add another; but you may replace the old one, on explicit permission from the previous publisher that added the old one.

The author(s) and publisher(s) of the Document do not by this License give permission to use their names for publicity for or to assert or imply endorsement of any Modified Version.

5. COMBINING DOCUMENTS

You may combine the Document with other documents released under this License, under the terms defined in section 4 above for modified versions, provided that you include in the combination all of the Invariant Sections of all of the original documents, unmodified, and list them all as Invariant Sections of your combined work in its license notice, and that you preserve all their Warranty Disclaimers.

The combined work need only contain one copy of this License, and multiple identical Invariant Sections may be replaced with a single copy. If there are multiple Invariant Sections with the same name but different contents, make the title of each such section unique by adding at the end of it, in parentheses, the name of the original author or publisher of that section if known, or else a unique number. Make the same adjustment to the section titles in the list of Invariant Sections in the license notice of the combined work.

In the combination, you must combine any sections Entitled "History" in the various original documents, forming one section Entitled "History"; likewise combine any sections Entitled "Acknowledgements", and any sections Entitled "Dedications". You must delete all sections Entitled "Endorsements."

6. COLLECTIONS OF DOCUMENTS

You may make a collection consisting of the Document and other documents released under this License, and replace the individual copies of this License in the various documents with a single copy that is included in the collection, provided that you follow the rules of this License for verbatim copying of each of the documents in all other respects.

You may extract a single document from such a collection, and distribute it individually under this License, provided you insert a copy of this License into the extracted document, and follow this License in all other respects regarding verbatim copying of that document.

7. AGGREGATION WITH INDEPENDENT WORKS

A compilation of the Document or its derivatives with other separate and independent documents or works, in or on a volume of a storage or distribution medium, is called an "aggregate" if the copyright resulting from the compilation is not used to limit the legal rights of the compilation's users beyond what the individual works permit. When the Document is included in an aggregate, this License does not apply to the other works in the aggregate which are not themselves derivative works of the Document.

If the Cover Text requirement of section 3 is applicable to these copies of the Document, then if the Document is less than one half of the entire aggregate, the Document's Cover Texts may be placed on covers that bracket the Document within the aggregate, or the electronic equivalent of covers if the Document is in electronic form. Otherwise they must appear on printed covers that bracket the whole aggregate.

8. TRANSLATION

Translation is considered a kind of modification, so you may distribute translations of the Document under the terms of section 4. Replacing Invariant Sections with translations requires special permission from their copyright holders, but you may include translations of some or all Invariant Sections in addition to the original versions of these Invariant Sections. You may include a translation of this License, and all the license notices in the Document, and any Warranty Disclaimers, provided that you also include the original English version of this License and the original versions of those notices and disclaimers. In case of a disagreement between the translation and the original version of this License or a notice or disclaimer, the original version will prevail.

If a section in the Document is Entitled "Acknowledgements", "Dedications", or "History", the requirement (section 4) to Preserve its Title (section 1) will typically require changing the actual title.

9. TERMINATION

You may not copy, modify, sublicense, or distribute the Document except as expressly provided under this License. Any attempt otherwise to copy, modify, sublicense, or distribute it is void, and will automatically terminate your rights under this License.

However, if you cease all violation of this License, then your license from a particular copyright holder is reinstated (a) provisionally, unless and until the copyright holder explicitly and finally terminates your license, and (b) permanently, if the copyright holder fails to notify you of the violation by some reasonable means prior to 60 days after the cessation.

Moreover, your license from a particular copyright holder is reinstated permanently if the copyright holder notifies you of the violation by some reasonable means, this is the first time you have received notice of violation of this License (for any work) from that copyright holder, and you cure the violation prior to 30 days after your receipt of the notice.

Termination of your rights under this section does not terminate the licenses of parties who have received copies or rights from you under this License. If your rights have been terminated and not permanently reinstated, receipt of a copy of some or all of the same material does not give you any rights to use it.

10. FUTURE REVISIONS OF THIS LICENSE

The Free Software Foundation may publish new, revised versions of the GNU Free Documentation License from time to time. Such new versions will be similar in spirit to the present version, but may differ in detail to address new problems or concerns. See http://www.gnu.org/copyleft/.

Each version of the License is given a distinguishing version number. If the Document specifies that a particular numbered version of this License "or any later version" applies to it, you have the option of following the terms and conditions either of that specified version or of any later version that has been published (not as a draft) by the Free Software Foundation. If the Document does not specify a version number of this License, you may choose any version ever published (not as a draft) by the Free Software Foundation. If the Document specifies that a proxy can decide which future versions of this License can be used, that proxy's public statement of acceptance of a version permanently authorizes you to choose that version for the Document.

11. RELICENSING

"Massive Multiauthor Collaboration Site" (or "MMC Site") means any World Wide Web server that publishes copyrightable works and also provides prominent facilities for anybody to edit those works. A public wiki that anybody can edit is an example of such a server. A "Massive Multiauthor Collaboration" (or "MMC") contained in the site means any set of copyrightable works thus published on the MMC site.

"CC-BY-SA" means the Creative Commons Attribution-Share Alike 3.0 license published by Creative Commons Corporation, a not-for-profit corporation with a principal place of business in San Francisco, California, as well as future copyleft versions of that license published by that same organization.

"Incorporate" means to publish or republish a Document, in whole or in part, as part of another Document.

An MMC is "eligible for relicensing" if it is licensed under this License, and if all works that were first published under this License somewhere other than this MMC, and subsequently incorporated in whole or in part into the MMC, (1) had no cover texts or invariant sections, and (2) were thus incorporated prior to November 1, 2008.

The operator of an MMC Site may republish an MMC contained in the site under CC-BY-SA on the same site at any time before August 1, 2009, provided the MMC is eligible for relicensing.

ADDENDUM: How to use this License for your documents

To use this License in a document you have written, include a copy of the License in the document and put the following copyright and license notices just after the title page:

```
Copyright (C)  year  your name.
Permission is granted to copy, distribute and/or modify this document
under the terms of the GNU Free Documentation License, Version 1.3
or any later version published by the Free Software Foundation;
with no Invariant Sections, no Front-Cover Texts, and no Back-Cover
Texts.  A copy of the license is included in the section entitled ''GNU
Free Documentation License''.
```

If you have Invariant Sections, Front-Cover Texts and Back-Cover Texts, replace the "with...Texts." line with this:

```
with the Invariant Sections being list their titles, with
the Front-Cover Texts being list, and with the Back-Cover Texts
being list.
```

If you have Invariant Sections without Cover Texts, or some other combination of the three, merge those two alternatives to suit the situation.

If your document contains nontrivial examples of program code, we recommend releasing these examples in parallel under your choice of free software license, such as the GNU General Public License, to permit their use in free software.

Index of Concepts

Index of Functions, Variables, & Directives